Michael Franzese

7-23-07

There's an old saying that the only way to leave the Mafia is in a coffin. Members are pledged to a lifetime of secrecy, and to quit would be to arouse suspicion that you are cooperating with the police or federal agents. Such breaches of faith the mob punishes with death.

Michael Franzese says he's willing to take that risk. He will not betray his former crime associates and then disappear into the federal Witness Protection Program....If he holds to what he has promised...it will mark the first time that a high-ranking member of the Mafia will publicly walk away from his past.

—Edward Barnes and William Shebar,
Life magazine,
December 1987

Investigative correspondent Brian Ross and producer Ira Silverman have been tracking the mob ever since they first hooked up as a team here at NBC fifteen years ago. They've met a variety of characters in their travels, but none as slick as the one they introduce to us tonight...a handsome and high-living young man as rich as royalty, and royalty he is—a prince—of the Mafia.

—Tom Brokaw,
"Expose,"
January 1991

Within a decade, Franzese had become...one of the biggest earners the mob had seen since Capone, and the youngest individual in *Fortune* magazine's survey of "The 50 Biggest Mafia Bosses."

—Fredric Dannen,
Vanity Fair,
February 1991

Michael Franzese has a lot to pray for. Before he was born again, he was a family man. The family was the Colombo crime family. And Michael Franzese was a captain, one of the richest and most powerful men in the mob.

—Bernard Goldberg,
"48 Hours,"
May 1991

I wouldn't want to be in Michael Franzese's shoes. I don't think his life expectancy is very substantial.

—Edward McDonald,
former attorney-in-charge,
Organized Crime Strike Force,
Eastern District of New York

He will get whacked.

—Bernie Welsh,
retired FBI organized crime expert
and legendary mob hunter

He's a fascinating person. What he did was intriguing. It took a lot of time and energy to dissect what he did.

—Jerry Bernstein,
former special attorney,
U.S. Department of Justice;
special agent,
Organized Crime Strike Force,
Eastern District of New York

I pray for Michael every night.

—Tina Franzese,
Michael's mother

That God teamed an ex-cop and an ex-Mafia capo is truly proof that the ground at the foot of the cross is level—and that God has a sense of humor. The evidence is compelling that Michael is the real deal—both who he was in the "life," and who he is today in the faith.

—Rob Michaels,
personal representative of Michael Franzese,
founder of Lord & Michaels Entertainment,
and former law enforcement officer

BLOOD COVENANT

MICHAEL
FRANZESE

HE QUIT THE MOB AND LIVED

WHITAKER
HOUSE

Publisher's Note: The first part of this book was derived from *Quitting the Mob*, © 1992 by Michael Franzese and Dary Matera. *Blood Covenant* brings the reader up-to-date with the story of Michael Franzese's life and ministry from the point where *Quitting the Mob* had concluded.

BLOOD COVENANT

Michael Franzese
www.michaelfranzese.com

ISBN-13: 978-0-88368-867-0
ISBN-10: 0-88368-867-0
Printed in the United States of America
© 2003 by Michael Franzese

1030 Hunt Valley Circle
New Kensington, PA 15068
www.whitakerhouse.com

Library of Congress Cataloging-in-Publication Data

Franzese, Michael.
Blood covenant : the Michael Franzese story / Michael Franzese.
p. cm.
ISBN 0-88368-867-0
1. Franzese, Michael. 2. Criminals—United States—Biography. 3. Mafia—United States—Biography. 4. Criminals—Rehabilitation—United States—Biography. 5. Converts—United States—Biography. I. Title.
HV6248.F674 A295 2003
364.1'092—dc21
2002156454

4 5 6 7 8 9 10 11 12 13 14 **ШJ** 14 13 12 11 10 09 08 07 06

Dedication

In loving memory of my dear mother-in-law, Irma Garcia.

Acknowledgments

To my friend and adviser, Rob Michaels, thank you for making this book possible.

To Harold McDougal, thank you for the hours of hard work you contributed to organizing my thoughts.

A special thank you to my valued assistant, Christine, for caring as much as you do and for being a true friend of the family. You are very much appreciated.

To Tina and Maria, my eldest daughters, who have endured all of the difficult times to become such lovely and talented young ladies. I love you both so very much. To my son John, whose strong support and dedication have made me proud to have him by my side. To my lovely daughter Miquelle, who came into this life when we needed you most. You have been a constant source of joy. To my lovely daughter Amanda, whose spirit so closely resembles my own. I love you dearly. To my namesake, Michael Jr. In you I see so much of myself. Use your abundant talents wisely. And finally, to my most cherished baby, Julia. You are truly Daddy's little girl, my bundle of joy. I thank God for blessing me with all of you.

To my most precious wife, Camille, my partner for life. I thank you for the past seventeen years. I thank you for never leaving my side. I thank you for being you. I love you, honey, "forever and ever and always."

And finally, thank You, God for allowing me to glorify You in my work.

—Michael Franzese

Cammy's Acknowledgments

To my beloved mother, thank you for your unconditional love, your patience, and your understanding. You were my very best friend. At times, I feel so lost without you. Your voice remains a constant echo in my ear throughout my day. I can hear you encouraging me to always be the woman that God wants me to be. I miss you more than you could ever know.

The seeds that you planted are growing so abundantly, you would be overjoyed. You were right about Michael, Mom. You had the vision long ago. Thank you for your faithfulness, your endless prayers, and for planting a seed in my heart when I was a little girl. I pray that I can be like you, Mother—a woman after God's own heart. You were the woman in Proverbs, "the wife of noble character." I will cherish the memories of our lives together until my last breath.

To my father, thank you for caring for me as much as you do, Dad. I know you love me and I will always love you. Thank you for being such a wonderful and caring grandfather to all of your grandchildren. They all adore you. I know how much you miss Mom. I will always do my best to care for you and to comfort your aching heart. From your "Skumpy."

To my beautiful children, thank you for inspiring me to be the best mother I can be. Miquelle, Amanda, and Michael Jr., thank you for carrying me through all the years we spent alone. My darling, Julia, thank you for being our thanksgiving gift to God for bringing Daddy home to us. You are all amazing gifts from God and I am blessed to be your mother. I am always here for you. You are all my heart.

To my dearest husband, thank you for all your wisdom, strength, and amazing courage in the face of all the obstacles you had to overcome. Thank you for always putting your family first. Thank you for allowing God to use you in such a meaningful way, all for His glory. You always have been and always will be my hero, honey. Thank you for loving me. I love you more then mere words can express. Forever, my love!

Contents

Note to the Reader

Dear Reader,

Please allow me to tell my story in the language of the street. Bear with me as I speak of "made men" and of being "straightened out," and as I talk about "cops" and "feds" and of someone "rolling over" on his friends. This is how I experienced it, and I speak here in the way of my former life because I want you, the reader, to experience it with me.

—Michael Franzese

Foreword by Dary Matera

> What lies ahead for Michael Franzese? A successful
> career producing movies and dealing in real estate?
> Personal appearances witnessing and giving his
> testimony as a born-again Christian? A seduction back
> into the mob? A bullet? Depending upon whom one
> speaks to, all are possibilities.
>
> —From the epilogue of *Quitting the Mob*

When I tapped out those words in 1991 to begin the epilogue
of Michael Franzese's first autobiography, *Quitting the Mob*, I
never would have imagined that I would be writing the foreword
to an updated version of that book a dozen years later. Actually, I
counted myself among those who wouldn't have taken the fat end
of a hundred-to-one bet that he would still be breathing.

But a funny thing happened on the road to Michael Franzese's apparently inevitable funeral: he never died.

To the contrary, most of the other possibilities for his life that
I put forth in the epilogue of *Quitting the Mob* have come true.
There have been movie projects, concert promotions, CD releases,
real estate deals, and speaking engagements. How has Franzese
pulled it off? Most mob-busting district attorneys and FBI agents
whom I've spoken with in the last decade insist that it's been
"business" as usual because Michael never really quit the mob.

But I've seen no evidence to support that theory. Quite the
opposite, actually. What I have noticed above all is that Michael's

Christian testimony has come to dominate his life, especially in recent years.

I have to admit, I was skeptical about his conversion for a long time. His first few years as a Christian were rough, and he had some notable stumbles when it came to living out his faith. Very few Christians I know have had Los Angeles Police Department SWAT teams burst into their homes with guns drawn, ordering everybody, including small children, to hit the deck. The "backward thinking" detailed in *Quitting the Mob*—wrong was right, gangsters were the good guys, and cops and prosecutors were the bad guys in Michael's world—appeared to be too ingrained in him to ever change. I was particularly dismayed that he hadn't cleaned up his *Sopranos*-like gangster street language. It wasn't uncommon to hear him talk about the love of Jesus one minute and then drop a string of obscenities the next.

When I expressed these misgivings to his longsuffering wife Cammy—the beautiful dancer who helped bring Michael to God and inspired him to give up his criminal empire—she would just smile and say, "Give him time, Dary. Rome wasn't built in a day." Cammy's unwavering belief in Michael made me recall what she wrote in her part of the *Quitting the Mob* epilogue: "I know I changed his life, but it wasn't me in the flesh....God said that through this woman I'll save Michael Franzese. God wanted to save him. God could see into Michael's heart."

Little by little, the seed Cammy planted in Michael's heart in 1985 has sprouted and grown into a sturdy tree, proving yet again that God is infinitely patient and has His own timetable. Michael's heavy-handed old ways and his paralyzing backward thought process have slowly receded. Along with them, the tough-guy street language also faded away.

And that was just the beginning. Eventually, Michael's all-consuming passion to make enormous amounts of money began to take a backseat. Replacing it was an intensified desire not only to walk the walk of a Christian but also to take an active part in spreading the Good News of God's abounding love and the gift of redemption through Jesus Christ. What prompted this was the courageous battle his mother-in-law, Irma, waged against an ultimately fatal illness that she came to accept as God's will. The firsthand experience of being with a cheerful, upbeat Christian preparing to "go home" moved Michael deeply.

Michael's charitable music and entertainment company, Breaking Out, was originally designed as an operation geared to help disadvantaged young men and women get a foothold in the music, motion picture, and sports industries. Today, it's been transformed into a full-fledged ministry that uses the Internet and personal appearances to get the message out.

In late 2002, I turned on the television one evening and was flabbergasted to see my old mob pal Michael giving his testimony on Paul and Jan Crouch's popular cable television show *Praise the Lord*. Seeing him sitting and chatting comfortably with guest host Dwight Thompson compelled me to circle back to the same nagging question that millions of others must have been thinking at that very same moment: how come this guy's still alive?

How indeed, especially considering that he's lived a very public life since quitting the mob. He never went into the Witness Protection Program, and he kicked off his public speaking career in 1995 after being released from prison. He traveled to the training camps of professional football, baseball, basketball, and hockey teams to warn wealthy young athletes about the dangers of gambling. The high-profile effort eventually moved to the collegiate level as well. I remember driving to Arizona State University one sunny afternoon in the late 1990s to watch him pace back and forth on the stage as big as life, telling the wide-eyed audience to stay away from people like he used to be.

"If the mob wants to waste this guy, he's sure giving them enough chances," I thought to myself at the time.

But as he bowed his head to pray on *Praise the Lord* that night, the mystery of his survival was revealed in an enlightening rush. Michael Franzese has been untouchable all these years because he's under the protection of Father God. God has plans for Michael, big plans, that are only now being brought to fruition.

The gangster turned baby Christian has matured rapidly. He has a powerful story to share, one about God's love and forgiveness. It's a story about even the most treacherous and violent of people being lifted out of darkness and into the light. If Michael Franzese can turn his life around, not only in words but also in deeds and a refocused dedication to what's really important, then anybody can. If Michael Franzese can reverse fifty years of backward thinking and finally get that good versus bad thing down, then no one is beyond hope.

Michael's is a story of a life pulled from the gloomiest pit and gloriously resurrected. Praise the Lord indeed!

Dary Matera
Chandler, Arizona

Introduction

There's an old saying that the only way to leave the Mafia is in a coffin. Members are pledged to a lifetime of secrecy and to quit would be to arouse suspicion that you are cooperating with the police or federal agents. Such breaches of faith are punished with death.

Michael Franzese says he's willing to take that risk. He will not betray his former crime associates and then disappear into the federal Witness Protection Program.... If he holds to what he has promised...it will mark the first time that a high-ranking member of the Mafia will publicly walk away from his past.

—*Life* magazine, 1987

It's been sixteen years since *Life* magazine published the story that included the above excerpt. I had granted *Life* an interview while serving time at the federal correctional institution at Terminal Island, California. But the article took even me by surprise.

"Quitting the Mafia!" the headline screamed, and there I was in living color, sprawled across two large pages. That was definitely not cool, considering that I had to share the prison yard with fifteen other fellow mob guys. As soon as the warden got wind of the article and the uproar it was causing, he called me into his office and asked me if I had a death wish. I had a very hard time convincing him not to lock me up in solitary for my own protection. In the end, he made me sign a waiver absolving the prison of any liability in the event that I met an untimely demise during my stay in his establishment.

It all began with an innocent enough statement I had made to the reporter who wrote the story. I was tired of a lifetime of battling law enforcement, I said. I had five prior indictments and five trials (albeit five victories). The last trial had been a six-month battle with Rudy Giuliani's cracker-jack organized crime lieutenants. And while all of this had been going on in one arena, I had also been battling to free my father from a fifty-year prison sentence he was serving because the feds had hit him with a bad rap in 1967. He had been a big catch, a superstar in organized crime.

With all of this, there had been endless investigations, grand juries, subpoenas, undercover operations, surveillance tapes, wiretaps, electronic bugs, and informants. At least the lawyers did well. The legal bills seemed to never cease. And it all gets to you after a while and wears you down—even if you are in the business of organized crime.

Just a year earlier, I had taken a plea to a ninety-nine-count federal racketeering indictment. I was fortunate to be able to wrap up in that one plea agreement all pending charges against me. In exchange, I would do a ten-year prison sentence and pay fines and restitution of $15 million. It was a pretty good deal, considering that the Justice Department had put in motion an unprecedented crackdown against the New York mob.

For the most part, the feds liked the deal, too. They were anxious to rack up some kind of conviction against me.

I had it all figured out. I could do five years in a place close to my new home in Los Angeles. There, my wife Cammy could visit me regularly. She would have enough money to last her until I got home. She had our baby daughter to keep her occupied, as well as another on the way. Five years away from her newlywed husband would not be a walk in the park, but she could survive it.

True, she was only twenty-one years old and drop-dead gorgeous. But she was very special, not like so many other young girls. She would make it because she loved me.

Cammy's mom was in my corner, too. What a great lady! She would help keep Cammy strong. Then there was my real ace in the hole...but I'll get to that.

And as for this "quitting the mob" nonsense, I wasn't concerned about that. The guys back in New York knew I wasn't quitting anything. It simply wasn't permitted. It didn't matter what I had said publicly. A few of the old hard-liners might get their feathers ruffled, but I could handle that.

In the old days, you could deny the very existence of the mob, but that was before wiretaps and bugging devices, and all you had was the uncorroborated word of mob turncoats. So you couldn't prove that this secret organization even existed. Not even J. Edgar Hoover believed it. Or so he said. But new surveillance and eavesdropping technology had changed all that. With their news toys in tow, the feds were definitely armed and dangerous, and soon the secrets of the Mafia were being brought to light.

Our own people were caught on tape, talking about most everything—the business, the sit-downs, the killings. Nothing was sacred. The feds even came up with a recording of our ultra-secret induction ritual. So, as far as I was concerned, admitting to my membership in the mob was a given. That was no big revelation, certainly not one worthy of a major headline. Besides, I had a plan.

I still had some cash left, even after the feds had taken their chunk, and the sunshine and beaches of the Golden State had become a lot more appealing to me than the coffee shops of Brooklyn. Plus, Cammy was there.

But after fifteen years in the mob, I knew what it was all about. Like it or not, I had taken an oath, and I would stand by that oath—even if I had my doubts.

So I would do my five years in the pen and then do five more on parole in L.A., a world away from the guys in Brooklyn. Everyone knew the feds were all over wise guy parolees. You associate with other "made" guys, and you're back in the joint. The judge had slapped another five years probation onto my own sentence with the same deal—no contact with the boys while under supervision.

So maybe we sneak a few meetings here and there, and I send in some cash when I make a score, but that's it. So I figured I had maybe fifteen years during which I would have to lay low, away from the bosses. I had gotten an excused leave of absence courtesy of the feds. At the end of it all, maybe they'd forget about me. You know, out of sight, out of mind.

The feds were slamming the bosses with huge indictments, and guys were turning informant left and right. Who would even be left at the end? I had a new life in L.A. and could live happily ever after with Cammy and the kids.

Yeah, I had it all figured out. What a plan! Everything seemed right.

But somehow it all felt wrong, and within days of the *Life* article, my well-thought-out "brilliant" plan began to unravel. Looking back now, I realize that nothing went according to my plan. That goes to show how smart I was. I could never have imagined the incredible turn of events that would shape the course of my life over the next fifteen years, events that would have nearly everyone in law enforcement who knew my story predicting that I would soon be another victim of a classic mob hit.

And why not? It happened to us "made" guys all the time. It was a part of the life I had come to know, the life I had sworn never to betray. Many of my former associates had met with that fate. At least three of my "brothers," those who took the oath with me that Halloween night in 1975, are no longer with us. This is serious business. It's a matter of life and death.

I'm not talking about the *Sopranos* here. There's no semi-dysfunctional mob boss calling the shots in this case. This is the real thing. When the boss says you're dead, you'd better be in hiding or in the Witness Protection Program, or you are dead. You violate the oath, you betray the family, and you're dead. That's all there is to it.

I never underestimate the power or ability of my former associates. We didn't control the underworld in this country since the turn of the century for nothing. In the real mob world, Tony Soprano would have been found dead in the trunk of a car soon after he spilled his guts to that cagey therapist. We can't take anything away from these men. They know their business, and they're good at what they do. No one knows that better than I do.

So why am I still alive? Why am I not in hiding?

After all, I violated the oath. I no longer live within the confines of the secret organization we call La Cosa Nostra (which means "this thing of ours"). What happened? Did I buy the right to live by paying the family $10 million from the stolen gasoline-tax money? Ed McDonald, the former strike force chief in Brooklyn, thinks so.

And what about my father, the legendary John "Sonny" Franzese? He's lived the life for fifty years now. A stand-up guy, as tough as they come, he proposed my membership in the family. So I let him down, too. The oath comes before everything in the life. It's a blood covenant, stronger even then the blood that binds a father to his son. Why did my own father allow me to live? Did the mob slip up big time?

Make no mistake. I'm alive by design, not by accident. Don't ever sell my former associates short. It could have been over for me a long time ago, a just reward for my past involvement in a life that was contrary to the laws of God and of man. And it might be over for me tomorrow. I take nothing for granted. But then again, it might be over for you tomorrow, too. Are we guaranteed even another breath?

For me, it no longer matters. Why?

The answer can be found in the pages of this book. My life has taken a dramatic turn. This turn has been described as "amazing," "unbelievable," "improbable," and "miraculous," but maybe it's none of these. Or maybe it's all of these. You decide. Whatever the case, it is my hope that by the time you reach the end of this book, your life will have changed, too. I searched for and found the truth, the truth that sets men free, and I found it in a blood covenant.

Michael Franzese
Los Angeles, California

Book 1

The Old Life

– 1 –

To understand me and the path I took in life, it is necessary to first understand my father, mob enforcer John Franzese, better known as Sonny. He, more than any other person, influenced the direction of my early life. Dad's friend Phil Steinberg tells a story of my dad's activities in 1964 New York that serves to introduce the flamboyant character who is my father.

Steinberg was sitting in his luxurious Manhattan office at 1650 Broadway one day, feeling on top of the world. The rock and roll record company he had started with two Brooklyn buddies had taken off. The Shangri-Las, a hot teenage girl-group, had hit No. 5 with a song called "Remember (Walkin' in the Sand)." A second group, the Lovin' Spoonful, was a year away from becoming a monster rock band that would release seven top-ten songs in a row. The record company itself, Kama Sutra/Buddah Records, was destined to become a giant in the industry.

Steinberg was only twenty-three years old at the time, and his partners, Artie Ripp and Hy Mizrahi, were just a few years older. Still, it appeared nothing could stop them. That is until Steinberg's secretary, an Ann Margret look-alike named Sandy, knocked on his office door one day.

"Phil," she announced, "you have a visitor. Morris Levy."

"Send him in," the boss said.

He smiled as he greeted Levy, a tough-guy record producer who had founded Roulette Records and would one day own

Strawberries, an eighty-store record chain. Levy didn't return the smile.

"We have a problem, Phil," he said.

"What's up?"

"The Shangri-Las," he said. "Nice kids! Great group! Great song!"

"Yeah, we got lucky," Steinberg said. "So what's the problem?"

"They're mine."

"No."

"They're mine, and I want my cut."

Steinberg felt the muscles in his neck tighten. A burly ex-football player, he suppressed an urge to toss Levy out of his office. That wouldn't have been a wise option. Steinberg knew the streets: Levy was an associate of Gaetano "Tommy the Big Guy" Vastola, a vicious soldier in the DeCavalcante Mafia family. He was also the childhood friend of Vincent "the Chin" Gigante, a menacing hood on his way to becoming the boss of the Genovese family. In short, Levy was big trouble.

"I'll discuss this with my partners, and we'll get back to you," Steinberg said, forcing a smile. "I'm sure we can work this out to your satisfaction."

"Make some calls. Check around," Levy advised. "I'm confident you'll do the right thing."

After Levy left, Steinberg called a meeting of his partners and explained to them what had just happened, and together they sank into a collective despair. Aside from his connections, Levy had legendary moxie, a boldness that bordered on insanity. He had once trademarked the term "rock and roll" and forced record companies to pay him a royalty to use those magic words. In the end, the government had to step in and stop his hustle by declaring the term "rock and roll" to be generic. With that kind of audacity and that measure of Mafia weight behind him, Levy wasn't about to back off of his claim on the Shangri-Las and Kama Sutra/Buddah.

The upstart record producers were in this state of depression when Dad passed by. His presence was not unusual, for he frequently dropped by.

Dad enjoyed popping into the record company as he made his Manhattan rounds. A few times, he even took Mom and us kids with him and showed us around the bustling recording studios. He liked checking on the progress of Phil and his friends. They were street punks from Brooklyn, just like him, and he admired their spunk. They had no business trying to crash the record industry, but they'd pushed their way in and hit it big. So more power to them, he thought.

"What's the matter with you guys?" Dad said that day. "You look like all your dogs died!"

Steinberg tried to brush it off. He didn't want his friend to know. Sonny might take it as asking for a favor, and Steinberg knew better than to ask. You ask for something, and you keep paying it back the rest of your life.

"Everything's okay. We're just a bit tired," was his reply.

Dad laughed. "Tired? You guys should be dancin' in the streets. What's wrong?"

Steinberg shrugged.

Dad grew serious. "Hey Phil, what? Am I your friend?" he said, tapping his chest with both hands. "You can't tell me your problems?"

Steinberg glanced up, and a smile cut through his rough but handsome features. This wasn't a "favor." It was a friend offering to help out a friend. And that was perfectly all right.

"Sonny," he confided, "Moe Levy came by today. He said he owns a piece of the Shangri-Las, and he wants his cut."

Dad raised his eyebrows in surprise. "Moe Levy said that? You must be kidding."

"No joke, Sonny."

Dad's deep brown eyes panned the room. He took in the worried faces of the three young men sitting at the table.

"You boys worked too hard to have the likes of Moe Levy shake you down," he said to them. "Don't worry about it."

And that was the end of the conversation.

Steinberg didn't see Moe Levy again until a few weeks later, when they bumped into each other at a nearby recording studio. Levy was all handshakes and smiles, complimenting Steinberg on the Shangri-Las' smash follow-up hit, "Leader of the Pack," along with a third hit Kama Sutra had produced, "Come a Little Bit Closer" by Jay and the Americans. When Levy made no mention of his cut, Steinberg searched his eyes for the slightest sign of indignation, any hint that a message had been delivered, but he couldn't detect a thing.

The Shangri-Las, Jay and the Americans, the Lovin' Spoonful, Sha Na Na, Gladys Knight and the Pips, and scores of other rock performers went on to bring tens of millions of dollars into Kama Sutra/Buddah's coffers. By the end of the 1970s, Buddah Records had become one of the largest independent record companies in the world. And no one ever came by demanding a cut again. Steinberg swore by this story, and it does seem typical of my father at work.

— 2 —

Those who knew Dad well in his heyday considered him to be something of a chameleon. He could change his colors so fast, over such a wide range of personalities, that he could have fooled any dozen psychiatrists into thinking he was certifiable. Actually, he *was* certifiable. His Army career was cut short in 1944 when the military shrinks made him for a "psychoneurotic with pronounced homicidal tendencies" and recommended that he be busted out of the service without delay.

He was.

The Army docs, however, had focused on a sliver of the Franzese psyche and failed to spot the seeds of the "other" Sonnys waiting to sprout. By limiting him to his baser instincts, they were the first to make the deadly mistake many of his victims would later repeat: they underestimated my father. Behind Dad's menacing eyes worked a shrewd mind honed to a razor's edge. His intellect, often purposely hidden, coupled with his cold-blooded fearlessness to give him an advantage over others.

Dad's chameleon ways extended beyond his personality. He was a powerfully built man, about five-foot-nine in height with short black hair sprinkled with gray. Early mug shots reveal a gruesome, bull-necked man with dark, close-cropped hair, a widow's peak, a boxer's squashed nose, dark stubble, and squinting eyes that seemed almost to burn demonically. He was a burly 200 pounds and, some said, pit-bull ugly. He looked every bit the street thug he was.

Other photos depict a man so different as to strain belief. Longer, styled hair speckled with dignified flecks of gray. Expensive, tailor-made suits draped over a leaner, 170-pound frame. Knock-'em-dead overcoats cut like a suit and fitting as snug as a blazer. Clean-shaven, meticulously groomed. Beaming smile. A crisp fedora with the brim cocked upward. And the Mafia prerequisites—a diamond pinkie ring and black pointed shoes.

At times, Dad resembled former middleweight champion Rocky Graziano, but as he matured, his features smoothed out more. His boxer's nose seemed to narrow and no longer dominated his face. In a *Life* magazine photo reprinted in 1988, he looked like singer Eddie Fisher, ex-husband of Liz Taylor.

Like the chameleon he was said to be, Dad's talent lay in adaptation. The higher he rose in the Colombo crime family, the more handsome and dignified his appearance became. Even his body movements changed over the years—from a plodding chunk of iron to an odd sort of grace, like a mountain lion who mesmerizes its victims with its athletic beauty before slashing them apart.

And Dad grew with each transformation. He was like a corporate executive rising from the mailroom to chairman of the board and looking the part every step of the way. From the streets of the Greenpoint section of Brooklyn (where he grew up riding shotgun on his Italian immigrant father's bakery truck) to the suburbs of Long Island, Dad soaked up each new surrounding and changed himself to fit it. On the streets, he enveloped himself in the image of the beast within and could paralyze the most fearless hit man with a stare. When he mingled with the moneyed of Manhattan, he could suppress the dragon and appear harmless. Not only did he learn to fit in, but he also came to dominate and control any circumstance and setting. Whether among the Mafia hierarchy, the affluent, or the nothing-to-lose street killers, Dad adapted, absorbed, and quickly controlled.

— 3 —

Dad was born in Naples, Italy, on February 6, 1919, the last son and next-to-last child of Carmine and Maria Franzese (they had eighteen children). Contrary to popular myth, Dad's parents (my grandparents) had established a foothold in America long before his birth. Grandfather was a baker, and he and Grandma traveled frequently between America and Italy to vacation in the homeland. After sixteen children, it became a tradition for Grandma to make the long voyage in the late stages of her pregnancies so that she could deliver in the homeland. Dad's birth has long given Mafia biographers and feature writers the mistaken impressions that he came to America as an infant with a newly immigrated family. It wasn't true.

What is true is that within the span of a decade, Dad rose from his father's bakery truck to become the underboss and heir apparent of the Colombo family, one of the five La Cosa Nostra crime families, established in 1931. These families were the Colombo, Gambino, Genovese, Bonanno, and Lucchese. The Colombo sect evolved from the Profaci-Magliocco family, though few today recognize the names of Joseph Profaci or Giuseppe Magliocco, the founding fathers.

Dad was brought into the Mafia by old-time Colombo capo Sebastian "Buster" Aloi. Little else is known about his recruitment and induction beyond the fact that tough street kids were frequently taken under the wing of founding Mafiosi as the five families built their armies in the 1930s, '40s and, '50s.

People's views on my father vary as widely as his personalities. Their feelings, then and now, are rooted in the circumstances of their acquaintance. Unfortunately, those who knew him at his most intense are not around to offer their insights. These would be the thirty-five or so individuals that, according to various law enforcement officials, he dispatched into another life, in assorted grisly ways, during his bloody rise up the Mafia ladder of success.

There remain enough of those who escaped his vengeance, who were true friends or hung out in the same neighborhoods, to paint a fascinating portrait of one of the Mafia's most powerful, most vicious, and, for a time, least publicized figures.

— 4 —

In the late 1940s, Dad purchased a parcel of land at Thirty-Seventh Avenue and Seventy-Sixth Street in Jackson Heights in Queens and constructed a personal playground he named the Orchid Room. The homey neighborhood tavern was a den of "made men" (men who had been formally initiated into the mob), and it doubled as the location of a thriving bookmaking operation. Dad's employees sold spirits and hope—and did well with each one of them.

In the decade following World War II, Jackson Heights was in its heyday. The Queens neighborhood was bustling with nightclubs, restaurants, pizza parlors, and ritzy apartments. Aside from the Orchid Room, things cooked all night at such places as the Dinner Bell, Bud's Bar, and the Blue Haven and Flying Tigers nightclubs. When the young and hip got hungry, they could grab a pepperoni pizza at fight announcer Angelo Palange's Savoy pizzeria on Roosevelt Avenue.

Despite the abundance of apartments and co-ops, Jackson Heights never was much of a family neighborhood, even at its best. As one longtime resident recalled, it was more of "the place everybody stashed their mistresses." Lots of things were "stashed" in Jackson Heights in the 1940s and '50s. Then, as now, the neighborhood was known for illegal activities. But the crimes of the 1940s sound almost romantic compared with those of today. Bookmaking (taking bets on horse races or other contests), shylocking (lending money at unlawful rates of interest), prostitution, shakedowns (extracting money by force), bar and restaurant skimming (illegally removing a portion of the sales), and tax cheating were the mainstays. The occasional "drop and drag" murder (killing someone in a bar or restaurant then dragging the body outside to avoid conflicts with the police) did little to keep the crowds away. And despite the unlawful activities, Jackson Heights was a safe area to take an evening stroll.

Not so today. Much of Jackson Heights has become the New York enclave of Colombian cocaine dealers and their desperate, crack-addicted clients. But that is now. This is about then. And then, Jackson Heights was happening.

"Sonny Franzese invaded the neighborhood like a one-man army," recalled Beau Matera, whose family owned the Dinner Bell Restaurant on Thirty-Seventh Avenue and Eighty-Third Street.

Dad's base had been Brooklyn, but Jackson Heights was hot after the war and began attracting the attention of everyone— from legitimate businessmen to nightclub operators and restauranteurs, and, as always, the mobsters. Dad's invasion was a bloodless coup because nobody was about to try and stop him. His reputation had preceded him.

"Funny thing," Matera continued, "Sonny's power had nothing to do with the fact that he was a 'capo' (captain) in the Colombo family. Most people didn't know, or didn't care, who he was connected with. His power came from within himself. The neighborhood didn't tremble at the thought of hidden Colombo armies keeping watch. They shook at the sight of Sonny Franzese walking down Thirty-Seventh Avenue."

The Matera family eventually sold the Dinner Bell to Tommy Grimaldi, one of Jackson Heights' top bookmakers, and Beau moved out West. The reasons behind this are interesting.

One of Grimaldi's activities was managing the Orchid Room for Dad. Matera befriended the gregarious, well-dressed, well-connected Grimaldi and frequently dropped by the Orchid Room to pass the time. He claims he wasn't there, however, the night it was Dad's turn to host a "drop and drag" party.

— 5 —

Those who were there recall it well. Dad was in a back corner talking with a slim young man. The patrons were aware of this because it was everyone's habit to keep one eye on Dad whenever he was in the room. Tensions were eased that evening because he and the visitor appeared to be friends. They were smiling, laughing, drinking, and talking. It was early in the morning, 2:00 or 3:00 A.M.

A shot suddenly pierced through the chatter and silenced the bar. The slim man crashed to the floor, his fingers still locked tightly around his own unused gun, drawn in an attempt to assassinate my father. Those who turned their heads say they saw Dad holding a smoking pistol. He quickly slid it back into the holster under his $500 suit and signaled for someone to take over. The slim man's body hardly hit the floor before it was dragged out of the place, and the fresh corpse was deposited on the sidewalk a block away. Before the drag men could make it back to the bar, the blood had already been mopped off of the floor.

According to witnesses, Dad then went about his business as if nothing had happened. No one prepped the crowd on how to handle what was to come. No one had to. Dad had reacted so fast that the would-be assassin never got his weapon aimed, but even a story of possible self-defense was not to be told to police. When cops arrived and questioned those remaining at the bar about the stiff down the block, no one in the Orchid Room seemed to have heard the shot. "Must have been dumped outta a car," more than one person helpfully surmised to the detectives.

Not much was ever known about the assassin. He was evidently some small-time hood nobody missed. Those at the bar that morning have trouble pinning down the exact year this happened—possibly sometime around 1948 or '49. What is significant, what they all remember, was Dad's reaction after the shooting. He sat in his usual corner, sipping a drink, talking with friends, laughing and enjoying himself, seemingly without a care in the world. He appeared oblivious to the fact that he had come within seconds of being killed, oblivious to the possibility that his life might lie in the hands of one person in the bar, one stranger, one out-of-towner who'd stopped by for a beer and didn't know the rules.

If even one person had talked about this incident, Dad would have been history. The police and the prosecuting attorneys wanted him bad. The shooting, regardless of who drew first, could have landed him a life sentence in prison. But nobody talked.

Soon after this incident, young Beau Matera was faced with the decision to either get into one of the crime families or to stop riding the edge. The reason he gave for his decision to move to Las Vegas was this: "I figured if you were gonna be a mobster, I mean really be a big-time mobster, you had to have nerves of steel like Sonny Franzese. You had to be able to take out your assassin, then sit there calmly sipping a drink while the police wandered about, asking everyone questions. I didn't have courage like that. Nobody had it like Sonny."

Nerves of steel! Those who knew Dad well nod at the description but quickly add that even that doesn't quite capture the strange measure of the man—or the power he commanded.

— 6 —

Bob Greene, a *Newsday* investigations editor, chronicled Dad's life in a riveting feature, "The Hood in Our Neighborhood," published on Christmas Eve, 1965: "He is a prototype of the rising young executive—aggressive, dynamic, moderate in his habits, a good family man, careful with money and so absorbed in his work that lunch, when he manages to find time for it, is usually a quick date-nut bread sandwich at Chock Full O' Nuts. He could be working for IBM, GM, or Chase Manhattan. But he isn't. He is John (Sonny) Franzese, 45...tabbed as the fastest rising young executive in the Cosa Nostra empire of crime. His business: supervision of underworld rackets in parts of Brooklyn, Manhattan, and Queens and in almost all of Nassau and Suffolk counties. The tools of his trade: greed, fear and, when necessary, the gun."

Sergeant Ralph Salerno, then the Mafia specialist for the New York City Police Department, added his expert opinion: "Sonny Franzese is the big corner in the Cosa Nostra. He has an extraordinary talent for organized crime. He knows when to compromise and when to get tough; he knows how to run a business and crime is a big business and, most important, he is an expert at not getting caught."

Greene continued, "The family boss is Joe Colombo of Brooklyn, an aging executive who is gradually paving the way for Franzese to take over completely. Operating under Franzese are six or more crime lieutenants, each of whom directs from ten to thirty crime *soldati* [soldiers], who in turn have their own individual criminal organizations."

This was Dad's world.

As diverse as his personalities were, Dad towed the line when it came to the Cosa Nostra's strict laws, even when it affected his private life. In the early 1940s, he met and married a beautiful German blonde named Ann Schiller. After a rocky start, they settled down, had three children, and were relatively content...that is until the mob became involved.

Dad received word that his higher-ups felt the independent-minded Mrs. Franzese, who longed to be an actress, couldn't be controlled. Dad was given the message that his career prospects would greatly improve in the mob if he found a more subservient Italian wife. Always the obedient soldier, he promptly left Ann Schiller, a process made easier by an obliging Mrs. Franzese.

Shortly afterward, he met my mom, Christina Capobianco, a slim, seventeen-year-old telephone operator who doubled as a coat-check girl and roving photographer at the renowned Stork Club in Manhattan. The exclusive restaurant and nightspot had a four-star celebrity clientele that included Marilyn Monroe, Grace Kelly, Ernest Hemingway, Damon Runyon, and radio broadcaster and journalist Walter Winchell. Genovese family boss Frank Costello was also a regular there, as were a healthy influx of other top-echelon mobsters. Mom was beautiful and dark-haired, and it is said that she was a pet of Stork Club owner Sherman Billingsley and a special favorite of frequent club guest Montgomery Clift, the brooding movie star linked in the newspapers with Elizabeth Taylor. Dad quickly replaced Clift, who was slow to scrap with an infamous killer over a skinny coat-check girl.

Dad and Mom fell madly in love, and according to one version of their romance, they capped a whirlwind courtship by getting married on July 24, 1951, one day after her eighteenth birthday. Dad was thirty-two. They were "the Mobster and the Coat-Check Girl," and had there been television movies back

33

then, their life together certainly would have made for a good one.

− 7 −

As young as she was, Mom had been married before. At sixteen, she had hooked up with a handsome, dark-haired soldier named Louis Grillo, and their teenage love affair, although it barely survived a year, had produced me. From the beginning of my Mom's second marriage, Sonny Franzese accepted me as his own, and he was, therefore, the only dad I ever knew.

Mom had to return the favor three times over when Dad's three children by his former marriage showed up on her doorstep one day after their mother left them to pursue a career. Whether this was of her own choosing or at Dad's request, no one ever knew for sure. Mom and Dad filled the house further by having three children of their own.

Despite what he did for a living, Dad was a doting father who played in the yard with us kids, took us to the local amusement park, and didn't favor any one of us over the others, despite the "yours," "mine," and "ours" nature of our brood. Sometimes he'd give Mom the night off, proclaim himself to be the world's greatest cook, and make an elaborate calzone dinner for the whole family. (This Italian delicacy consists of stuffing dough with cheese, sausage, pepperoni, peppers, and tomato sauce, or any variation of the above, and baking it in the oven.) The excitement of "Daddy's making dinner!" always made for a joyful evening.

When he wanted to discourage us from various harmful activities, Dad would resort to making up wild stories. We sons, for instance, were discouraged from owning or riding motorcycles by his vivid tale of a grisly accident that transformed a handsome athlete into a drooling, brain-dead paraplegic. His anti-drug speech was dressed up by the tragic story of another "friend" who descended from being a successful businessman with a beautiful wife and family to being a crazed freak who crawled the gutters, coughing, vomiting, and debasing himself a dozen different ways to feed his habit. These stories had their desired effect because they frightened us.

— 8 —

Dad's ability to adapt, learn, and then control every situation can be seen in how he operated his "other" family, especially in how he handled their interests in the entertainment industry. He had a piece of the infamous Linda Lovelace film *Deep Throat*, which revolutionized the motion-picture industry by bringing hard-core pornography out of the shadows and into neighborhood theaters. He also had a cut of the classic blood-and-gore horror film *The Texas Chainsaw Massacre*.

But his strongest suit was recognizing very early on the changes coming to the music industry and becoming a pioneer of sorts in the record business.

In January 1964, the record music industry changed dramatically when the Beatles hit No. 1 on *Billboard's* music chart with "I Want to Hold Your Hand." The song stayed there for seven weeks and was finally toppled by another Beatles song, "She Loves You." By the time the mop-haired Englishmen crossed the Atlantic to appear on *The Ed Sullivan Show*, they were already a sensation here. And their appearance on that television show marked the long-awaited explosion of rock and roll (which had been burning like a lit fuse all during the previous Elvis decade).

Most of the entertainment-minded mobsters rejected this new longhaired music. They deemed it a passing fad, preferring to place their bets on the continuing success of the kind of music being recorded by Frank Sinatra, Dean Martin, Tony Bennett, Sammy Davis Jr., Steve Lawrence, Perry Como, Nelson Riddle, Andy Williams, Connie Francis, Brenda Lee, and the McGuire Sisters. But Dad saw the future, and the future rocked. He made

New York's famous Tin Pan Alley part of his rounds, as we saw earlier. He kept a close watch on what was happening in the infant rock business, made friends, and took notes. Then, in the mid-1960s, he formed a lucrative booking agency with Norby Walters, which began with popular New York area performers and rock groups, and later branched out to include a glittering array of black superstars. However, it was Dad's relationship with Phil Steinberg and his upstart record company that provides the most insight into this multidimensional man.

As we have seen, during his Tin Pan Alley rounds, Dad befriended Steinberg, and he subsequently allowed the young record producer to become one of the few people outside the Mafia who were close to him

Steinberg's own story is not without drama, so much so that it was optioned as a television miniseries. Much of the drama involves how his life intertwined with my father's. Steinberg was a dead-end Brooklyn street kid who teamed up with his two partners to form a record company in the early 1960s. They were in the right place at the right time, and the company took off. Along with the previously mentioned superstar acts, the Kama Sutra/Buddah roster included the Isley Brothers, Lena Horne, Rod McKuen, Paul Anka, Charlie Daniels, Curtis Mayfield, Bill Withers, Captain Beefheart, Melanie, and dozens of others. By 1975, the company had crashed and burned, a victim of sex, drugs, bad business, vicious infighting, relentless investigations, and its ominous reputation as a mob company.

The improbable rise and fall of Buddah Records was aided by my father all right—but not in the way it was commonly believed. And not in the way the IRS, the FBI, and the New York State attorney general's office, which hounded Buddah for years, suspected.

Dad admired Steinberg and became, for lack of a better description, his guardian angel. According to Steinberg, it was all on an unspoken level. To this day, he doesn't even know for certain that Dad intervened in the Moe Levy incident.

"Who knows?" Steinberg said. "You never knew. He was my friend, a close friend, but I never knew. That was Sonny's way. He had a thousand people who owed him favors. But he had ten thousand who thought they owed him a favor but weren't sure. You had to go through that dance in your own mind. That was one of Sonny's strengths, the illusion that a debt was owed to him."

Steinberg's description of Dad was filled with the usual contradictions. It was easy to see that he considered Dad to be a benevolent father figure in his life, and yet he stated, "Sonny was what we called an 'iceman.' When he walked into a room, everyone's blood ran cold."

Sometimes the two sides of Dad could be seen at once. Steinberg recalled, "We were going to a boxing match at Sunnyside Gardens one night. I'm walking with Sonny, and he bumps into some big guy in the crowd. Nothing hard, nothing intentional, just a typical bump. The guy freaks out and starts screaming and yelling and calling Sonny vile names. I couldn't believe it. I'm figuring Sonny's going to blow him away any second or rip out his throat with his bare hands. Instead, Sonny just calmly walked away.

"So the idiot follows, still cursing and threatening Sonny. Now I'm getting mad. I'm about to deck the guy when Sonny holds me back. He shakes his head, shrugs, and talks in a soft, calm voice: 'Phil, let it go. Let it go. Who cares? He's nothing. We don't have to do anything. Guys like that, somebody will do it for you.' I was amazed at how calm Sonny was and how, with all his power, he didn't let the guy call his hand."

"Of course," Steinberg added, "for all I know, Sonny had the guy followed and seriously harmed before he got home."

— 9 —

Another incident that was burned into Steinberg's mental file could have imperiled their relationship.

"It wasn't long after I first met Sonny," Steinberg remembered. "How we met I can't really remember, but at the time, we weren't that close. We were at a party, and I brought my wife. She didn't drink much, so when she had a drink at the party, it loosened her up. Sonny came over, and I introduced them. My wife stared at him for a couple of beats, then brightened up and became animated.

"'I know you!' she exclaimed. 'I've seen you in the newspapers!' She then brought her arms down like she was holding an imaginary machine gun. 'You're the guy who goes *rat-tat-tat-tat-tat-tat!*'

"I cringed, as the room suddenly went silent. It was like one of those E. F. Hutton commercials where everybody shuts up and leans in to listen. Only this time everyone was holding his breath. The silence lasted for what seemed like an eternity. Then Sonny started laughing. Relieved, everybody else started laughing. Sonny put his arms around my wife and said, 'Phil, you got yourself some lady here.'"

Dad's power extended beyond Brooklyn, Jackson Heights, Manhattan, and Tin Pan Alley. It coursed throughout the Colombo family, was felt by the other families, and even reached across the country. Famous people knew and respected him.

"We were out at Al and Nick's in Manhattan one night, having dinner and watching one of the shows," Steinberg recalled. "Sonny was in good spirits, enjoying himself to the hilt. Joe Colombo comes in, and he and Sonny started getting playful. Before you know it, Sonny had Joe's head in a headlock. One flexed muscle and Sonny could have snapped the boss's neck like a stalk of spaghetti. Sonny could have climbed the final rung to the top, but that wasn't his way. They were just playing. And, anyway, Sonny already ran the family.

"A little later, Frank Sinatra comes over to our table. Sinatra leaned down, took Sonny's hand, and kissed his ring. Kissed his ring! Right in front of Colombo. Unreal!"

There was more than one reason that Sinatra was so respectful to Dad that evening. Dad usually had a ringside table whenever Sinatra, or Sammy Davis Jr., or any number of entertainers opened anywhere in New York. He was a regular in their dressing rooms backstage. He was not an unwanted presence, because the superstars were keenly aware of the power Dad wielded.

Another reason Sinatra paid his respects to Dad that night was because Dad had treated his son so well. In 1963, some years before the incident Steinberg witnessed, Frank Sinatra Jr. was playing at the San Su San nightclub off the Jericho Turnpike in Mineola, Long Island. The crowds were thin, and the young singer, struggling to step out of his father's immense shadow, was bombing. A call came to Dad from Chicago. The next night and for many nights afterward, it was standing room only at the San Su San. The crowd, made up mostly of hit men, mob soldiers, bookmakers, and extortionists accompanied by their floozies and favorite prostitutes, cheered wildly and treated every Frank Jr. number as if it were the greatest thing they'd ever heard. Standing ovations followed virtually every song. Buoyed by this boisterous response, young Sinatra cranked it up a few notches and gave a rousing performance equal to the unexpected adulation. The entertainment press was alerted to the San Su San happening, captured the unrestrained enthusiasm in the room, and dubbed Frank Jr. a hit. That brought in the legitimate crowds and, no doubt, the elder Sinatra's ring-kissing gratitude. It wasn't the first or the last time Dad packed a house for a struggling entertainer, and if Dad had a good time, there was no favor to repay.

– 10 –

"Hey," Steinberg continued. "I know everything about Sonny. Things I can't even tell you. I knew what he was and who he was and even who he killed. He was a hitter—*the* hitter. He swam in the biggest ocean and was the biggest, meanest, most terrifying shark in that ocean. Still is. I don't care how long he's been in jail or how old he is. He still is. He was an enforcer, and he did what he did better than anyone.

"And he was a great friend. My friendship with him caused me enormous problems with the police, district attorney, IRS, FBI, SEC. You name it, but it was worth it. He was always there for me. Always! Artie, Hy, and I were just kids from the Jewish ghetto running a record company that exploded into a $100 million operation before we learned what we were doing. But Sonny kept the wolves away, and he never asked for anything in return. That's why I love the guy so much."

I know it sounds so Hollywood: Sonny Franzese as the mob enforcer with a heart of gold, the benevolent godfather hovering protectively over some fellow Brooklynites trying to stake a claim in the record business and protecting them for no other reason than to be a pal. Yet from all accounts, Steinberg's improbable story checks out. The government agencies that tried so hard to figure Dad's angle in Buddah Records consistently came up empty.

There are those who laugh derisively at the image of my father as a benevolent godfather—or a benevolent anything. To them, he was a madman and a killer. And although his victims can't offer their opinions, there remain those who insist they were on his hit list and survived, or at least survived long enough to record their stories.

The best of these can be found in James Mills' twenty-nine-page *Life* magazine article published in August 1968. The epic story chronicled Dad's murder trial. Mills shadowed the Queens County, New York prosecutors for nine months, and, as Bob Greene did with "The Hood in Our Neighborhood," produced a lasting work of journalism.

Particularly engrossing were the sections detailing the terror of the witnesses testifying against Dad. As the trial date neared, the witnesses, including four convicted bank robbers, demanded to be taken to the courthouse in helicopters or armored cars. Their drivers reported that they cringed on the floor of the back-seats as they rode to the trial.

The stress of testifying against Dad and his fellow defendants is not hard to imagine. Nearing hysteria, one particular witness, John Rapacki, a convicted robber, told the prosecutors prior to testifying, "If Sonny hits the streets, he'll kill my wife. I know they'll kill her....They know they can hurt me by killing her.

"They're going to kill me. They're going to poison me right in prison. You don't know how powerful they are. They're more powerful than you....If Sonny beats this, he's gonna figure no one can touch him."

Not long after Rapacki expressed these views, the jury returned with its verdict of not guilty, and Dad walked away a free man.

– 11 –

I was so young when much of this took place that I can't say for sure what's true and what's not, but all this talk of murder, blood, guts, and savagery has always struck my mother as a complete fairy tale. Her views of the man she fell in love with, married, and has waited for with a devotion that would make Odysseus' wife, Penelope, blush, are startling in their contrast to the harsher images promoted by law enforcement officials.

"Boss of this, boss of that...the 'family.' What family?!" she exclaims. "I was Sonny's family. My children were his family. Sometimes, when I read the papers, I thought he had another wife and kids somewhere, because they were always talking about his 'family,' and it wasn't us.

"And this stuff about his being a killer. He couldn't stand the sight of blood! If one of the kids scraped their knee, Sonny turned his face away. He couldn't deal with it, and I had to take care of it. Then the next day I'd read in the newspapers about what a bloodthirsty killer he was.

"I didn't know that man in the newspapers. He wasn't my husband. He was the work of somebody's imagination."

Killer. Madman. Army psycho. Capo. Enforcer. King-in-waiting. Unselfish guardian angel. Gentle lover. Squeamish father.

Who was Sonny Franzese really? What is certain is that when my mother married him, she set an interesting and undeniably confusing course for my life. Was I destined to follow in my father's footsteps?

— 12 —

My mistrust of law enforcement officials had its roots in my childhood. One incident that occurred when I was only ten serves to illustrate this point. It was a warm afternoon in the late summer of 1961, and I was playing catch with a neighborhood friend in the front yard of our Long Island home.

"Throw it high. I want to jump for it!" I shouted to my friend.

He obeyed, hurling the baseball just above my head. I leaped and snagged it in the webbing of my leather glove.

"Throw it higher," I said, tossing the ball back. "I want to catch it like Mickey Mantle did against the Red Sox!"

This time the pitch was too high. The ball skittered off the top of my glove and rolled down the street. I chased after it and found it under the brown wing-tipped shoe of a big man with a craggy face wearing a tan overcoat. He opened his coat, flashed a badge, and pulled a huge black pistol from a shoulder holster.

"See this gun," he growled, shoving the barrel in my face. "This is for your father. Bang! Bang! He's dead!"

Those words and the sight of the massive weapon froze me in place. The thought of my father being killed paralyzed me with fear. I hated that evil detective, just as I would eventually grow to hate all the policemen and FBI agents and United States attorneys who, I believed, wanted to hurt my father.

"Go on, you little punk, get outta here," the cop said, waving the gun to shoo me away.

I ran off as fast as I could, but I remember that officer and his gun as if it happened yesterday.

That encounter was just the beginning of some tough times for us in the Long Island suburbs. There were other problems, some of them at home. After dinner one evening, about three months after that incident, I hid in the den and listened as my parents argued heatedly. I hated spying on them, but fear made me hang on their every word.

The topic of their discussion was my stepbrother and stepsisters. Mom wanted them returned to their own mother. Dad explained for the umpteenth time that his ex-wife wasn't cooperating.

"What am I supposed to do—throw them out in the streets?" my father shouted. "My hands are tied."

My eyes widened as I saw my stepbrother, Carmine, wander by on his way to the refrigerator. Carmine had heard this argument so many times before that he had become immune to it. Suddenly, Mom grabbed the barefooted Carmine and pushed him out the door into a blanket of fresh snow that had gathered on the porch. I ran from my hiding place and peered out the window. There I saw my stepbrother hopping up and down on the ice and snow. A wave of terror shot through me, for I figured I was next.

My mind began working. I wasn't about to be heaved out into the snow by my father without a fight. I rushed over to Mom and grabbed her around the waist. "Stop! Stop!" I cried. "Don't do that to Carmine. Let him in! Let him in!"

My strategy was to show my father that I didn't agree with what my mother had done. Technically, he was my stepfather, as I said, but since he was the only father I'd ever known, I had never thought of him or referred to him in that way. At the time, however, I was just beginning to understand the difference. That's why I hid and listened to their arguments, and why I felt moved to act. I wanted Dad to know that I was on Carmine's side. Whatever childish logic was in this, the tactic seemed to work. Mom cooled off, and a shivering and perplexed Carmine was allowed to come back inside the house.

I had done my best to diffuse an ugly scene, but it hardly eased my mind regarding my status in the family. Later that evening, I cornered Mom in the kitchen and pleaded with her to accept my stepbrother and two stepsisters for my sake. I felt that I was in a particularly precarious position, one that made me uneasy for much of my early life. Of the seven children in our house, I was the only one who didn't have Sonny Franzese's blood running through my veins. I reasoned that if my mother wanted my father's previous children out of the house, where would that leave me? The most obvious solution to the arguments appeared to be a compromise that banished both the "yours" and the "mine" from the family, leaving only the "ours," the three younger children Mom and Dad had together.

Mom gently assured me that my status was secure, that the union between a mother and her child was unbreakable. She explained that it was that precise union she felt my stepbrother and stepsisters needed in their lives. Her explanation did little to ease my anxiety.

As my parents continued to debate this issue over the ensuing months, I became so anxious that I tried to run away and live with my grandmother. I guess that I was so afraid of being kicked out of the house that I left voluntarily. But the action reveals what I feared the most: I didn't want to be there the day my father—whom I absolutely idolized—finally turned on me.

He never did. No matter how coolly Mom treated my stepbrother and stepsisters, and how much she believed that "a child belongs with its mother," Dad never withdrew an ounce of love from me. And I never forgot that fact.

— 13 —

Dad's rapid rise in the mob enabled our family to make a succession of moves during my first nine years of life. We hop-scotched from Brooklyn to New Hyde Park, Long Island, and finally, in 1960, settled in a two-story home in Roslyn, Long Island, a bedroom community twenty minutes from Manhattan. Our spacious home, purchased in 1960 for $39,000, was one of my father's better investments. When Mom finally put it on the market, it brought nearly $500,000.

As a child, my parents told me, I was every bit the future doctor they dreamed I would become. I was helpful and obedient to my older brothers and sisters, never a "brat," and I hovered protectively over the younger siblings. My only flaw, according to Mom, was a fierce determination to have my way.

"He could wear me down like you wouldn't believe," she once told a friend. "If he wanted something and I wouldn't let him have it, he would sit there with those puppy-dog eyes and just burn a hole through your heart. I'd almost always cave in."

Even so, she concedes that I demanded little and used my persuasive power sparingly.

Dad schooled me in athletics. He taught me how to hit and catch a baseball by playing a game called "pepper" in the back-yard during the summer. The game entailed hitting ground balls to each other from close range. He was a firm but encouraging taskmaster, ordering me to bend my knees and keep my body in front of the ball until I could scoop up the sharply hit grounders in my sleep. When it was my turn at bat, I was told to keep my swing level, keep the Louisville Slugger trademark up, and place the ball where I wanted it.

When the weather cooled and the leaves began to turn, we put away our Roger Maris bats and Mickey Mantle signature gloves and brought out a Joe Namath football. The sport was dif-ferent, but the lessons continued. Dad taught me to fake one way, cut sharply in the opposite direction, then cradle the spiraling leather-and-lace ball into my arms. He taught me how to lead a receiver so that the football could be caught on the run without breaking stride.

Whenever the family went to my mom's parents' house in nearby New Hyde Park, Dad and I frequently slipped away from the gathering and retreated to the backyard to play a game of our own creation we called "Off the Wall." We bounced a pink rubber ball off the chimney and tried to catch the rebound before it hit the ground. A catch was worth a point. Hitting the ledge where the cement base merged with the red brick chimney was worth five points. The first one to earn five hundred points won the game. We played this game for hours at a time.

As I entered my teens, the chimney game became fiercely competitive, and most matches went down to the wire. We each hated to lose, and we each won our share. If Dad fell behind, I had to stay on top of him to make sure he didn't inflate his score. He loved to cheat.

We argued and laughed and tossed the pink ball against the chimney until the sun set over Queens and it was too dark to see the rebounds. Our competitiveness only heightened our enjoyment of the game.

These backyard contests and training sessions went on for more than a decade. Dad was never too busy to play with me. In my eyes, he was the world's greatest father, and I cherished every minute we spent together.

— 14 —

When Dad wasn't grooming me to be a good shortstop, the Catholic schools were trying to mold me into a responsible citizen. I started at St. Ann's Grammar School in New Hyde Park, then graduated to Holy Cross High School in Flushing. I spent two years as an altar boy at St. Ann's Catholic Church in Garden

City, frequently rising at 5:00 A.M. so that I could get dressed and ride my bike to the church for six o'clock Mass. Early risers could spot me tooling down the road, clutching the handlebars with one hand and holding my black and white vestments outstretched in the other.

At St. Ann's, I found myself in the minority. Four out of five students there were Irish, and the Irish and the Italians clashed. Playground fights were frequent, and sports teams were usually divided along ethnic lines. When we played "keep away," it was always the Italians against the Irish. There would be forty Irish guys on one side and about ten of us Italians on the other. Needless to say, we usually got creamed.

Fighting and playing against stacked odds toughened me and further elevated my athletic ability so that, by the time I reached junior high, I was pretty good. Despite facing yet another hurdle—all the coaches were Irish—I worked my way to starting roles as shortstop on the school's baseball team and halfback on the football team. Despite my small physique (five-foot-eight and one hundred thirty pounds), I was quick enough to dodge bigger, slower players and tough enough to burst through those my own size. These two attributes enabled me to win a junior varsity Most Valuable Player trophy, which Dad proudly displayed in the kitchen. Whenever a new associate came over for a breakfast or coffee meeting, he'd first have to pay homage to the gleaming trophy and listen while Dad bragged about my accomplishments.

"He should have three trophies up there!" I once heard him say to a group of associates. "He should have won it the last three years, but those dirty Irish coaches kept stealing it from us. This year, he was so good, they couldn't take it away from us!"

He spoke knowledgeably about my athletic achievements because he rarely missed a game. From the time I donned the ice-blue hat and stretch socks of the "Nuzzi Brothers" Little League team in New Hyde Park, through my tenure as Big Jock on Campus at St. Ann's and Holy Cross, Dad was a constant fixture

47

in the stands or on the sidelines. Sometimes he'd come right into the dugout, wearing his standard summer outfit of black nylon socks, sandals, and Bermuda shorts—a dowdy contrast to his dapper Manhattan suits and diamond rings. Often, he brought his close friends, "nice" men who in another world were notorious figures. My cheering section included Jo Jo Vitacco, "Johnny Irish" Matera, Red Crabbe, Felice "Philly" Vizzari, Whitey Florio, Salvatore "Sally" D'Ambrosio, Anthony "Tony the Gawk" Augello, and Fred "No Nose" DeLucia.

I always knew when my father arrived at the stadium or ballpark in his understated red Plymouth Valiant or, later, his green Buick Electra, and I took note of where he sat in the stands or stood along the sidelines. It was as if I were performing for one person—my father.

At an eighth-grade all-star football game, I broke through the line and jitterbugged down the field for sixty-five yards before being tackled at the five-yard marker. When I got up, I searched the sidelines for Dad. I spotted him running down the edge of the field, leaping up and down and throwing his fists in the air. His friends trailed behind. When they caught up, they slapped his back and congratulated him on my heroics. Two plays later, I took it in for what would be the game-winning touchdown, causing more sideline celebrations.

Pumped with adrenaline, I followed by kicking off, dashing down the field and leveling the ballcarrier near the twenty-yard line. The public-address announcer reported that another player had made the tackle. I glanced over to the sideline and saw Dad run to the broadcast booth, wave his fist in anger, and shout at the announcer. The announcer quickly corrected his mistake.

"You see, Rock," Dad said to my grandfather, as they stood behind the bench, "I knew Michael would make that tackle. He ran sixty yards, scored the touchdown, kicked off, and made the tackle! He's a one-man team! That's my boy!"

My athletic success and the pleasure it gave my father led to a changed role for me in the family. Instead of being the outsider, I was emerging as a star at home, as well as on the ball fields. My single-minded desire to please my father in every way was paying off. I brought home report cards filled with A's, stayed out of trouble, scored touchdowns, and piled up base hits.

As I succeeded, my insecurity over being a stepchild eased. Nothing was ever said between us, but my father's unqualified acceptance of me as his son had made an indelible impression. His love and attention were added to the other qualities I saw and admired in him. I admired the power that surrounded him, his force, and the way he controlled all the bigger men around him. He was fair, kind, and rarely lost his temper, no matter how tense the family situation became. My father was a role model I felt I could emulate, and I made it a point to observe and copy the qualities in him I so admired.

— 15 —

Handling my mother was a problem of another stripe. Although Dad provided her with a live-in maid, Mom was a fanatic about cleanliness and preferred doing most of the cooking, dishwashing, laundry, ironing, and vacuuming herself. Her frequent cleaning frenzies stirred tension in the household. For instance, we children were sometimes forbidden to use the showers and tubs for days after she had scrubbed them to a shine. I once became so exasperated with this practice that I took a bar of soap out to the backyard swimming pool and bathed there. We were also not allowed to enter our bedrooms after the rugs had been vacuumed and raked, and I had to wear my Catholic school uniform long into the evening so as not to soil a second set of clothing.

As clean as the house was, the battles that went on there were anything but. My spirited mother's hands-on approach to disciplining her noisy brood included threatening us with wooden spoons, table legs, a guitar, the metal chimes from a grandfather clock—or anything else within her reach. She kicked, scratched, and, on at least one occasion, bit me. She was quick with her hands, I used to warn my friends, describing her as one might a good prizefighter.

Mom was similarly spirited in her periodic spats with Dad, but her weapons of choice with him were psychological. She argued like she cleaned—furiously and repetitively. She could beat a dead horse into dust, resurrect it the next evening, and then beat it to dust again. No issue was ever settled, no argument was too redundant, and no matter what subject initially set off a new round of arguing, the verbal sparring almost always shifted to the two main issues of conflict—my stepbrothers and sisters, and money.

I guess one can sympathize with Mom's feelings toward the extra children. She had been just a teenager herself when she met Dad, and her head was swimming at the time with the excitement of the Stork Club. She thought she was marrying a powerful figure with heavy ties to the entertainment business, but along with the thrilling nights on the town and the ringside tables at the big shows, she was suddenly swamped by four, five, six, then seven children.

The money conflict resulted from their opposing attitudes about money. Mom was as loose with a buck as Dad was tight. He had grown up in the Depression, and like many who struggled through that dark period, he could never shake the thought that those bleak times might return—no matter how much money he later made. Mom harbored no such memories, and she loved to spend, particularly on clothing and home furnishings, both of which she was forever changing.

I often wondered what kept my parents together. Once, when I was older, I went as far as suggesting to Dad that they divorce for his peace of mind (an unusual stance for someone to take against his own mother, but that shows where my loyalties were). But Dad wouldn't hear of it. From his perspective, Mom's few eccentricities were a small price to pay. She was gorgeous, a characteristic that, in his eyes at least, could cover a multitude of sins, and each new expensive outfit she bought only made her look more ravishing. It was comforting for him each evening to come home to a beautifully kept house filled with children who were expected to toe the line. What's more, to the outside world, Mom defended him and his children—all the children—with a ferocity that made all of the internal conflicts meaningless.

— 16 —

Although I struggled to maintain my focus on science (biology at the moment) and on fielding ground balls and eluding linebackers, Dad's notoriety kept intruding. I was only twelve when articles first began to appear on the inside pages of the local newspaper. The stories would announce that Sonny Franzese had been arrested for some minor crime. Invariably they went on to refer to him as a "Mafioso" or "organized crime chief." But Dad would show up at home a day or so later and act as if nothing had happened. No explanation was ever offered to us. Up until then, I had always thought he was just a successful businessman— which he was. He owned or had interests in many legitimate businesses, including a dry cleaner, numerous bars, nightclubs, restaurants and diners, a sportswear company, and a pastry shop. He even had a piece of a major record company and was involved with professional boxing.

I didn't understand the stuff in the newspapers about organized crime. It was finally our English maid, Pauline, who sensed my dismay and confusion. She sat me down one afternoon and, without being judgmental, explained to me what the terms "Mafia," "La Cosa Nostra," and "organized crime" meant. I was grateful to Pauline, but I remained perplexed. As the stories increased, I wondered why Mom and Dad didn't just call a family meeting and explain to us what was going on. They never did. They ignored it, so I ignored it, too.

I was fourteen, just getting started in high school and serious athletics when the stories leaped from the back pages to the front. On December 24, 1965, many of my neighbors and classmates discovered for the first time that I was the stepson of "The Hood in Our Neighborhood," as the article called Dad. Our family brushed off the long, damning story and proceeded to revel in a typical Christmas Eve, feasting on seafood and spaghetti at Mom's parents' house.

Nothing seemed different that evening. At midnight, we sat in a circle around the tree and, one by one, opened a mountain of presents. Dad gave me a gold, ten-speed English Racer bicycle that year. The sight of that sleek bike made my blood rush. To my utter dismay, two days later it was stolen from in front of a Great Eastern Mills department store, where I had parked it so that I could go inside and explore.

When I returned to school after the holiday break, there were stares and whispers about the newspaper story, but not as much as there could have been. I attended school under my birth name, Michael Grillo. Mom explained that it had been a condition of her divorce that I go by that name until I was eighteen. After that, I could decide for myself which last name I wanted. The Grillo name worked to shield me from those who didn't know my background. The ones who did were mostly friends, and they kept their feelings to themselves. I was a football star and a popular student and had my own identity.

But there's always someone who has to make trouble. In this case, it was a fat Irish kid who took it upon himself to bring one of the articles to school and flash it around the hallways and the playground. He informed everyone within earshot that "The Hood in Our Neighborhood" was none other than my father. Encouraged by the attention he was getting, he decided to taunt me directly. "Hey, Michael, I hear your dad's a gangster," he said in the hall.

I stayed cool at first, pretending to shrug off the embarrassing incident, but inside I was furious. It wasn't so much the personal insult that bothered me, but the way the fat kid and his snickering friends were portraying my father. I shadowed the guy for the rest of the afternoon, caught him on the playground after school, and beat him bloody.

That quieted things down for a while. Unfortunately, both the press and the prosecutors stayed on my father's tail, and the stories continued. At baseball practice that spring, one of my teammates, jealous over being beaten out of the coveted shortstop position, christened my victory with a cutting jab: "So what? At least my father's not a hood," he said. I tore after him, but the ensuing fight was broken up by the other players and coaches before any serious damage could be done.

— 17 —

Around that same time, I was given a brief glimpse of Dad's darker side. One afternoon, I went with him to Manhattan to visit Kama Sutra Records, check in with Phil Steinberg, and see if I could catch a glimpse of the teenage sisters Mary and Betty Weiss, who made up half of the hot rock group the Shangri-Las. We were picked up by Johnny Irish Matera and Red Crabbe, two bruisers. On the way, Dad ordered Matera to pull down a side street where a stocky, balding man about six feet tall was waiting. Dad told Matera, Crabbe, and me to wait by the car as he went for a walk with the stranger. The two were about fifty feet away when I heard Dad yelling and cursing. I looked over and saw him grab the bigger man around the collar with both hands and literally lift him from the pavement. He held the man there for about thirty seconds, then dropped him to the ground. I had never seen him so furious, and I marveled at the almost superhuman strength he had displayed.

I noticed that Crabbe and Matera were extremely tense through all of this.

"This ain't right," Matera kept saying. "This don't look right. We better stay close."

The confrontation ended as abruptly as it had started. Dad returned, jumped in the car, and ordered Matera to hit the gas. "That dirty bum," he mumbled as we drove away. Nothing further was ever said of this incident.

A second encounter occurred inside our home in Roslyn. A hapless neighborhood carpenter, a distant cousin with a reputation for laziness, picked the wrong house and the wrong woman to irritate. Mom was unnerved by his delays in her latest paneling and redecoration project and got on Dad about it. When the mammoth carpenter finally showed up to complete the job, Dad confronted him in the kitchen. The carpenter offered some excuses, and my father responded by firing a right cross to his eye, tumbling him to the linoleum. The carpenter got up and tried to slink away, but Dad wouldn't let him go.

"Get back here," he shouted. "I haven't finished talking to you!"

Despite the intensity of the incident, I had to stifle a giggle. I looked at Mom, and she too was fighting to keep from laughing. Dad had barked at the big carpenter the same command he so often used with us kids.

After the carpenter had gone, Mom took Dad to task about his actions.

"I can't believe you punched the guy right here in my kitchen!" she complained.

"I did it for you," Dad explained. "Now stop nagging me about him!"

"Dad, you treated him like one of the kids," I said.

We all ended up laughing about it—everyone except the carpenter, of course.

— 18 —

By the early 1960s, law enforcement officials had placed Dad under constant surveillance. Detectives sat in unmarked cars at various locations near our home, disturbing neighbors and making a general nuisance of themselves.

It was no picnic for the officers either. Their job was boring and mentally numbing, and they grew to hate the family who had put them in that position. During the hot summers, the detectives baked inside their cars and struggled to contain the anger this misery caused them.

One neighbor, a woman known for her eccentric behavior, became so sick of the grumpy officers parked in front of her house that she decided to take action. She walked to their car, brandishing a garden hose.

"You guys hot in there?" she asked. "Maybe you need to cool off."

And with that she sent a blast of water inside the open car window, soaking the men and their detailed surveillance records. None of the surveillance vehicles ever parked in front of that house again.

Other incidents were more serious. One evening, Dad decided to take us to dinner at the nearby Silver Moon Diner on Lakeville Road. A beefy Nassau County cop with a bad attitude decided to make a point with us, so he rode our bumper, flashing his headlights. He would back off for a little while, then speed up and ride the bumper again. This frightened the younger children and made them cry. Through all of this, Dad kept his cool, but I could tell he was furious that the officer was making a scene in front of the family.

Once we had arrived at the diner, Dad calmed the younger children and seated everyone. Within minutes, the beefy detective walked in with his partner.

"There's the tough guy and his worthless family," he said as he passed.

Dad had heard enough.

"You degenerate bum!" he said to the officer. "You bother my family, and I'll kill you!"

The diner went deadly silent, and everyone inside it froze in place.

Startled, the detective turned and started to go for his gun. This only enraged my father further.

"Go ahead. Go for it! Go for your gun. I'll kill you before you get it out of the holster!" he shouted.

Mom and I jumped up and held Dad back while the second detective grabbed his partner. Dad and the offending officer continued to trade insults over their shoulders before finally settling down.

Dinner proceeded without further incident, and the next day, the loose-cannon detective was taken off the assignment and was never seen in the neighborhood again. His replacements were less overt, but the harassment continued.

— 19 —

Fighting boredom, the officers began hassling Mom and the rest of us. A confrontation on the lawn led to a detective calling Mom a dirty name. I charged the man but was held back by Mom and my brother Carmine. Infuriated, the next day I quietly got in Dad's Buick, sped out of the driveway, and took two teams of Nassau County detectives on a wild chase around the neighborhood. Once I had lost them, I returned to the house.

The detectives circled back, spotted the car, and went right to the door and reported my behavior to my father, and he was not amused at all. He explained to me that as unnerving as the unwanted surveillance was, this was no game. The policemen were dangerous and were not to be trifled with. He was very serious, and I got the message.

But the harassment of our family continued. Just as I arrived at the door of a high school date's home one evening, I found myself engulfed in a blinding spotlight from behind. When I turned, a voice bellowed from the beam: "We just wanted to see which scumbag it was, the little one or the big one."

Before I could answer, my date came to the door. "What's going on, Michael?" she asked.

"Nothing. Go back inside," I said, pushing her into the house. "I'll handle it."

By the time I turned to confront the detectives, the light had been turned off, and they were leaving. I told my date that it had all been a mistake, that the officers had the wrong address.

A short time later, another teenager from the neighborhood, a cute Jewish girl named Leslie Ross, tearfully informed me that her parents had forbidden her to date me. Rightly or wrongly, I blamed the police for this. Thus I grew up with a strong sense that they were the villains, not us. They were the bad guys. They were crude, nasty, and obnoxious, and they were always hassling and suffocating us. They were the enemy, and this concept was enforced by the fact that our whole neighborhood hated them. Many supposed that my parents taught me to hate or disrespect law enforcement officials, but that wasn't true. My thinking concerning them was a result of what I experienced.

For instance, when our whole family went out somewhere, detectives and/or FBI agents sometimes broke into our house and snooped around, planting bugs, adjusting those that were already planted, or randomly searching for evidence of some criminal activity. They tried to accomplish this without leaving a trace, but Mom's relentless cleaning had this one benefit: she could spot the presence of a long-gone intruder the instant she walked in the door. On one occasion, the footprints across the freshly raked carpet were so obvious that even the youngest children could spot them. Mom was enraged, but not just because her privacy and civil rights had been violated. The law enforcement officers had committed a far greater crime: they had walked on her freshly raked carpet!

— 20 —

One afternoon when I was sixteen, I was blindsided by a confrontation of a different sort. I was working after school at a drive-in hamburger shop called the Big Bow Wow on Rockaway Boulevard near Kennedy Airport, when a thin man with salt-and-pepper hair came in and asked for coffee. I stared at him, and he stared back at me. Our eyes locked, but neither of us said a word. He sat at a small table and slowly sipped his coffee. Then he quietly left.

After work, I went to my maternal grandmother's house instead of going home.

"I think I saw my real father today," I told my grandmother. "I'm not sure, but I think it was him."

Seeing that the uncertainty of this was eating at me, Grandma made a few calls. She confirmed what I already knew: Louis Grillo had paid me a visit. He had wanted to see what his son was like as a teenager. For a long time after that, I wondered why my birth father hadn't said anything to me and also why I had been unable to speak to him, although I had sensed who he was. I came to realize that neither of us had anything to say to each other.

When Dad learned of this brief encounter, he became very angry. I had long noticed that any mention of Grillo upset him, but I had never understood why. In the days to come, I chose not to dwell on the strange meeting with my real father or on Dad's odd reaction to it. The memory of that ghost from the past was quickly pushed aside by the growing public pressure coming down upon the only man I knew or wanted as my father.

Although Dad continued to beat arrest raps and maintain his freedom, the police and prosecutors were stepping up their harassment. This reached a climax one evening shortly before I graduated from high school. My parents had decided to throw a party in my honor and had set up a tent in the backyard and put out an impressive spread. Scores of classmates attended. That evening, I gave my first public speech, thanking my father for my success.

Near the end of the celebration, Dad signaled me to come over near the side of the house where we could be alone. There he handed me a small package.

"This is for you," he said. "I want you to have it. You deserve it."

I opened the neatly wrapped box to find a $10,000, eighteen-carat-gold Lucien Picard watch embedded with diamonds. My jaw dropped when I saw the extravagant gift. Dad smiled and opened his arms. His eyes glistened, and we embraced for nearly a minute.

"You've been a good kid, Michael," he said. "I'm proud of you. I'm proud that you're my son."

In that moment, I had to fight to hold back my tears.

Within days of the graduation party, a shower of subpoenas rained down on my high school and neighborhood. All the cars driven to the celebration, from teenagers' hot rods to their fathers' Oldsmobiles, had been photographed and their license plate numbers recorded. The subpoenas, summoning the registered owners to a Nassau County grand jury, went out to high school students, their parents, and unknowing friends who had loaned out their cars for the afternoon. Our phone rang incessantly for several days with calls from frightened teenagers and anxious parents wanting to know what was happening and how they should respond.

This airing of our dirtiest laundry in public was terribly embarrassing, but Dad seemed to take it in stride. He advised everyone who called to appear before the grand jury and tell the truth. The police and prosecutors surely knew that nothing of substance would result from this tedious and expensive effort, but in the annals of government harassment, it was a move worthy of the *Guinness Book of World Records.*

A few weeks before I turned eighteen, Dad called me into his room and handed me some legal papers.

"You're changing your name," he said. "It's all been taken care of. I want you to go see the lawyers."

I found it peculiar that he hadn't asked me if I *wanted* to change my last name to Franzese. In fact, I did, and I was overjoyed that he had arranged it. Still, I was curious about why he hadn't asked me first.

Especially right then. The previous year, the Franzese name had been back in the headlines as we suffered through a series of highly publicized trials, the charges ranging from extortion to murder. A law enforcement blitz led to a further spate of newspaper and magazine articles starring my father as a mob king-in-waiting. I again fought to ignore the stories, ignore the stares of my classmates and the insults of the policemen, and lead a normal teenage life. I had, for the most part, succeeded.

I wasn't nearly as successful in ignoring the effects of the trials themselves. The court proceedings and their aftermath made a very deep impression on me, one that would eventually alter the course of my life.

— 21 —

My father's downfall began with the arrests of four low-level bank robbers in 1965 and their implication of him in a case in which he was, strangely enough, innocent. Two of these bank robbers, John Cordero and Charles Zaher, were heroin addicts, and the other two, Jimmy Smith and Richard Parks, were criminals of minimal style. Their *modus operandi* was to sweep into a targeted bank, freeze everyone in the sights of their guns, and send Smith, the designated "jump man," bounding over the counter to grab all the loose cash he could. Then they'd split, usually in a waiting car driven by Zaher or Cordero's wife, Eleanor. The fact that the critical "wheel man" was often one of the heroin addicts didn't speak well for the group's mental abilities. After completing a half-dozen or so of these reckless robberies, the gang had grown important enough to be targeted by an opportunistic snitch. Their arrest was the first step in what would be a classic example of the criminal food chain.

In prison, the four bank robbers banded together and decided to do some snitching of their own. They agreed to offer up a mid-level mob associate named Tony Polisi as their mastermind. Polisi was promptly arrested, tried, and convicted.

But the bank robbers were not happy. They had been cooperative, but what they got in return was rather small. Although some time was shaved off of their sentences, they still faced long years in prison. It was never hard to surmise what happened next. Their comrades in prison no doubt chided the robbers for having played their trump card for so small a pot. If you're going to sell somebody out, the jailhouse logic goes, you might as well sell out somebody big and go for a reduction of the entire sentence.

It wasn't long before the four robbers called the prosecutors back into their cells and said it was all a mistake. Tony Polisi had only been an errand boy. Sonny Franzese was the *real* mastermind. On the basis of this testimony, Dad was arrested and charged with conspiracy to commit bank robbery, and he was given the police treatment afforded mob superstars. Everywhere he went, from booking rooms to court hearings to jail cells, he was escorted by a dozen or more shotgun-toting, uniformed officers, prison guards, police detectives, or federal agents.

The charges against Dad were difficult for us to believe. It was unthinkable that he would have thrown in with a band of drug addicts and losers. I didn't realize it then, but the two heroin addicts were proof of his innocence in this matter.

A strictly enforced La Cosa Nostra policy at that time forbade a member's involvement with narcotics, under penalty of death. And Dad was unfailingly loyal to his La Cosa Nostra oath. This is illustrated by a story I learned years later. When Buddah Records began coming unglued, Dad could have marched in and taken over. Inwardly, he would have liked nothing better. He enjoyed the music scene, with its stars and excitement, and the entertainment business had long been a source of relatively clean income. Buddah was a money factory, and, as I said earlier, Dad was a close friend of the owners. Still, when the lucrative record company was at its most vulnerable, Dad backed off. The reason for this was that his friend, Buddah co-founder Phil Steinberg, had gotten himself addicted to speedballs, a potent combination of pharmaceutical speed and cocaine.

"When I became an addict, any plans Sonny and the Mafia had for Buddah Records disappeared," Steinberg confirmed. "They used to be everywhere, all over the building. Then *boom,* they vanished. We had our corporate throats exposed, and suddenly they were gone."

Unfortunately for my father, such dramatic testimony could not be offered at his trial. In the cagey world of the law, defense attorneys would never consider going into court and saying that their client had sworn a blood oath to the mob that forbade him to have any dealings with drugs or drug addicts. Nor would the attorneys add that if such were the case, the jury need not trouble itself with a verdict. If the accusation were true, then my father's own "family" was sworn to swiftly enact the death penalty upon him. Such a courtroom strategy would have been too risky and far too subtle for a jury to comprehend. The legal rule of thumb back then was that if it came out during the trial that the accused was a mobster, the jury would convict—regardless of how the facts of the actual case stacked up. This did not bode well for my father.

— 22 —

The trial commenced, and the four felons repeated their synchronized stories about meeting with Dad in a Long Island motel room in July 1965 so he could map out their reckless bank robberies. Few people believed this testimony, not even the journalists who had hounded my father for years

"That's not the way it's done," flatly stated *Newsday's* Bob Greene. "The guys at Sonny's level, they insulate themselves. They have a soldier deal directly with robbers. Even if he were involved, he would have worked through an intermediary."

Greene had said something similar in his story "The Hood in Our Neighborhood": "Franzese follows a basic Cosa Nostra policy of protection, police say. It is a policy called insulation. The man who makes book or robs a motel is five persons removed from Franzese himself. Franzese gives the orders over a public phone or in a walking conversation, and they are then transmitted down the line through three to seven people before they reach the man who commits the actual criminal act.

"So even if the criminal is caught, it would require three to seven people to admit that the original orders had come from Franzese. Somewhere along the line, one of those people would keep silent. This, authorities say, accounts for the inability of law enforcement agencies to imprison him for crimes they know he is masterminding."

Many years later, Greene stated, "It's my own personal feeling that the testimony was entirely out of context. Having seen the way Sonny operated in the past, having investigated him, and having talked with law enforcement officials who had Sonny under surveillance, it just didn't add up. Sonny was extremely careful. He was the rising star in the Colombo family. At the time, the family was in disarray, and Sonny was the guy everyone expected to straighten it out and emerge as the boss. He had brains, he conducted himself with dignity, and he was highly regarded among his associates. For him to do something like that, sitting down with a bunch of flaky guys, masterminding minor bank robberies, something so out of control like that, it didn't fit.

"Sonny was one of the highest-profile mobsters around at the time. He was being written about a great deal and was being looked on as a comer. The feds might have targeted him."

Another *Newsday* reporter, the late Tom Renner, monitored the trial and sat in on some of the testimony. Renner, regarded as one of the foremost organized crime writers and authors in the nation, supported his colleague's view.

"I was shocked—really shocked," he said. "That was not Sonny's bag. He didn't get involved with clowns like that. He had such a strict sense of carefulness on who he dealt with and how he dealt with them. This was low-level crime, and Sonny was a high-level criminal. Gambling. Entertainment. Bookmaking. He wasn't a two-bit bank robber. It didn't make sense, and it still doesn't make sense."

The government tried the case, the bank robbers testified, and the defense attorneys did their best. But in the end, Dad was convicted. Judge Jacob Mishler completed the dispensation of justice by sentencing my beloved father to fifty years in prison.

This was an extremely harsh sentence. In early 1990, a judge in Phoenix, Arizona, sentenced a bank robber to no jail time at all, just 240 hours of community service.

"Fifty years is definitely a long sentence for bank robbery," Greene said. "Sonny got the years because of who he was. Back then it was different. That was before the *Godfather* movies came out and humanized the Mafia. Before that, they were thought of as inhuman thugs who had to be put away. *The Godfather* was the best thing that happened to the Mafia."

Marlon Brando and Al Pacino came along five years too late to help Dad. The general feeling was that justice had been served, and the details were said to be unimportant. A "bad man" got what was coming to him, a "bad man" the government feared was becoming too big and powerful. He was being put away for the rest of his life so that he could not later emerge and continue his climb up the ranks.

It was a big win for the guys in the white hats, but no one considered the impact the trial and its proceedings would have on a teenage boy who watched part of the trial from a seat in the front row. At the time, I was an honor student heading to college and medical school and a career as a doctor.

I had struggled all my life with the confusing concepts of good and evil and how they related to our family. I idolized Dad, and despite the fact that the newspapers had often said that he was a criminal, I refused to believe it. I knew him as good. I knew him as the strong, honorable man I saw every night at the dinner table, the man who treated my often demanding mother so tenderly, and who loved my brothers and sisters so intensely, the man who embraced an insecure stepchild and treated him as a blood son.

If he was evil, then I wanted proof. I wanted to see facts presented that would show who was right and who was wrong. I wanted to see for myself who was just and who was unjust. Surely a trial in an American courtroom would serve that purpose.

I sat in that courtroom and waited for evidence of the alleged evil that justified portraying my father as such a horrible man in the eyes of the whole world. I waited, and it never came.

I also wanted to see, in comparison, the good in the upstanding citizens who were pitted against my father—the judges, prosecutors, and law enforcement officers. I had to understand who was right and who was wrong so that I could know which side to choose.

Sadly, what I observed during the trial were federal judges and prosecutors who accepted without question the improbable and self-serving statements of junkies and robbers. I heard police officers and FBI agents swearing to God to tell the truth in a court of law and then telling lies so transparent that even a teen-age boy could see through them. The trial left me totally confused.

Later, I listened as my father's associates spoke of a system that worked on the theory that the ends justified the means. I listened, and I remembered.

— 23 —

Within months of his bank robbery conviction, while free on appeal, my father was arrested again. This time the charges were much more serious—murder.

Dad was held in jail without bond and brought to trial, charged with ordering the 1964 gangland slaying of veteran hit man Ernie "the Hawk" Rupoli. The Hawk had been shot six times, stabbed twenty-five times, bound, fitted with cinder blocks, and buried in the waters off a Long Island beach. Despite this "expert" work, his mangled body had surfaced three weeks later.

Dad swore that he had never even heard of the man. The witnesses against him were the same four bank robbers who had testified against him in the previous trial. And after deliberating for only three hours—a very short time for a three-week murder trial—the jury found him and his codefendants innocent. His friends gathered at our house, and we threw a big champagne party to welcome him home.

The next morning, and every morning afterward for the following six weeks, Dad awakened at six, as he had been forced to do in jail. He'd walk down the hall into our bedroom and wake me in the upper bunk. He used the ruse that he needed someone to make coffee (Mom being a late sleeper) and designated me for this task. I suspected that he was just lonely, so I never complained. I loved spending the quiet morning hours alone with him, watching the sunrise, talking sports, trading jokes, laughing, and telling stories. By the second week, my eyes would pop open at 5:45 A.M. as I eagerly awaited Dad's summons to the coffee machine.

His court victory didn't stop the prosecutors in an adjacent district, Nassau County, from trying to get some headlines of their own. Also using some of the same bank robbers as witnesses, they charged my father with masterminding a particularly heinous home burglary that had been highlighted by the robbers tying up the children in the basement. Dad was infuriated that he would be linked to a crime against children, but he also understood that the bigger the smear, the better the chance of conviction against him.

He decided that Mom should stay out of the courtroom this time. He didn't want to risk any more stories about her threatening the witnesses with hand gestures. I took her place and watched most of the proceedings, usually sitting up front with a Colombo family capo named Joey Brancato, a World War II hero with a wooden leg.

As the jury announced its decision, Brancato was so nervous his peg leg began knocking loudly against the bench. He grabbed my hand and squeezed it tight.

The jury found Dad not guilty. He turned around and winked, embraced his attorney, then walked from the defense table and hugged me. Outside the courtroom, Dad, Brancato, and I waited for the jury so that we could thank each member individually. One of the jurors, an older, gray-haired man, walked over to me and said, "You take care of that father of yours and keep him out of trouble."

It was a very large order, one that I was incapable of obeying.

— 24 —

Dad's attorneys managed to delay his bank robbery sentence for three years while they appealed the case. During that time,

Mom worked feverishly trying to gather evidence that would reverse the verdict. But as hard as she tried, she couldn't come up with anything to sway the judge.

On Holy Thursday, 1970, when I was nineteen, the day of reckoning finally arrived, for Dad's lawyers had exhausted all but one appeal, and a ruling on that final appeal was imminent.

Before my father left home that day, he took me aside.

"They might remand me today, Michael," he said, using the legal term for being handed over to the prison system. "If they do, I'm depending on you to take care of your brothers and sisters and mother for me."

As he expected, his appeal was rejected. He was taken into custody and transported to Leavenworth, Kansas, where he began a fifty-year sentence for a crime he never committed.

The whole family was stunned. Our beloved father and husband had remained free on bail for so long after the initial conviction that we had come to believe he would probably never have to serve time. Following the first trial, there had been two court victories and big, post-verdict celebratory bashes. It was now hard to comprehend that the long-forgotten, bogus bank robbery conviction, which seemed like little more than a bad dream, could take him from us. I drove around and around the neighborhood that afternoon trying to come to grips with my grief.

By then I was in my first year of premed studies at Hofstra University, and classes had finished for the day. After driving around aimlessly for a while, I somehow found my way to my grandfather's house. There I searched the backyard barbecue cabinet until I found a pocked and fading pink rubber ball in a drawer where my grandfather kept paper plates and plastic forks, and I began throwing it against the chimney.

I did this softly at first, then harder and harder, until the ball hit the ledge with such force that it sailed over the neighbor's seven-foot hedges. I didn't bother to search for the tunnel I had burrowed through the hedges when I was younger in order to retrieve errant rebounds. I had other things on my mind.

"Five points, Dad," I said to myself in a voice choked with emotion. "We'll get you out. I won't rest until we do."

— 25 —

Returning home, I was dismayed to realize that my parents had never sat any of the children down and prepared them for this moment. Dad had walked out of the house that morning and had never come back, and we would each have to deal with this loss in our own way.

With Dad behind bars, Mom began working even harder to dig up some nugget of evidence that could prove he had been framed, but her understanding of the often frustrating intricacies of the law was limited. In her eagerness, she had her attorneys rush into the courtroom with motions based on bits and pieces of evidence that appeared important to her but that, in reality, held little legal value. We all tried to get her to slow down and let the attorneys build a better case, but she wouldn't listen. From her perspective, the frame-up that had put our father behind bars was so obvious and the evidence in his defense was so compelling, why make him sit in jail one day longer?

While we debated among ourselves what our next move should be, I received a call from Joey Brancato. He said that family boss Joe Colombo was furious over the FBI's arrest of his son, Joe Jr., on the flimsy charge of melting coins for their silver content. Colombo was planning to counterattack by picketing the FBI's Manhattan office at Sixty-Ninth Street and Third Avenue, and, Brancato said, Colombo wanted Mom and me to join him.

The pickets began with just a handful of people, including Colombo himself. That was unprecedented. Suddenly, one of the most powerful leaders of a legendary secret society had surfaced from the darkest shadows and was out in the open, walking a picket line and chatting with reporters. Colombo's two other sons, Vincent and Anthony, joined Joe Jr., out on bail, in supporting their father.

At the start of the second week of protests, someone handed me a sign to carry, which read, "I am the victim of FBI Gestapo tactics. My father was framed and is serving fifty years."

The clean-cut college freshman waving the sign was a natural for the media, so I received Colombo's blessing for giving interviews and talking about my father's case. A number of newspapers, including the *New York Post*, wrote feature stories about it.

Each day, as word of the street action spread, the number of picketers increased. Colombo reacted by creating an organization called the Italian-American Civil Rights League. The purpose of the group was said to be to combat stereotyping and ethnic slurs against Italians, particularly the belief that all Italians were mobsters. The fact that the group's leader was himself a bona fide Cosa Nostra don and might do more to foster the stereotypes than fight them was brushed aside.

The picketing went on for months. Colombo, a short, polished man with dark, thinning hair, was tenacious. As the Italian-American Civil Rights League grew in numbers and popularity, his determination grew with it.

— 26 —

I walked the picket line every chance I could, attending biology, chemistry, Italian, English, and sociology classes at Hofstra in the mornings and picketing in the afternoons. We hounded the FBI agents as they moved in and out of their offices, cursed them, painted them as villains, and generally made them as uncomfortable as possible. I found it ironic that the tables had turned. Our family had suffered harassment by law enforcement officials for many years. Now we were harassing them. I loved it.

My involvement with the league had a second, subtler effect. I began striking up friendships with Colombo's soldiers and their associates, and they educated me on their operations and even offered me slices of the pie. I wasn't about to commit myself at that point. I still had plans of becoming a doctor, but I took it all in and stored it in the back of my mind for possible future retrieval.

A few months into the protests, I was standing in front of a nearby coffee shop one day with Mom and another woman when two men in a convertible approached. They slowed down as they drew near.

"Hey, you dago," they called and cursed me.

"Come over here," I yelled back.

Before anything could happen, a uniformed officer approached out of nowhere and grabbed me.

"You should get *them*," I said, pointing out the men in the convertible. "Why are you jumping on *me*?"

"Shut up, Franzese," the officer growled. "You're just a troublemaker. Get across the street with the rest of the greaseballs where you belong."

Twenty years of what I considered abuse from policemen suddenly spun like a scratched record through my mind. I felt my blood rush and my anger swell. I clenched my fist and threw a straight right that dropped the cop to the pavement. Within seconds, a half-dozen officers were climbing all over me, throwing me against a storefront wall, and pounding me with their nightsticks. I fought them back as hard as I could, cursing and lashing out.

The officers finally subdued me and proceeded to snap a pair of handcuffs around my wrists. Then they stopped traffic on Third Avenue, ushered me across the street, and shoved me rudely inside a paddy wagon. I was on my way to jail, and I was only nineteen years old.

— 27 —

When Mom saw what was happening to me, she ran screaming to alert the other picketers. Joe Colombo was quick to act. He ordered the picketers to surround the vehicle in which I had been placed and prevent it from leaving the scene. For thirty minutes, the cops and the Italians had a tense standoff, with the mob demanding my release and the cops holding firm and refusing. Finally, Colombo relented, gave the signal, and the crowd dispersed. I was taken to the precinct station, photographed, fingerprinted, and placed in a cell.

Infused with anger and pumped with adrenaline, I couldn't help taunting the processing officers. For instance, a detective told me that my father was outside and wanted the keys to the car. Knowing that it was my grandfather, not my father, I answered that it wasn't true. My father wasn't out there, and I refused to hand over the keys to him. The detective went into the lobby, returned, and repeated the request. I again refused, insisting that I knew my father wasn't there. Finally, the detective caught on.

"Okay, wiseguy," he said, "your *grandfather* wants the keys to the car."

With that, I turned over the keys, but I couldn't resist the taunt, "I told you it wasn't my father!"

Within the hour, Barry Slotnick, a famous New York defense attorney, was in the station house arranging my release. Slotnick, at the time, was Colombo's attorney, and he retrieved me from the cell and escorted me to a waiting car. I was surprised to find that inside the car was Joe Colombo himself.

"Are you okay?" the boss asked.

"I'm fine," I said defiantly.

Colombo laughed.

"You're bold, kid. But you have to learn. You don't fight with cops. You can never win."

I shrugged.

Then Colombo did something that changed my life.

"You're a good kid," he said, reaching into his pocket and pulling out a button. "I'm making you a captain in the league."

The experience left me with a far greater sense of destiny than the small gesture might have indicated. I was impressed by Joe Colombo. I was impressed by the way he had commanded his forces to stall the paddy wagon and by the way he had dispatched a prominent attorney to handle things at the jail. For the first time, I was getting a feel for both the power and the "family" aspect of my father's mysterious life. The "family" had taken care of me, and I liked that.

What I had done that day, hitting a police officer, was a serious offense, and some have done hard time in prison for less. My case actually was much worse. I had assaulted a half-dozen officers and verbally abused them, and yet I was out of jail within the hour. The charges were later downgraded from felonious assault to harassment, and I was slapped with a small fine of $250.

I was impressed indeed.

— 28 —

When Dad learned of my arrest, his reaction was odd. The only thing that bothered him about it was that I had been identified in the newspapers as his stepson. "Where do they get this 'stepson' stuff?" he growled over the phone from Leavenworth. "Why do they write that?"

I said I didn't know. I also didn't know why it bothered him so much—since it was true.

But where did I go from there? Despite my promotion within Colombo's fringe organization and my first taste of family power, I was quickly becoming disillusioned with the Italian-American Civil Rights League. I had joined solely to help Dad, and I wasn't seeing any progress on that front. When I visited him at

Leavenworth and told him about what the league was doing, he cautioned me not to expect too much. As usual, he didn't spell out what he meant by that. What he knew and wasn't saying was that few of his associates were in a big hurry to see him get out of prison. With him in jail, the rest of them could move up a notch. And they could have a share of his former cut. In addition, Joe Colombo himself had to be breathing easier, for Dad's power had begun to rival that of the boss himself.

The press had touted my father as the future don, going so far as to proclaim him the real force behind the family. Although the newspaper stories said that his rise had come with Colombo's blessing and that he was being groomed to take over, those inside the mob knew differently. Dad wasn't being groomed for anything, except maybe a coffin or a prison cell. This explains why he advised me and Mom to focus on the legal details of his case instead of wasting time and energy with the false hope of help from Colombo's league.

Since Dad wouldn't explain this, I had to figure it all out for myself, and that took time. Meanwhile, I was lost when it came to understanding the treacherous inner workings of the organization. It was hard to conceive of the fact that Dad's loyal confidants would turn their backs on him at a time like this.

A month later, at one of the league's Tuesday night meetings, my eyes were opened. Between scheduled speeches, a squat Jewish man with a gravelly voice stood and made an important point.

"What you are doing is great," the man said, "but what about Sonny Franzese? What's being done for him?"

I recognized the speaker as Artie Intrada, a friend of my father's outside the mob who often invited us over to his spacious home for Passover dinner. Intrada, a shop steward for the laborers' union in Manhattan, had slid me into the closed union the previous two summers so I could work in construction for union wages of $400 to $500 a week—not bad for a teenager.

Anthony Colombo was standing at the podium as Intrada spoke that night. After fumbling for a second, he started saying that my father was important and was to be remembered. Before he could finish, however, Joe Colombo sprang from his chair, took the microphone, and changed the subject. The boss signaled for Joey Brancato, who was responsible for Artie, to muzzle his charge. I watched in confusion as Brancato, the peg-legged war hero who had been my father's closest blood brother, removed Intrada from the meeting. Intrada later reported that he had been given a verbal thrashing.

Apparently, that wasn't punishment enough. Two months later, I received a call from Artie's hysterical wife. Through her sobs, she told me that her husband had been murdered. I drove to her house in Queens to see what I could do to comfort her.

— 29 —

At the funeral of Artie Intrada the following day in a temple on Queens Boulevard in Forest Hills, a friend of the Intrada family took me by the arm and ushered me up front. We stopped in front of a closed casket surrounded by red, yellow, and blue flowers.

"I want you to see what these animals did to Artie," the woman said, lifting the coffin lid.

I recoiled in shock. Artie's head was bluish purple and swollen to three times its normal size. Even his neck and hands were rubbed raw and bruised. The tough union steward had apparently gone down fighting. His body had been dumped among the flies and rotting fruit in a trash heap on a side street in Manhattan. Besides being beaten half to death, he had been shot once through the back of the head.

As I sat through the ceremony, the horrifying image of Artie's swollen face spun through my mind. I was further unnerved by the piercing wails of Artie's son, who, at four, was just old enough to sense that something terrible had happened. I stared at Artie's wife and his pretty teenage daughter, two formerly happy, outgoing women who now sat in a trance, the life drained from their faces.

The air was thick with grief and fear that seemed to radiate from the casket. I felt queasy and wanted to run outside into the fresh air. It was all I could do to make it through the sullen ceremony.

Few inside the temple understood what had happened. Artie had not just been murdered. His death was being used to send a message. My father's reign was over. He was in prison, where the family apparently wanted him to stay. And anyone who questioned this would end up in the garbage with Artie.

At the time, I refused to accept or believe what seemed obvious. But I immediately made reservations to fly to Kansas and consult with Dad, pushing up a scheduled visit two weeks.

"I couldn't even recognize him, Dad," I said in the visitors' area at Leavenworth. "Artie spoke out for you at the meeting, and they're saying that's why he was killed. Could it be true?"

"I don't know, Michael," he said with only a trace of emotion. "Could be. Could be that hurt him."

"Why?" I asked incredulously. "Why would they go that far? What's going on? Why did they do this?"

As always, Dad measured his words in the careful manner I sometimes found so frustrating. He always spoke as if every conversation, even those with his family, was being recorded by the FBI.

"Don't think that these people, this league of Joey Colombo's, don't think that they will do anything for me," he said. "You keep working with the lawyers."

On the plane back to New York, I struggled to comprehend what was happening. What mystified me were the actions of Joey Brancato. Joey would have given his life for my father without hesitation. How could he have turned? It would take years for me to understand. Brancato was a good soldier, and regardless of his decades of friendship and loyalty, if the word from the top was that Sonny was to rot in prison, that was the policy he must follow. This was the way of the family.

I continued being active in the league and continued believing the family that had so easily rescued me from jail could do the same for my father. I wasn't afraid that my efforts might cause me to suffer the same brutal fate as Intrada. A son was expected to fight for his father—at least until directly told to do otherwise.

— 30 —

The Italian-American Civil Rights League expanded rapidly, and by 1971, membership had soared into the thousands. Frank Sinatra, Sammy Davis Jr., Vic Damone, and Connie Francis, among others, lent their celebrity to the cause and gave benefit concerts to raise a war chest. The donations coming in totaled millions. Unwittingly, Joe Colombo had stumbled upon a vast new source of clean revenue. Italian pride apparently equaled big bucks.

But not everyone was overjoyed about what was happening. Colombo's bizarre social activism was frowned upon by the ruling commission of the five Cosa Nostra families. The remaining bosses, led by Carlo Gambino, were aghast at what Colombo was doing and that he was operating so openly. They were seeing him give interviews on the evening news and reading about him in the newspapers. They were also suspicious of what he was doing with the donations that were pouring in and that he wasn't sharing fairly with the other families.

In time, the commission met and ordered Colombo to curtail his civil rights activities and get back to the business of organized crime, but Colombo refused. Not only did he rebuff the commission, he made plans for the biggest gathering yet by organizing an Italian unity day rally for Columbus Day, 1971, at Columbus Circle in Manhattan.

Colombo nailed up posters and sent out a kingly proclamation that all stores in the surrounding area should close for the holiday-like celebration, but both Gambino and rival Colombo capo Crazy Joe Gallo ordered the stores to remain open. Gallo and his men went around ripping down the posters promoting the rally. The merchants, caught in the middle of a vicious tug of war, didn't know what to do. Most made their decision based upon whose men were in their store last.

On the morning of the rally, I was surprised when my mother decided not to attend. She was a longtime friend of Colombo, was active in the organization, and had been anticipating the big event. That all changed when she awakened that morning shaken by a vivid nightmare of Colombo being gunned down. She reasoned that if she went, it would happen as she had dreamed.

Others received more direct warnings.

"Don't go to the rally," Crazy Joe advised FBI agent Bernie Welsh, one of the few feds the mob guys respected. "There's gonna be a stampede."

Welsh reported the tip to his superiors and discovered that there was a loud buzz on the streets that something bad was going to go down during the event. The rumors proved correct.

— 31 —

When I arrived in the square that day, nearly fifty thousand people had gathered. Colombo, flush with victory, was standing at the podium, going over his speech and preparing for the grandest moment of his life. He spotted me and called me over. Handing me a stack of programs that outlined the afternoon's events, he asked me to distribute them.

"Look at this crowd," Colombo beamed. "Let them try and stop me now."

I nodded, turned, and was walking down the steps when I was suddenly rocked by two successive explosions. They were so loud that I instinctively covered my ears. My first thought was that someone had tossed a pair of bombs into the crowd, but I turned my head just in time to see Colombo drop to the floor.

"Joey's been hit! Joey's been hit!" someone yelled.

Then I saw some men pounce on a black man clutching a pistol. The "explosions" had been only gunshots, but I had been so close to the discharging weapon that the sound had been deafening.

I heard two more bangs, almost as loud but from another direction. FBI agents on the scene later explained the second set of shots. In a scene reminiscent of Jack Ruby and Lee Harvey Oswald, one of Colombo's soldiers had stuck a pistol through the legs of a policeman and blasted the black man while he lay handcuffed on the pavement. Once he had fired, the soldier dropped his gun and vanished into the crowd. Within seconds, a half-dozen more revolvers bounced like live hand grenades on the pavement as Colombo's associates rid themselves of their guns before police backup could swoop in.

Meanwhile, the crowd screamed and ran in every direction, crashing into each other and nearly creating a deadly stampede—just as Crazy Joe had predicted.

My first thought was to find my sister Gia and my girlfriend, a blond Hofstra student named Maria. I spotted them standing dazed in the surging, panicked crowd near the stage and directed them into a nearby coffee shop. Ordering them to stay inside, I went back out to see if I could learn what had happened. The word among the family was that everyone should go home. Joe Colombo had been shot and was on his way to the hospital. He was alive, but barely. The man who had tried to assassinate him, Jerome Johnson, was dead. There was nothing more anybody could do.

I returned to the coffee shop, rounded up my charges, and drove them home. There I found Mom distressed both by

Colombo's attempted assassination and by her eerie dream that had foreseen it.

— 32 —

Although I was not yet an initiated member of the family, I was close enough to learn two prevailing theories of what had happened that day and why. The first theory was the most obvious. Colombo's unprecedented activity with the Italian-American Civil Rights League had heightened his profile and that of La Cosa Nostra. This was bringing heat down upon the five families. The mob's high commission had ordered him to cease and desist, and he had refused. That was a capital offense.

Crazy Joe was known as an opportunistic guy. Still smarting from losing to Colombo in a power play for the family's leadership a decade earlier, he perhaps now sensed an opening. Colombo's grip on the family had eroded, and his support among the other families was now either thin or nonexistent, so Crazy Joe may have seen it as the opportune moment for taking his revenge.

In truth, few imagined that Crazy Joe had aspirations to take over the family. A prison term had weakened his power, and his soldiers had never been very loyal—a factor attributed to his tightrope walk with sanity. The general feeling was that Crazy Joe, who had met Jerome Johnson in prison, had paid his friend to take out Colombo for the sheer joy of it.

But again, the Colombo family was, at the time, in its most vulnerable position in its forty-year history. Colombo was off in left field, fancying himself the Martin Luther King Jr. of Italians. His two most powerful "caporegimes" (underbosses), Carmine "the Snake" Persico Jr. and Sonny Franzese, were in prison. With Colombo out of the picture and my father and the Snake locked away, maybe Crazy Joe really did think that he could make one last mad dash for family leadership. Who knows for sure?

The second theory, the one supported by Persico, the man who eventually took over the Colombo family, was that the government had set up Johnson to kill Colombo because they were afraid of the power he was gaining through the Italian-American Civil Rights League. The plan was, as Persico saw it, that after the shooting, Johnson was supposed to be arrested, not killed. He was then set to "roll over" on some specified La Cosa Nostra target, possibly Persico himself. Johnson would get immunity to testify, go into the Witness Protection Program, and would never have to do a day for the murder. The feds would have Colombo dead and his replacement indicted for murder, a one-two blow that might have destroyed the family.

Whatever the truth in all of this, one thing is certain: Jerome Johnson's bullet, which turned Colombo into a vegetable, burst the bubble of the Italian-American Civil Rights League. The organization quickly crumbled into dust. But not before my participation in its affairs had sown seeds in my life that would one day bear evil fruit.

— 33 —

As Joe Colombo lay in his bed, stripped of his mental capacity, his crime family spun out of control. Because Colombo had focused on keeping my father in jail and disbanding Dad's loyalists, Carmine Persico's soldiers were allowed to stay together. That placed Persico in a position to mount a successful coup from behind bars. He installed Thomas DiBella, an aging, low-keyed capo, as the acting don, pending his own parole.

Following the assassination attempt on Joe Colombo, my personal life also seemed to become unfocused. I now found it very difficult to concentrate on my studies. Counting the years that would be required for medical school and internships, I suddenly realized that I faced a decade of intense study before I could become a doctor. This fact was brought into focus by what now appeared to me to be a much quicker route to success.

As frightening as the Intrada hit and the Colombo shooting were, there were aspects of the mob that I found intriguing. The stories I had heard on the picket line about the money that could be made through various legal and illegal business ventures excited me. I needed money because I had come to believe that money was the key to winning Dad's release from prison. And I didn't have ten years to wait. I decided that I would continue to study, but with a reduced class load, so that I could take a stab at a few business opportunities—legitimate ones at first.

Among my father's many scattered business interests was an automotive body shop in Mineola, Long Island. I had once worked there after school and learned how to paint and restore car exteriors. I figured that might be a good place to start.

I paid a visit to the new owner, an upbeat man named Frank Cestaro, and explained that I had worked for the previous owner and was interested in a job. This approach was mostly a ruse to see, meet, and scrutinize the person who had taken over the place. Cestaro, no doubt making the connection, called me the next day. I admitted that I wasn't really interested in working for him as an employee and offered to lease half the shop and operate my own business there. Cestaro agreed.

I began digging wrecked Ford Pintos and Chevy Vegas out of junkyards, restoring them, and selling them for a healthy profit. The two makes, America's first attempt to counter the successful small Japanese cars, were so flimsy and cheaply built that it took little more than a fender bender for an insurance company to total them. Many junked Vegas and Pintos were actually in relatively good shape and could be fixed in a day or so and sold for $1,500 to $2,000. Although this effort did turn a profit, I quickly realized that a half-interest in a body shop wasn't going to buy me a mansion on a hilltop, so I began looking for other opportunities.

About that time, I received a call from Tony Morano, a stout man in his late thirties with a head of curly sandy-blonde hair. Morano had experience in the auto-leasing business (along with a criminal record, although he wasn't connected to La Cosa Nostra). Morano and I hit it off, formed a partnership, and rented a corner lot on Cherry Valley Road in West Hempstead.

Next, we needed some financing. We approached Mel Cooper, a man I knew in the finance business, and asked him to direct us to a company that would assist with our start-up financing. Cooper sent us to a man named Vince who was in the garbage business. Vince heard us out and recommended Equilease, a company run by two brothers. We talked the brothers into giving us a $500,000 line of credit to begin our West Hempstead automobile leasing operation. Within a few months, M.B.E. Leasing was turning over ten to twenty automobiles a month, and I was pulling down $500 a week.

Meanwhile, Frankie Cestaro was struggling to turn a profit with the body shop. I took over the entire operation and moved the equipment to the West Hempstead lot. The business, now in a better location, started turning around, and from that operation, I was soon putting another $500 into my pocket each month.

Six months later, during my sophomore year of college, Tony and I sectioned off a corner of our Cherry Valley property and opened a used-car lot. This segment of our rapidly expanding operation started kicking another $1,000 a month into my swelling kitty.

My success in West Hempstead did not go unnoticed. Some of Dad's friends started coming around, looking over the operation and trying to figure how they could get a piece of the action. I played them nice and easy, giving up nothing, but leaving doors open and making sure no one left insulted. Pretty soon, instead of trying to squeeze their way in, they came to me with partnership offers on other ventures.

One such offer, for instance, was for a pizza restaurant in Lindenhurst, Long Island. Vinnie Perozzi told me about a location he had scouted in a shopping center near the commuter railroad tracks there. I checked it out and saw what Vinnie had seen—lots of hungry people waiting for trains. I kicked in a month's take from the leasing business and opened a small pizza place. I named it Sonny's Pizza. I instructed Vinnie to open early and serve breakfast during the morning rush hour. The strategy worked, and the restaurant was soon turning a profit of $800 a month for each of us.

In twelve months of part-time work, I had started four successful businesses and was pulling down close to $5,000 a month in profits.

— 34 —

Around this time, another part of my life began to take form—my love life. Early in my freshman year at Hofstra, Leslie Ross, the neighbor who was forbidden by her parents to date me, introduced me to a coed named Maria Corrao. Maria, the daughter of a well-off Italian jeweler and his Polish wife, favored her mother. She had long blonde hair, blue eyes, and the sparkling look of the proverbial all-American girl.

An education major, Maria was far more intelligent and refined than the party girls I was accustomed to dating. She was also more mature and serious. I was surprised to discover that she lived within a mile of my home in Roslyn. Although we were the same age, we had never met. I had dated her best friend for a while but had never even seen Maria around the neighborhood. She explained that she wasn't the type to wander the neighborhood checking out the guys.

At the time Maria and I were introduced, I was dating an archaeology major from Holy Cross named Barbara DeVito. Leslie Ross despised Barbara and thought that if I went after

Maria, at least I wouldn't be with Barbara. I took her bait and asked Maria to a college dance. Although the relationship got off to a slow start and wasn't grounded in romantic fireworks or a burning physical attraction, I was drawn by Maria's character. Everything about her was very nice. It was a quality that my parents picked up on immediately. Mom, who could be a "pill" when it came to my dating girls she didn't like, approved of the squeaky-clean Maria from the start, and Dad liked her, too. Shortly before he went to jail in 1969, we all spent a happy New Year's Eve together at the Copacabana.

Maria had appeared during the most stressful point in my life (and my mother's), and she turned out to be the perfect salve for us both. Instead of being frightened away by the family's reputation and deepening troubles, she drew closer. A nurturing type, she comforted me during my worst days of anger and frustration over my father's conviction and was there to help my mother any way she could. Often, while I was working or out doing other things, Maria would be at our house visiting or babysitting the younger children to allow Mom to work on Dad's case.

The more stressed and turbulent our lives became, the more understanding Maria seemed to become. After the Colombo assassination, a salient event that would have telegraphed to a thousand girls that this wasn't the kind of family to get involved with, Maria responded by hanging tough. In doing so, she soared beyond nice in our estimation and into the realm of sainthood.

Everybody loved "Saint" Maria—my mom, my dad, my brothers, my sisters. I cared for her a whole lot, too, and with my time divided between school and the expanding business interests, a thoroughly undemanding girlfriend like Maria seemed ideal for me.

Although Maria and Mom were as thick as thieves, what impressed me the most about Maria was how unlike Mom she was. She was low-keyed, easy to please, and, most of all, quiet.

She had minimal concern for fancy clothes and material things, knew little and cared less about furniture, and had a healthy notion about the acceptable standards of household cleanliness. She never complained or asked anything of anyone, and she was always there when anyone needed her. She was, in essence, the kind of woman who would never give her boyfriend any reason to break up. There was no doubt that Maria would make a perfect wife and mother, a quality Mom pointed out to me what seemed like a few hundred times a day.

Maria and I were engaged in 1973, and we set the date for our wedding for the following year. As that date neared, however, I became increasingly nervous about the whole matter and eventually canceled the wedding. I liked Maria and cared for her, but I still wasn't sure if I loved her and wanted to spend the rest of my life with her. Also I wasn't quite ready to give up the less saintly girls I occasionally dated, the kind who overflowed with passion and little else.

Maria was crushed by my decision, but, true to character, she didn't show it. She just waited for me to come around and set another date.

— 35 —

With all the business deals I was now involved in and the domestic drama whirling around me, I never lost sight of my primary goal—freeing Dad from prison. Everything I did was geared toward that, and every dollar I saved was reserved for it. When a private detective named Matthew Bonora, a former police detective, contacted me about the possibility of getting his hands on my father's missing police surveillance records, I jumped at the opportunity and paid $5,000 to Bonora as a retainer.

Some time later, Bonora called and told me to come to his office at the Mineola Courthouse. The first thing I noticed when the detective greeted me was that he was wearing white gloves.

Inside the office, he acted nervous and spoke softly, as if he possessed something so secretive that we were in danger merely by being in the same room with it.

Bonora opened a locked drawer and gingerly removed a stack of papers. He told me I could look at the material but couldn't touch it or change the precise order of the pages. He explained that they were the original records and were there only so I could confirm that they existed. They would have to be returned that same day, and we couldn't even risk copying them. He explained that if the records were stolen, they wouldn't be allowed in court.

I looked the papers over, and they appeared to be exactly as Bonora had represented them. There were names, times, and dates of every place my father had gone and everyone he had met. I was certain that somewhere in that stack of papers was a sheet covering the exact time and date the bank robbers had said they met with Dad. This was the critical evidence that had mysteriously vanished during the bank robbery trial. I was equally certain that this information would place Dad at a completely different location.

The detective said we would have to try to find a way to legally obtain the papers. I left the office more confident than I had been since the day Dad left home that this would help him. I told Mom, and she, too, was elated.

Unfortunately, Bonora could never get his hands on the records again. He told me that his source had dried up and that the papers had been moved. Meanwhile, prosecutors and police continued to deny the very existence of the papers. I kicked myself for not having grabbed them when I'd had the chance, especially when Bonora later told a newspaper reporter that the entire incident had never taken place.

− 36 −

Just as that door slammed shut, another one opened—seemingly by accident. Next to Sonny's Pizza in Lindenhurst was a bar called the Village Pub. Although I didn't drink, I occasionally dropped by the bar to sip a club soda and talk with the owners. In this way, I became friendly with a waitress there named Dee.

One afternoon, Dee's latest boyfriend, a seedy-looking dude with dark hair and a bushy mustache, was in the pub talking about the wild and crazy time he'd had with his previous girl-friend. She was a woman named Rusty who wore red wigs and had a habit of marrying serious criminals. He said she had told him that her husband and his friend had framed some big mob guy and were in serious trouble.

I had been listening to him halfheartedly until he mentioned the framing of a "big mob guy," and then I perked up. I let the man go on for a while, then I asked him if the mob guy that had been framed might possibly be Sonny Franzese.

"Yeah, that's him," the man said. "Franzese."

"That's my father," I said.

The poor man nearly had a seizure. I told him I wanted to meet Rusty, who I was sure must be Eleanor Cordero, widow of the slain hit man Ernie "Hawk" Rupoli and now the wife of John Cordero, one of the bank robbers who had testified against my father. After some arm-twisting, the ex-boyfriend gave me his name, address, and phone number and promised to arrange a meeting.

The following day, he called. He said that the woman had agreed to meet me that night. We would meet at midnight in the parking lot of a diner on the Sunrise Highway in Lindenhurst. She would be in a red Mustang parked in the back of the lot.

I told Mom about this possible breakthrough, and we con-tacted a family attorney, Herbie Lyons, to seek advice. The attor-ney advised me that it might be beneficial to wear a recording device to the meeting because I might never have the opportunity to talk with Eleanor Cordero again. I considered this, but some-thing inside told me "not this time."

When I pulled into the diner a few minutes after midnight that night, sure enough, there was a red Mustang in the back of the lot. As my headlights flashed through the car, I could see the figure of a woman sitting in the passenger seat. I parked my car, walked over, and got into the Mustang on the driver's side.

Although the woman was wearing a new wig, I recognized her instantly.

"Hello, Eleanor," I said.

Without the usual formalities, Eleanor pulled out a .32 and pointed it at my head.

"If you're wired, you're dead," she said.

Then, with her free hand, she searched my chest, thighs, crotch, and armpits—anywhere the recording device could be concealed. I remembered the debate earlier in the afternoon and breathed a sigh of relief that I hadn't used the device.

"I'm clean," I said.

"You're lucky. What do you want?" she growled.

− 37 −

I stared at Eleanor Cordero. She was one tough, ugly woman, about five-foot-five, chunky, totally unappealing. She had scars on her arms and hands, markings I didn't remember her having before. I marveled at the fact that she had never lacked for husbands or lovers, even if they were hit men and junkie bank robbers.

"I want the truth, Eleanor. I need your help," I confided.

She relaxed her grip on the gun but still held it to my head.

"Your father's innocent. They set him up. I know everything, and I can get him out. But I want money, and I want protection from my husband and from the government."

It was clear that Eleanor feared the FBI as much as she did her criminal husband, and I understood that.

Before I answered, it occurred to me that maybe *she* was wired. I would have to choose my words carefully.

"I'll help you any way I can," I ventured, "but I can't give you money. That would make it appear that I had bought your testimony. But if you do this for me, I'll be very grateful."

"What about protection?"

"I can protect you. Don't worry about that. But you'll have to come to the lawyer's office and make a statement."

Eleanor thought for a moment then pointed the gun barrel between my eyes. She was squeezing the handle so tightly I was afraid it would go off any second.

"If you double-cross me," she said, "I'll blow your brains out. Do you understand?"

"I just want the truth," I replied, fighting to stay calm. "That's all I ask."

I gave her my number and told her to call me.

Eleanor called the next day, and we met again. She was less afraid this time, but still armed. To reiterate the importance of her demands, she explained her scars. One weekend her husband, John Cordero, in a particularly mean mood, had mixed sex, drugs, and an axe, alternating between the three. He had fed her tranquilizers, chopped on her with the axe, and then made love to her. He repeated this trio of activities for two days, until she nearly bled to death.

Eventually, when he told her that he was going to the basement to sharpen the axe so he could chop her up into little pieces, she managed to crawl to the phone and dial 911. The police arrived, arrested her husband, and summoned an ambulance to take her, barely alive, to the hospital. She required more than two thousand stitches to mend her body. Still, her husband had been released, something she attributed to the fact that he had ratted on my father.

"So I need money and protection," Eleanor repeated. "I can't help you unless I have money and protection."

What could I say? She had me over a limb.

— 38 —

For the next seven months, the most miserable months of my life, I baby-sat Eleanor Cordero. I rented an apartment for her in Hempstead, then later moved her to a house in Huntington. I bought her a car and paid the living expenses for her and her twelve-year-old daughter. I even placed myself at her disposal twenty-four hours a day. Soon, she was making sexual advances, and I had to fight her off.

Time after time, during those months, I felt that I'd about had it with this woman's constant demands, but I couldn't end it. She seemed to be cooperating with the attorneys, giving them everything they needed. They advised me to keep her happy a little longer because they needed her to testify at a hearing.

I knew that if I was to keep Eleanor happy any longer, I would have to find her a good man, so I desperately flipped names through my mind. Who did I know who could be compatible with this strange woman? I decided to call a friend by the name of Jerry Zimmerman. Jerry, who was six-foot-five and weighed two hundred seventy-five pounds, was a shaggy dog of a guy, a happy-go-lucky con man by trade. Could he be Eleanor's type? As it turned out, Jerry liked Eleanor, Eleanor liked Jerry, and I was thrilled.

For a time, Eleanor seemed to calm down, but as the months dragged on, she continued to make constant demands for money or other material things.

If that wasn't bad enough, Mom kept pressing me to meet Eleanor and get involved in the process. I imagined that these two headstrong women would clash like Siamese fighting fish, and I saw no reason to dump them into the same bowl. But Mom was so persistent that I eventually relented.

As I had predicted, the two women instantly despised each other, and after Mom's visits, all Eleanor could talk about was how my mother drove a Cadillac, wore expensive clothes and jewelry, and lived in a big house. And then she began demanding similar clothing, transportation, and accommodations.

Despite the insanity and misery of putting up with this woman, in the end, she came through for us. She swore out affidavits, outlining everything she knew about my father's case and swearing that he had been framed. She even introduced me to Charles Zaher, another one of the bank robbers. After being released early from his bank robbery conviction, Zaher had gone straight and was working for a phone company. He was uneasy about meeting me but eventually agreed. What he said backed up Eleanor's claims, and he agreed to cooperate with our defense lawyers, too.

I was also able to get my hands on a letter it had long been rumored that Zaher had written to his wife from prison, a letter that admitted he and his partners were planning to frame my father. Things were beginning to take shape. As horrid as my experience of baby-sitting Eleanor had been, it appeared to be paying off.

— 39 —

The afternoon prior to the hearing in which Eleanor was to testify, I was at a body shop I owned in Deer Park, Long Island, when I spotted legendary FBI mob hunter Bernie Welsh lumbering toward me. Welsh, a giant of a man whose size and girth contrasted with his baby face and friendly demeanor, was an old-style *Untouchables*-type agent who liked to go toe-to-toe with the toughest mob enforcers. Far from just shadowing his targets, he sometimes hounded them in an exaggerated fashion. For instance, he'd go to a mob hangout, spot a made man or two, and make a big show of shaking their hands and offering to buy them drinks. Sometimes, he'd try to sit down and have dinner with them. The men involved always hated this act. It killed their conversation and made them look like informers. Invariably, mobsters would disappear into dark corners at the first sight of Bernie.

Welsh loved being an agent, and he loved the mob beat. As annoying as he was, he was respected because he was a straight shooter. When he busted a guy, he did it by the book.

"I'm gonna get Joey Brancato, and I'm going to get him honest," he'd tell me, alluding to his long battle to turn or convict my father's associate.

"That's a switch," I'd shoot back. "After you guys framed my father, now you're going to start doing things honestly?"

Welsh would just shake his head and laugh, never confirming or denying the setup.

"Michael, come on out. We gotta talk," Welsh shouted from the front of the body shop that afternoon.

"No way, Bernie," I said, in no mood for the agent's games.

He persisted, and I reluctantly walked over to meet him. Welsh immediately went into his theatrics. He slowly shook his head and peered at me like a high school principal looking at a truant student.

"You're getting out of hand, Michael. You've been doing some bad, bad things."

"What now?" I said, figuring it was another famous Welsh stunt.

"We've received information that you were at a meeting and that you ordered the kidnapping of Judge's Mishler's daughter."

"What?" I shouted, my blood heating. "I didn't even know he had a daughter. What kind of nonsense is this?"

Then it struck me. "Did you tell the judge this?"

"We had to," Welsh said, shrugging like he hated to do it but was duty-bound.

"A day before the hearing you tell the judge I'm gonna kidnap his daughter? You jerks never let up, do you?"

I called our attorney, who contacted Judge Mishler. The judge confirmed that the allegation had been brought to his attention.

Our attorney quoted the judge as saying that he hadn't necessarily believed the story but neither could he discount it.

What effect the FBI's underhanded tactics had on the subsequent decision is impossible to determine. Under the law, judges are ordered to remove themselves from a trial or hearing if they believe a threat, or even an unconfirmed report of a threat, may cloud their judgment. In practice, however, judges rarely take this step. What is known is that my family received a devastating lesson in the law. We entered the hearing with what we confidently felt was an open-and-shut case—recanted testimony, sworn affidavits, a critical piece of written evidence that spoke of the plot to frame my father before the fact. How could we lose?

As it turned out, it was easy to lose. Eleanor had demanded and received too much from me, and therefore the judge felt that she wasn't credible, especially after the state produced a witness who claimed Eleanor had bragged that she was selling her testimony. Regarding Zaher, a witness reversing prior statements holds little weight in the eyes of the law. Except for rare instances, the only thing that matters is what is said during the trial. Plus, there were three other witnesses who had not yet recanted their testimony. Since the Zaher letter hadn't been mentioned during the trial, a legal loophole held that it was insignificant. Besides, the judge felt that there was some debate over the meaning of the word "frame" in the letter.

The bottom line was that the government felt the Franzese family was too powerful, and our image too menacing, for anyone to believe that we hadn't frightened, coerced, or bought the testimony of the witnesses. So the appeal was rejected.

To say that we were shattered doesn't quite capture our feelings that afternoon. The time, the money, and the agonizing effort spent baby-sitting Eleanor had all gone for nothing.

As usual, Maria was right there, comforting me, calming my mother, encouraging us to go on, and assuring us, in her cheerfully innocent way, that the truth would eventually prevail. I wasn't so sure, but I also wasn't yet ready to give up trying.

— 40 —

Despite these personal reverses, things were going well for me on at least one front. The auto-leasing business in West Hempstead was expanding so rapidly that I decided to seek a larger line of credit to float more cars. Our original deal had topped off at $500,000, but we wanted to fly higher.

A friend introduced me to a banker who was being strangled by a mountain of medical bills because of a paraplegic son, and I was given to understand that if I took care of the banker, he would feel obligated to push through my credit application. Strangely, all the banker required, initially at least, was for me to purchase from him a $2,500 mink jacket he claimed to have won in a church raffle. I figured it was a small price to pay for a $2 million line of credit.

I was wrong. That fur coat would haunt me for the next two years, leading to my arrest, three trials, and the destruction of my entire business structure. It would also forever brand me as a mobster—a distinction I had until then escaped.

I didn't know anything about furs, but fortunately I shared a roof with an expert—my mother. She loved mink coats and was excited to hear that I was buying one, and she wanted it. She assured me that the coat was worth the price.

I was having a hectic day at work when my friend Vinnie arrived with the coat. After waiting around as I took one phone call after another, Vinnie signaled that he would just hang the fur on the door. I indicated that I understood. As the day proceeded, I forgot all about the coat. At 5:30 that afternoon, I locked up the office and drove home, leaving the mink hanging on the door exactly where Vinnie had left it.

The instant I set foot in the house, Mom greeted me by saying, "Where's the coat?" When I told her that I had forgotten it, she ordered me to go right back and get it. Exhausted from the activities of the day and in no mood for another long round-trip through traffic, I tried to refuse, but she was persistent. She simply wasn't willing to wait another twenty-four hours for her mink. I finally called an associate and asked him to pick up the coat and bring it over.

When the man arrived at the office, he couldn't find the coat, so he called me and relayed this information. Figuring that someone had put it in a closet or somewhere else, I told him not to worry about it.

"We'll find it tomorrow," I assured him.

A thorough search of the office the following morning failed to locate the mink, and then I knew that something was amiss. I suspected a young mechanic who we believed had been taking things from the shop for months, so I called the man in, confronted him, and after some tense moments, he confessed. He said that he had already moved the fur on the black market, and I advised him that he'd better "move" it back. He promised to try.

When the man said that he needed his Camaro, a beat-up car he had been working on in the shop for more than a week, it made me think that he was about to disappear like the coat. I decided to hold the Camaro and its registration as collateral until the fur had been returned.

During the confrontation with the mechanic, an old friend and business associate of my father's, Philly Vizzari, had been in the office. A few days passed, and the mechanic called me. He had changed his story. He hadn't taken the coat after all, he said. I reminded him that he had already confessed to taking the coat, so if he would just tell me who he sold it to I would get it back. In the meantime, I was holding the car.

The next day, I was out of the office, and at one point, I called to check for messages. I was told that the place was swarming with cops. They had impounded the Camaro and were looking for the registration!

I asked to speak to the lead detective. I told the officer that I had the registration with me and would bring it. I arrived a half-hour later, peeled it out of my wallet, and handed it over. The detective grabbed it and ordered the troops to retreat.

The next morning, a Friday, I received a call from a local used-car dealer.

"The cops were over here asking if you tried to sell me some beat-up Camaro. What's this all about?"

What it was about was that the police were trying to build a case against me.

I called my attorney, John Sutter, and made an appointment to see him.

"Don't worry about it," he said when I explained to him the whole matter. "It's nothing. I'll take care of it."

I wasn't so sure.

– 41 –

I drove from Sutter's office back to mine, a ten-minute drive, and the phone was ringing when I walked in. It was Mom. She said there were cops all around the house, searching for me, and she advised me to make myself scarce. As those words left her mouth, the door of my office was crashed open, and a squad of cops, guns drawn, burst inside.

"Get away, quick!" my mother repeated on the phone. "They'll be there any minute."

"Too late, Mom" I said.

I was arrested and charged with conspiracy, grand larceny, and two counts of possession of stolen property (the police viewed the car and the registration as separate entities). The charges, altogether, were punishable by up to ten years in prison. Tony Morano was also arrested.

It was a strange arrest. Because of nothing more than an in-house employee/management hassle, I had been slapped with serious felonies. The newspapers and television stations covered it as big news. I was Sonny's son—a Franzese—so I had to be a mobster. Enhancing that image was the fact that Philly Vizzari, the mildly interested observer, was also arrested under the same charges. Philly drove a long Cadillac, smoked a fat stogie, and fancied himself a modern-day Al Capone. He was not the kind of guy with whom a college premed student wants to get arrested.

What didn't help, and what no doubt led to the Gestapo-like police action, was the fact that a parade of mobsters and organized crime associates had been observed coming in and out of the leasing office for months. Aside from those hanging around, many of my father's old friends figured they could at least get a good deal on an auto lease from me. Street guys have a difficult time getting credit, so I accommodated them—a kindness that proved to be a massive headache.

More times than not, these men lapsed on their payments, or made no payments at all. Included among these scofflaws was Philly, who I had always called Uncle Philly. Not only did Uncle Philly beat me out of a car, but he also tried to make a deal with Tony Morano behind my back to create a competing leasing company in a neighboring town.

These experiences taught me a lesson I would never forget: friendship and business don't mix, at least not when it came to Dad's friends. On top of the aggravation, my association with the mob soldiers had also brought the police down on me. Monday, after being forced to spend the weekend in jail, I was released on bail.

– 42 –

A week after my arrest, another Friday, I entered my office and came upon an ugly incident in the making. Morano was having a heated argument with two "bruisers," John "Big Chubby" Verrastro, thirty-four, and his brother Robert "Little Chubby" Verrastro, twenty-nine. Big Chubby was six-three and weighed three hundred pounds, and Little Chubby was six-four and weighed three hundred fifty pounds. Standing behind them was a third mobster, Albert Strauss, thirty-one, six feet tall and weighing two hundred ten pounds. A fourth man, Oscar Teitelbaum, twenty-nine, six-two, and a tightly muscled two hundred thirty pounds, waited outside in the car. The "Chubby Brothers" were threatening to tear Morano apart. At issue was an old man's car: Morano had sold it on consignment and then decided to keep the money, and the Chubbys and crew had come to collect.

I learned what the problem was, did my best to resolve it, and then withdrew into my inner office. Inside, I put my feet up on the desk, settled back, and called Maria.

Then suddenly, *Boom!* The door slammed open again, and the office filled with men carrying shotguns. I didn't know what to think. Was it a hit? A robbery? What now?

"Freeze!" one of the men shouted. "You're under arrest."

The words came as a relief. Of all the possibilities, cops were the best. There were fifteen to twenty police officers this time, twice as many as before. They were inside, outside, in plainclothes and in uniforms. They swept up everyone in sight—me, Morano, the Chubby Brothers, Al Strauss, Oscar Teitelbaum in the car, and two of my employees who chose the wrong time to be hanging around, Jerry Zimmerman and Peter "Apollo" Frappolo.

I was handcuffed to Big Chubby, who was acting like a caged bull. The big man yelled and cursed the cops and dragged me around like a rag doll. I yelled at him to mellow out, but Big Chubby continued his frantic act all through the ride to the police station.

Once there, I heard the familiar voice of one of the officers. "You need anything, Michael?"

"Yeah," I answered. "Get me away from this maniac!"

The officer smiled and uncuffed me.

It took five hours for the police to come up with their charges, and I figured I was in the clear. All I had done was pass through the office where an argument was in session. I didn't even know some of these men.

When the charges were sorted out, an officer read them: "Conspiracy, grand larceny, extortion, and coercion, against Franzese." I couldn't believe what I was hearing.

At the arraignment the next day, I stood in the middle, completely dwarfed by the monstrous gang. Aside from the Chubby Brothers and their crew, Zimmerman was six-five, two hundred seventy-five pounds, and Frappolo was five-eleven, two hundred forty pounds. In the middle of the prosecutor's impassioned reading of the charges, he stopped, turned with dramatic flourish, pointed at me, and blared, "And that one in the middle—Michael Franzese—he's the ringleader!"

His theatrics backfired. The judge and most of the gallery burst out laughing. Here I was, a twenty-two-year-old college kid, five-ten, one hundred sixty pounds, and I was supposed to be the big boss?

The judge, stifling a laugh, admonished the prosecutor, "Are you sure you got your facts straight?"

When it came my turn to speak, I was equally impassioned.

"Your Honor, I'm going to college and trying to make a living. I don't know what I'm doing here. Every Friday, the cops come in and break down my door and stab guns in my face. Now I'm here with a bunch of guys I've never seen before in my life, and I'm their leader?"

The judge was sympathetic, but not sympathetic enough. I was arraigned on a $25,000 bond.

— 43 —

The situation at the leasing office remained tense. At midweek, Morano and I had a brief argument. I had discovered that he had a weakness for gambling and had been skimming money from the business to support his habit. I'd overlooked it at first, but now I'd had enough.

"You go back there in the shop and work it off," I said. "I don't want to see you in this office again."

I installed Zimmerman and Frappolo as the leasing agents and went about business as usual. The plan was to send Morano a message and get him to stop his pilfering.

Three days later, Friday afternoon, I arrived at the office with two of my father's friends, Jake and Vinnie Perozzi. As I went into the office, I saw that the place was crawling with police officers.

"What's with you guys?" I said. "Every Friday you come to arrest me."

I turned and looked for the Perozzi brothers, and they were nowhere to be seen. Although they had been only a step behind me, they were veteran players and had made the cops and disappeared without a trace.

Zimmerman, Frappolo, and I were arrested and charged with coercion for attempting to squeeze Morano out of his business. The charge began to make everything clear. Morano, in deep with his gambling debts, had borrowed $10,000 from Philly Vizzari. Unable to pick a fast horse, he had squandered the loan. As a trade-off, he agreed to be wired in an attempt to set up both me and Vizzari.

This explained the commotion the previous Friday. The detectives, listening in, had heard the Chubby Brothers going wild and making threats. They had swarmed in, only to discover that it was just two giant hotheads trying to collect a small debt. This also explained their long delay in filing charges. The whole elaborate setup had been intended to catch me. Instead, they had netted a separate gang. Figuring that their cover had been blown, they jumped on my disciplining of Morano and tried to cover their losses with the weak coercion charge.

The whole Chubby Brothers incident turned out to be a lucky break for me. Had the brothers not bullied and blustered their way in that Friday and frightened the police into taking indeliberate action, Morano might have worn a wire around me for months, pressing me and goading me into doing something illegal. (I later became friends with Big Chubby and the rest of the guys.)

At the precinct station, a grim-faced detective sat me down in an interrogation room.

"If anything happens to Tony Morano, we're coming after you," he threatened.

Weary of the harassment, I shot back, "I can't control what happens to liars."

I paid yet another bail bond, this one for $10,000, and was released again.

At 5:00 A.M. the following Friday morning, I was rocked out of the upper berth of the bunk beds I shared with my brother John by a voice blaring from a megaphone outside the house: "Michael Franzese, come out with your hands up."

I looked out the window. The lawn was covered with the flashing lights of police cars. It looked like a discotheque, only these people weren't dancers but an army of police officers. A thought pierced my brain: *Tony Morano must have been killed, and I'm going down for his murder.*

The next thing I saw was my mother outside on the porch.

"He's not here," she lied.

"We know he's in there," the megaphone responded. "We'll break the door down if he doesn't come out soon."

"He's not here!" my mother defiantly repeated.

Having been forced to clean and repair my office three times in as many weeks, I dreaded seeing the police bursting in and marching through the house. I pushed up the bedroom window and shouted, "I'm coming down. Just let me get dressed!"

"You have five minutes," the response came.

Outside, the officers roughly cuffed my hands behind my back. They were serious and nasty. I was more sure than ever that Tony Morano must be dead, and that I was being blamed for his murder.

At the precinct house, I spotted Zimmerman and Frappolo sitting in a detective's office, leisurely drinking coffee and eating doughnuts. I couldn't believe it. Here I was, cuffed and shackled, and they were enjoying doughnuts?

"What are you guys doing here? Having breakfast?" I inquired.

"The police called us and told us to come down," Zimmerman said.

What was more incredible was the upshot. I had been dragged out of bed and arrested merely because a second count had been added to the coercion indictment. It was something that could have been accomplished with the stroke of a pen and then mailed to my attorney. Instead, it had been decided that the blue army must invade under the cover of darkness, ready to break down the door and trample my mother's freshly raked carpets.

It was no coincidence that all these arrests had occurred on Fridays. This is a common police tactic used when they want to get under someone's skin. Since judges work Monday through Friday, nine to five, like the majority of people do, a Friday arrest, especially a Friday afternoon arrest, results in a Monday arraignment, which means a weekend in jail for the suspects. There was definitely a method to their madness.

— 44 —

In 1974, I went to trial three times on the fur coat caper. Prior to the proceedings, Uncle Philly sold me out, blaming everything on me in an attempt to free himself from the charge. Visiting my father at Leavenworth, I informed him of his buddy

Philly's "loyalty." The news infuriated him, but it didn't surprise him.

"What did you think he was, a stand-up guy?" he said.

"But he was always around the house. I called him Uncle Philly. I don't understand," I insisted.

Dad just shrugged.

I sensed my father's dismay over my legal problems, so to ease his mind, I tried passing it all off as "no big deal." But that only made him angrier.

"No big deal! You see my clothes," he said, grasping his prison uniform. "You see these bars. You're telling me it's 'no big deal'? You got more indictments at twenty-two than I've had in my entire life!"

Calming down, Dad asked me how school was going, and that led to more bad news. I explained that I'd had too many distractions recently and wasn't able to concentrate on my studies. At that point, I confessed, it didn't look to me like I could handle the long grind of becoming a doctor, especially now with all the legal and financial problems resulting from my recent arrests.

He looked away, for he knew in that moment that the sins of the father were being visited upon the son. He had been so proud when I legally took his name instead of Grillo's, but now the Franzese name was working to cripple me.

Despite Philly's undermining my case, the charges against me were weak. The jury hung several times, 7-5, 10-2, and 11-1, all favoring acquittal. The fact that the case was tried a third time after a 10-2 acquittal vote was a legal rarity (and a waste of taxpayers' money), but it spoke of the prosecutors' intense desire to feather their caps with the conviction of another Franzese.

During the third trial, Mom spotted an attractive young woman from the neighborhood on the jury. She was a substitute teacher who had taught my brother John and sister Gia. Mom alerted me, and I started giving the young woman the eye. We traded glances and smiles the whole time the trial was going on, and I figured that I was assured of another hung jury because of this.

Unfortunately, Maria was a regular visitor to the courtroom. Near the end of the trial, I made the mistake of giving her a quick hug and kiss in view of the jury box. When the jurors were unofficially polled outside after the 11-1 verdict, it turned out that the only one who had voted to convict me was the substitute teacher I thought I had befriended.

— 45 —

The "Chubby Brothers" indictment went to trial in the hot summer of 1974. We were dubbed "the West Hempstead Seven" by the press. The prosecutor's case was even weaker than that of the fur coat caper. Even so, the trial became a major ordeal. With seven defendants and six attorneys, such mundane activities as choosing a jury took nearly a month.

One problem was my dress and demeanor. I sat among my massive codefendants in a crisp suit and often entered the courtroom carrying my attorney's briefcase. The prospective jurors kept mistaking me for one of the lawyers.

A few days into the trial, one of the jurors wrote the judge a disturbing note, and the judge promptly declared a mistrial. It was never revealed what the note said, but it's not hard to imagine. The juror must have suddenly realized he had a relative who knew one of the defendants, or something similar, and could therefore be considered biased. The result was that the attorneys had to start over.

After another tedious period of jury selection, the trial chugged along in fits and starts. The courtroom was hot, and the stress was intense, and my hefty codefendants started dropping like flies. First the Chubby Brothers went down, fainting and hyperventilating. Then Jerry Zimmerman, Peter Frappolo, and the others fell ill. Everyone but me. The paramedics had to keep rushing in with oxygen, and this resulted in the judge delaying or canceling the proceedings for the day.

"This trial must be sponsored by the Red Cross," someone cracked as yet another defendant plopped to the floor.

At one point, the prosecutor made a dramatic announcement that someone had confessed and implicated a codefendant. A rumble was heard among the defendants. Zimmerman was certain it must be Frappolo. He began ranting in my ear.

"I knew it. He's no good. I knew he wouldn't last. The man's a pathological liar. I knew he would break. Let me at him!"

The prosecutor made his announcement. "The man who confessed is Jerry Zimmerman!"

I nearly doubled over with laughter.

Jerry shot up out of his chair and began screaming that it was a lie, that he was no rat. He was so agitated that he had to be restrained.

As it turned out, the prosecutors had leapt to conclusions because of a vague statement the verbose Zimmerman had made during his police interrogation. It had not been a confession at all, and the judge promptly threw it out.

The star witness of the trial was Tony Morano. I figured Morano was the state's entire case. Get to him, and the ball game would be over. My attorney didn't share this view and advised me against it. I chose to ignore this advice and had a friend set up a meeting with Morano.

Tony was apologetic. He explained that he had gotten in deep with his gambling debts, was being squeezed by Philly, and saw no way out.

"Don't worry," he assured me. "I'll bail you out of this. You watch."

And Morano came through. He took the stand and double-crossed the prosecutors by testifying in a manner that cleared me and virtually the entire gang.

After that, all the Nassau County prosecutors had left were the tapes from Morano's body mike, and the quality of the recordings was terrible. The jurors could clearly hear the words "maim," "kill," "strangle," "murder," and "break you apart" as the Chubby Brothers performed their tough-guy tag-team act, but no one could fill in the gaps. And no one could determine who was threatening to kill or maim whom.

When the tape evidence fell through, the prosecution's case started unraveling to an embarrassing degree. Before the prosecutors finished presenting their evidence, Zimmerman's and Frappolo's attorneys interrupted and moved that charges against their clients be dropped because of lack of evidence. When the prosecutors couldn't come up with a single reason the judge shouldn't grant the unusual motion, the two men were freed.

After the prosecutors finished the state's case, my attorney made a similar motion, and the judge granted it as well. That left Big Chubby, Al Strauss, and Oscar Teitelbaum. (Little Chubby had been unable to complete the trial for medical reasons and was scheduled to be tried when he recovered.) The defense presented its case, and the whole gang was acquitted.

The sad irony is that the person least involved, Oscar Teitelbaum, ended up doing time. Although he was acquitted, he had been just twenty-nine days out of jail when the cops invaded the leasing company. Consequently, the state slapped Oscar with a parole violation. All he had done was go for a ride with the Chubby Brothers. And what a long ride! It cost him two years of his life.

The final indictment, the one based on the banishment of Morano to the body shop, eroded, and the prosecutors dropped the coercion charge down to a misdemeanor. I refused even the misdemeanor, and the prosecutors dropped it further, down to a violation. I paid a $250 fine, and the matter was ended.

— 46 —

Although I had successfully dodged a whole volley of law enforcement bullets, the damage to my businesses proved fatal. The bad publicity surrounding the arrests and trials, the six months spent fighting the case and the legal expenses involved dried up the leasing operation and caused us to lose our critical credit line. The body shop went down with it.

My savings were all depleted, and I was suddenly down to my last $10. I sat in a Greek restaurant with Maria, scrutinized the menu, and tried to determine how we could both eat, tip the waitress, and stay within my limited budget. I found the need to think that way depressing, as I did the fact that I walked out of the restaurant with only thirteen cents in my pocket. That day I vowed never to have to face such an afternoon again.

With some doors closing on me, another interesting one suddenly opened. Vinnie Vingo, a friend from the Italian-American Civil Rights League, was operating a bustling weekend flea market on the grounds of the Republic Field Airport in Farmingdale, Long Island. He asked me to help manage it and offered me a salary of $300 a weekend. I accepted and soon found the flea market to be a great opportunity.

There were six hundred spots available in the flea market and a list of two thousand vendors trying to get in. Since I was in charge of handing out locations, I began fielding offers of $20 to $100 to reserve a prime spot. I told Vinnie about it, and we shared the bonus.

But I had an even better plan. Many of the vendors who rent spaces needed money to replenish their stock, so I figured that the market was ripe for a good loan-sharking operation. Most of them were regulars whose livelihoods were tied to their slots, so they could be depended upon. I began farming out my salary, charging a point a week on any loan more than $1,000 ($10 a week until the principal was paid) and up to ten points on smaller loans in the range of $100 to $300.

Although I had been repeatedly arrested, indicted, and brought to trial, this was the first time, aside from punching the cop, that I had ever broken the law. Still, lending money to mom-and-pop flea market vendors didn't make me feel that I was in the same league with Jack the Ripper. Truthfully, it didn't feel like crime at all. I looked at it as providing investment capital for my clients' small businesses. It was a service they happily lined up to take advantage of.

I guessed right about the vendors' dependability. They were good customers, paid back their points on time, restocked their stands, and dutifully paid back their principals. Within six months, I was clearing $1,000 to $2,000 a weekend in shylock interest, and I could look at a restaurant menu again without worrying about having enough to pay the tab.

The flea market shylock operation had a limited life. Police officials continued to track me and started snooping around Vinnie's market. That made Vinnie nervous. He didn't need the attention my presence attracted, especially since I was operating a lucrative loan-shark operation. He suggested that I take time off, and I didn't argue. Vinnie had done enough for me, and it was time to move on.

— 47 —

I decided to make an attempt at getting back into some legitimate business. The auto business still intrigued me, and I now went in search of a bank or credit company to finance a new leasing operation. In the process, I kept hearing the same thing—banks preferred new-car dealerships, so I set about trying to get my hands on one. I put out feelers and got wind of a Mazda dealership on Main Street in Hempstead that was for sale. Mazda had introduced its bold new rotary engines in the early 1970s, but by 1974, the cars were dying with startling regularity. The problem proved to be faulty seals between the five pancake-like engine sections. As immobile Mazdas began littering the countryside, the public became wary of buying Mazdas, and business hit the skids.

Because of this situation, I was able to buy the Hempstead dealership from a man named Joe Aveni for the fire-sale price of $75,000. I put down $25,000 (flea market shylock cash) and financed the rest. I then found a new partner, a wild kid named John Marshall who was making a mint with a fleet of "roach coach" sandwich trucks. I sold Marshall a partnership for $50,000 gleaned from the pockets of hungry workmen on construction sites. His money provided me with some working capital.

The problem we faced now was how to make money with cars no one wanted, and the answer proved to be from factory warranties. While everyone was deserting Mazda, I saw gold hidden in all those broken-down cars. I refurbished the dealership's service area, beefed up the staff, and then phoned Mazda and said that I wanted my shop to be the main service point in the district.

Mazda, fighting a public-relations disaster, was ready to stand behind its warranties and was paying dealerships $1,200 per car to repair the hemorrhaging seals. The materials cost next to nothing, and the repairs took about five hours. So, after paying the mechanics, there was still a profit of $900 on each repaired engine. Within weeks, our service bays were full, and we had broken-down cars backed up all over our lot.

Getting the sales division going proved to be a much greater challenge. The previous owner had promised that his bank would continue to provide the floor plan financing. They would buy the new cars as they came in and hold the titles until they could be sold off the lot. But no sooner had the transfer papers for the dealership been signed than the bank backed out of this commitment. I learned of this just as a carrier truck with eight new cars pulled onto our lot. I called Mazda headquarters and was able to convince the regional sales manager to leave the automobiles without receiving the $80,000 bank draft he had been expecting.

"Give me a month to get a new floor plan," I pleaded, and he agreed.

So now I had to go shopping for a new bank, and it was a great challenge. Personally, I was twenty-four years old and had no credit history, and the business was so new that I had no way of producing a financial statement. I had nothing but a trail of negative newspaper articles that I was hoping the bankers hadn't read. I was turned away at bank after bank until time began to run out on me.

I went back to Mel Cooper, the financier who had helped start me in the leasing business. I was desperate.

"Give me some names," I pleaded. "Anybody."

Cooper directed me to the Small Business Administration (SBA), a government agency, and the Small Business Investment Corporation (SBIC), private lenders who are supported ninety percent by the government. I figured I'd have my best luck with the SBIC. Cooper gave me the name of SBIC agent Thomas Scharf of Lloyd Capital Corporation in Edgewater, New Jersey, and I paid him a visit.

"Who makes the final decision?" I asked the affable Scharf.

"Me," he said. "I'm the loan committee."

Scharf was intrigued by my description of the Mazda operation, and he made arrangements to visit the dealership the next day. He arrived with his accountant as scheduled. Despite Mazda's troubles, our place was impressive. The showroom was large and beautiful, and the service bay was hopping. Scharf and his accountant went over the existing books and reviewed the entire operation.

"Let me and my accountant meet in private for a moment," he then suggested.

"Sure," I said, directing them to the manager's office.

They emerged fifteen minutes later to say, "We've got a deal."

Some deal it was! Scharf offered us a $250,000 line of credit, but at fifteen percent interest, about three percent higher than

Michael Franzese

the banks were offering. And, on top of that, he wanted a $75 to $150 "consulting fee" per car sold.

"Tom," I said, protesting these near-usurious terms, "this is expensive."

But he was the only game in town at the moment, and so I had to agree to his terms.

Despite the financial burden, the dealership prospered. Mazda upgraded its line, began producing conventional piston engines, advertised heavily, and regained a reasonable share of the market. Within a few years, the operation began taking in $100,000 a month, $25,000 of which was profit. Everyone was happy.

When the SBA began a routine investigation of Scharf, I spoke up for him.

"Without his 'consulting' advice, I'd have never made it," I lied. "He's important to my business."

— 48 —

As word of my financial rebound spread, many criminal types again began to visit me. Among them were some prison-fresh entrepreneurs directed to me by my father. The first was Jimmy. Jimmy was said to be a wizard at the fruit-and-vegetable business, and Dad had highly recommended him. I put up $25,000 to open a market in Suffolk County, called Sonny's Farm Circle. The market promptly went under since Jimmy made off with most of the capital.

Next came Joey, a burly truck driver. Joey told my father about all the money they could make in the long-haul trucking business. All they needed was the tractor.

"Michael, I love your father," he told me. "If anybody hurts you, I'll bring you their head on a platter."

I bought Joey a $12,500 tractor, painted it shiny black, and added new chrome bumpers. Joey nearly cried when he saw that truck. He was so happy he hugged and kissed me and again vowed his undying loyalty. He then got into the truck, threw it in gear, rolled down the road—and was never seen again.

"Dad," I said during my next prison visit, "don't send me any more of your friends. Please."

Undaunted, Dad tried again. Another ex-con, Ronny the Shark, came with impeccable credentials as "the best loan shark in town," and I fronted $100,000 to put him on the street. Despite getting up to four points a week, I got back only $80,000 at the end of the year instead of receiving the expected $300,000. The guy, without question, was a great shylock, and he had generated a couple hundred grand in interest. The trouble was that he was a lousy handicapper. He had gambled away all of the interest, and part of the principal, on the ponies.

"Dad, *please*—no more of your guys," I pleaded anew.

In June of 1975, I finally ran out of excuses and married Maria. She had stood by me through all the arrests and trials, never wavering once in her love, and I had come to care for her in a way that was deeper and more meaningful then the cheap thrills I thought I wanted. There was no question that she would make a perfect wife. She would be devoted and faithful and never give me a moment's worry.

The reception was held at Queens Terrace, a catering hall in Queens that was a mainstay for mob marriages. Six hundred people attended, including a battalion of Cosa Nostra soldiers. Among the people paying their respects was Al Gallo, Crazy Joe's brother. That was ironic: it had long been rumored that my father had ordered the hit on Crazy Joe. Apparently, it was all just business.

But this was just a sidebar to the events of the afternoon and evening. Maria and I were the stars of the moment, and ours was a union that made both my mother and father very happy.

— 49 —

The year 1975 marked yet another milestone in my life. It was the year I decided to get involved in Dad's businesses. I was desperate to earn enough money to pay lawyers and private investigators to help get him out of prison, so I decided to tell him the next time I visited him at Leavenworth that I was giving up my hopes of becoming a doctor to dedicate myself more seriously to business. We argued about it in the visiting room for some time, but when he saw that my mind was made up, he took another angle.

"Michael," he said, "if you're going to be on the streets, you need to do it the right way. I'll send word downtown, and you'll be contacted by one of my associates. He'll tell you what to do."

I wasn't exactly sure what my father was getting at. He had sheltered me from his business affairs for most of my life. We lived in the suburbs, not in the city or in Brooklyn, where mob guys were everywhere and were viewed as celebrities and big shots. I knew the designations "goodfellow" or "made man" meant that someone had been inducted into La Cosa Nostra as a soldier, and that trusted mob associates were often called "wiseguys," but I only had a vague sense of what the secret brotherhood was all about. What I did know was that the organization was my father's heart and soul. If he wanted me involved, it was an honor I could not take lightly.

"Okay," I responded, emotionlessly.

"What would you do if you had to kill someone?" he asked.

I was taken aback by this question.

"If I had to, I could," I heard myself respond.

"Would it bother you?"

"Depends upon the circumstances."

Dad smiled. Apparently, that was the correct answer.

I wasn't completely naïve. I knew what my father was saying. Before one could be invited to go through La Cosa

Nostra's secret, time-honored induction ceremony, a recruit had to "make his bones." Making one's bones meant doing some "work" for the organization, and "work" included the possibility of killing someone. As with most mob terms, the special language was developed to thwart hidden listening devices and to confuse the courts.

Typically, there was never a clear explanation of why my father decided at that particular moment to "straighten me out." This phrase itself is one of the more quizzical of mob euphemisms and means the opposite of what it might seem. "Straighten out," no doubt, developed from the idea of taking a wild, cunning street criminal, embracing him into the mob, and putting his talents to more productive use.

This may explain why I was being invited to join La Cosa Nostra. Despite my history of legitimate business success, I had showed no timidity in venturing over the legal line. My shylock operation at the flea market had proven that. I already had a long history of arrests, grand jury indictments, and trials. I had been branded a mobster by the press while I was still clean and serious about becoming a doctor. Also, the word among the families was that I was "a comer," meaning that I was aggressive, motivated, and determined to be successful. I was also proving to be resilient. The Nassau County police and prosecutors had tried to destroy me, and I had survived.

I assumed that Dad was afraid one of the other four families might "straighten me out" before he had a chance. He figured that if I wasn't going to become a doctor, and I was determined to play both sides of the business world, legal and illegal, I might as well operate under the protective wing of the Colombo family.

A tougher question to answer is why I accepted Dad's proposal. I didn't need the mob. My parents had given me an education, I'd had the opportunity to become a doctor, and I was doing well in my own business ventures. I wasn't a street punk from a broken home in search of the "family" I had never known. I didn't even believe in that stuff. I was a regular guy with a nice wife and a successful auto dealership.

But I was my father's son, and my desire to win favor with him remained as intense as ever. If he wanted me to become a member of La Cosa Nostra, I wasn't going to question it. And I never did.

I never asked Dad why he wanted me to take over his businesses, and I never asked him why he chose that particular moment in time to do it. All I knew—and was comforted in knowing that *he* knew—was that it would draw the two of us even closer together. Being close to my father, winning his respect and approval, and, more importantly, being accepted as his "son" remained my prime motivation.

— 50 —

There was another unspoken benefit in joining the mob. The way I saw it, my father had been forgotten by the Colombo family because of his long prison sentence. Although he understood the life and never complained, I had a hard time dealing with that fact. With me in the family, I might be able to use La Cosa Nostra's influence and vast network of contacts and associations to help free him from prison.

My induction was made possible by a mob high commission decision. From 1955 to 1972, the mob was a closed shop. Virtually no one was inducted during that period. This ironclad policy was developed to keep the families tight and secret and to eliminate the possibility of informers or undercover agents infiltrating. By 1972, with the ranks thinning because of death, old age, and imprisonment, the doors were opened. It was time for fresh blood.

I was formally proposed as a member of the family by Jo Jo Vitacco, a longtime friend of Dad's. Jo Jo was a mite of a man, barely five-foot-four, but he walked with a tough-guy swagger and looked every bit the street soldier he was. Jo Jo spent more time behind bars than free, and in prison he worked as a barber. He could drink with men twice his size, and up to the time of his death, he ran five miles a day. In his later years, he owned and operated a bar on Metropolitan Avenue in Brooklyn called the JV Lounge.

Jo Jo took me to a house on Carroll Street in Brooklyn. It was a burglar's home that was being used as a meeting place. There, Jo Jo introduced me to Colombo family acting boss Thomas DiBella, a big, lumbering man who had spent fifty years working the unions and the docks. DiBella was seventy-two years old. He had survived in the mob by making sure he never stepped on anyone's toes. It was that quality, along with his advanced age, that had prompted Carmine Persico to install DiBella as boss until he himself could get out of jail.

After acknowledging my father and how warmly everyone regarded him, DiBella's speech to me that evening was similar to the standard line given to all prospects. "I want you to understand that La Cosa Nostra comes before anything. You are your own man. If you are inducted into our life, you and your father would then be equals. Fathers have no priority over sons, and no brother has priority over another. We are all as one, united in blood. Once you become part of this family, there is no greater bond among men. Stay close to Jo Jo. Whatever he says, you do. When and if we are ready for you, you'll know."

By this I understood DiBella to be saying, "When and if we feel that you have proven yourself worthy and have earned the privilege of becoming a member of the family, we'll let you know." (Some men waited more than twenty years to be deemed worthy, and their call to join the family never came.)

After the meeting, my name, along with those of the other potential inductees, was circulated around the five families. This was the mob's version of a standard credit check. If anyone had any reason to object to me becoming a member of the family, he would let DiBella know quickly.

The name circulation also had a second purpose. If anyone in another family felt he had a claim on a prospect, he was to let that be known as well. That's exactly what happened with me. Pasquale "Paddy Mack" Marchiola, a Genovese soldier, raised an objection. He argued that I had done some business with one of his friends, and that made me his recruit. Paddy Mack gambled that this would counter my own father's claim and negate the time I spent walking a picket line with family boss Joe Colombo. The mob commission overruled Mack's claim.

A curious factor in the name circulation period was that I was never called in to confirm the heritage of my biological father. La Cosa Nostra only inducts Italians, and stepsons don't count. For all they knew, Louis Grillo could have been Irish, Jewish, or Greek and changed his name. Normally, a recruit would have been scrutinized on that subject, but I was never called in to explain. It was thought that someone must have known that Grillo was Italian or that perhaps my father had cleared the matter.

— 51 —

My assigned caporegime was Andrew "Andy Mush" Russo, a cousin of Carmine Persico, and one of my first activities during my "pledge" period was to invite Russo in on a nightclub deal I had in the works. The owner of a discotheque on Long Island needed some cash to book star acts into his youth-oriented club. Russo and I kicked in $7,500 each on the promise of getting a percentage of the weekend take until the debt could be repaid. The percentage could go as high as $2,000 if the place was packed—a return that equaled a healthy 13.3 loan-shark points a week.

Norby Walters, a partner of my father's, booked the acts into the club. He provided such national superstars as the

Spinners, the Stylistics, the O'Jays, Harold Melvin and the Blue Notes, the Trammps, the Drifters, and the Supremes. These big acts provided a windfall, while the lesser-known groups produced less revenue. Regardless, I made sure that Russo got his thousand every week, often kicking in my entire share to bring his take up to the maximum. Sometimes, after healthy weekends, I still gave my captain my own take, handing over $1,500 to $2,000. I'd explain that it had been an unusually free-spending crowd.

My generosity was a calculated move. I wanted Russo to spread news around that when you made a deal with Michael Franzese, it would pay off. That, in turn, would open the door to bigger stakes for me in the future.

This "pledge" period lasted nearly a year. The family took this time to train the recruits in discipline and carefully measure their character, all the while waiting for the right low-level "work" to present itself. I spent most of my indoctrination acting as a chauffeur and gofer for DiBella. I was called upon to drive the acting boss around on his daily schedule, usually to meetings and restaurants. Ironically, they almost always used my cars because, in this case, the chauffeur owned better automobiles than the boss.

Through this minimal activity, I was able to meet various upper-echelon Colombo family members, along with the bosses and captains of the four other New York families. Almost everyone who greeted me paid tribute to my father. The meets were brief encounters in hallways, lobbies, or on sidewalks, and I was never invited to attend the actual official meetings.

Outwardly, I performed my functions like the eager hopeful I was supposed to be. Inwardly, however, I was bothered by the servile duties and was not happy about the time they took from my business operations. I also didn't particularly care for Brooklyn, where DiBella's activities were centered. I preferred wide-open spaces. Wisely, I kept those feelings to myself.

As boring as gofering for DiBella was, Jo Jo Vitacco also made frequent use of the yo-yo string I was on. He would summon me to his bar merely to have someone to talk to. I was in the process of building an assortment of businesses and disliked having to spend my afternoons and evenings watching Jo Jo get drunk. But, again, I kept my mouth shut and accepted all of this as part of the process.

On one occasion, things did get interesting. Jo Jo was lathered and in mean spirits when I arrived at his place as ordered one day. He was having trouble with his latest girlfriend, a barmaid half his age. After grousing about her for an hour or so, he leaped off a barstool and decided to go a few more rounds with her over the telephone.

He lost again, and when he did, he slammed the receiver down, retreated into his office, and emerged within seconds waving a .38 Special. Next he started firing wildly at the telephone and cursing his girlfriend. The phone was set against a concrete wall, and bullets ricocheted off the wall and began whizzing around the bar, shattering mirrors and whisky bottles. I ducked and lunged for him, afraid that any second a bullet was going to bounce back and catch the little gangster right between the eyes. I grabbed him, wrapped my arms around him, and, after a struggle, was able to calm him down.

On other occasions, Jo Jo's lounge was as dull as a graveyard. These would be the nights that FBI agent Bernie Welsh made an appearance. He would waltz in, set himself down in the center of the bar, begin to drink as only an Irishman can, and loudly greet and glad-hand any mobster who entered the place. As soon as any mobsters spotted him, they'd get out of there as quickly as possible.

"Welsh, you no-good bum, you're killin' my business!" Jo Jo would rant, bobbing up and down like a cork.

Welsh would laugh, order another drink, and settle in for a long night.

Whenever Welsh saw me at Jo Jo's, he would really become animated.

"Hey, it's my old buddy Michael Franzese! Put it here, man!" he'd shout, extending a meaty paw.

Once, when I refused to shake his hand and ducked into a nearby restaurant, the FBI agent tracked me down.

"Michael, I'm insulted," he said, hovering over the table like a storm cloud. "Why didn't you shake my hand?"

"In front of all those people? You jump in like you're my best friend? You must be kidding!"

"You can still shake my hand," Welsh said, standing firm.

"All right," I said, standing. "I'll shake your hand. Now go over to the bar and leave me alone."

"You sure you don't want me to eat with you guys?" he'd ask.

"We're sure, Bernie," I said. "Go to the bar. The first drink's on me."

— 52 —

Careful as I was, I made two mistakes during my training. The first occurred when I dropped off DiBella at Junior's Restaurant on Flatbush Avenue. Instead of waiting in front of the restaurant by the car, I became edgy and started pacing up and down the block. When DiBella came out, I was on the opposite corner. DiBella chewed me out. "If I tell you to wait out front, you wait out front! You wait there for three days if you have to. You don't walk. You don't go to the bathroom. You stand right there. How did you know I wouldn't come running out and need to leave immediately?"

The second mistake was arriving ten minutes late for an appointment on a cold winter morning. Because of it, I was left standing on Carroll Street for six hours. I asked the family members who passed by what to do, and they explained that I had to keep waiting. DiBella passed by twice but left me shivering on the corner. After that, I learned that a 3:00 P.M. meeting meant arriving at 2:30, a 4:00 P.M. meeting meant arriving at 3:30, and if you expected any difficulty arriving at a meeting the next day, you camped out on the spot the previous night. If your car broke down on the way to a meet, you abandoned it and jumped into a taxi or stole another car in order to make it on time.

Aside from the usurious rates on the nightclub loan, I did nothing illegal during my indoctrination. I was invited to go on various stickups and burglaries by soldiers and fellow recruits, but I always declined. That was accepted. The mob never chose a job for its members. A numbers runner who came in remained a numbers runner. An auto thief continued to steal cars. A loan shark continued to lend money and a bookie to take bets. The mob never tried to make a numbers runner into a loan shark or a bookie into an auto thief. Since I was a businessman, I wasn't expected to rob convenience stores. I was free to decline to participate in any activity that wasn't my specialty. However, when it came time for a recruit to do some "work," he usually had no such option.

Fortunately, my case was unique. I never received the order. From what I could guess, there were two reasons for the rare break with Cosa Nostra tradition. First, there was such a rush to induct new recruits, especially in the severely weakened Colombo family, that the initiation murder was waived and instead marked down as debt to be paid at a later date. Secondly, the number of recruits the mob wanted to train far exceeded the number of people the bosses could think of to kill. That made for gangs of eager recruits who were all dressed up with no one to "knock off." Whatever the reason, I was spared—thankfully.

— 53 —

The moment of my formal induction into the mob finally arrived. It was Halloween, 1975, and I was about to shed the mantle of the legitimate businessman and figuratively costume myself in the pinstripe suit and wide-brim fedora of the world's most notorious secret criminal organization—but I didn't know that yet.

Jo Jo called and told me to meet him at his bar on Metropolitan Avenue in Brooklyn and to wear a suit. I was given no indication about what was to transpire. We drove to a catering house in Bensonhurst. There I was escorted to a small office down the hall from the main ballroom where five other recruits were nervously waiting. I knew three of the five men, including Jimmy Angellino. As I sat and waited with them, I looked around the room. If the pattern was to mix two guys from each hit squad, and the initiation requirement hadn't been waived for the others, that meant three people had been murdered, maybe more, to uphold the tradition that brought the six of us there.

I was the third recruit called. Jo Jo came out, a big smile cutting through his tight, hard features, and he nodded for me to follow him into another room.

The lights in the room were dim, and the mood was as solemn as the darkness. In the center of the banquet hall, the hierarchy of the Colombo family sat on folding chairs spread out in the shape of a U. As I walked inside the U, I recognized the stern faces of the men sitting around me. The captains were on the edges, and the closer one sat to the center, the more powerful his position. I recognized John "Johnny Irish" Matera, one of my father's soldiers who had risen to be a captain himself. Matera gave me a nod.

In the exact middle of the U was Tom DiBella, the family boss. To DiBella's left was the family consigliere, Alphonse "Allie Boy" Persico, Carmine's brother. (Normally, the family underboss would have been to DiBella's right, but at that time there was no underboss.)

I stood in front of DiBella.

"Are you ready to take the oath of La Cosa Nostra?" the big man asked.

"Yes," I answered.

"Okay, cup your hands."

I did as I was told, and a small piece of paper materialized in DiBella's hand. DiBella lit it and dropped the flaming paper into the pocket formed by my hands.

"If you ever violate the oath of La Cosa Nostra, may you burn in hell like the fire burning in your hand," he warned.

I felt only a tinge of heat as the paper was quickly consumed. The act was purely symbolic, not, as some believe, a show of toughness or of the ability to withstand pain.

DiBella grabbed my right hand in his big, rough hand, held up my thumb, and pricked it with a pin. It stung. As the blood formed into a fat drop, DiBella squeezed my thumb. The drop of blood became too heavy and spilled to the floor. Looking down, I could see the splattered drops of blood from the two recruits who had come before me.

"This is a blood tie," he intoned. "Your allegiance to La Cosa Nostra is bound by blood. Should you ever violate this oath, your blood will be shed."

DiBella squeezed again, harder this time, and another fat drop of blood fell to the floor. The point was made. I could feel the breath of death in the room. Violate the oath, and my blood would spill in quarts, not drops. That's what it was all about—life or death. Humanity at its most instinctive level. Follow the rules or die.

The oath, we were told, included the following: keep the secrets and traditions you will hear and learn about. Do not violate another member's wife, sister, or daughter. Never raise your hand against another member. Carry out orders. La Cosa Nostra comes before anything and everything in your life.

"Michael Franzese, do you accept and understand the blood oath and blood tie of La Cosa Nostra?" DiBella asked.

"Yes," I answered solemnly.

"Good. Now you have been born again. You are *amico nostro* [a friend of ours]."

I shook DiBella's hand and kissed him once on each cheek. Then I repeated this procedure with Allie Boy, Johnny Irish, Andy Russo, and the rest of the captains. The congratulations were just as serious as the rest of the ceremony. The air remained thick and tense. Any one of the men I was shaking hands with and kissing might one day be called upon to kill me. Or I might one day be called upon to kill him. That's what struck me the most about the entire ceremony. Instant capital punishment, often without trial or jury. It was the central theme of the evening—death, murder, and spilled blood.

Yet, as I was leaving the dimly lit room that night, I found that I was excited. This feeling grew until it became exhilaration. I was now part of an army of blood brothers. I was locked into a brotherhood few would ever experience or even understand. And more importantly, I had become one with my father. I had bonded. I could never be rejected now, never be banished from the house. That's all that really mattered. My father had accepted me as blood, blood spilled in drops on a wooden floor, but blood nonetheless. It was a joyous moment for me.

— 54 —

After the last recruit had been sworn in, we all, new family members and old alike, sat down at a large banquet table and shared a meal of pasta, veal, and chicken. In the course of the meal, the solemnity that had been felt so strongly in the air slowly lifted.

Later, outside in the foyer, Jo Jo appeared at my side.

"Now you can pick up your bag of money," he quipped.

My fellow inductees who overheard this raised their eyebrows, and Jo Jo and the men around him started to howl. It was mob humor, an old joke played on the recruits. I got the joke and would never forget the meaning behind it. There was no bag of money waiting for newly made men. There never had been, and there never would be.

We were not automatically given a salary or put on some-body's payroll. It was up to each man to make his own way. In fact, it was up to each man not only to carry his weight but also to kick a healthy share of his earnings back into the family kitty. Essentially, from a purely business standpoint, the mob was an elaborate criminal pyramid scheme.

As I drove home that night, the seriousness of what I had just done began to overwhelm me. Did I know what I was doing? I had given over my life—not for a few weeks or months or years—but forever. What if I didn't like this new life? What if I *hated* it? There was no easy way out. No excuse. I couldn't just say "take this job and shove it" when I felt like it. You couldn't quit the mob. If you quit, you died.

I wasn't like the others. It had not been my lifelong dream to be in La Cosa Nostra, and I didn't "get off" on the violence like some of the others did. I suddenly wondered if I had made a ter-rible mistake. Had I just signed my own death warrant?

No, I decided. It was the right move. I was now part of a pow-erful organization that stretched out across the world. Anywhere I went I would be welcomed and sheltered by my special brothers. Knowing that was a great feeling.

Besides, my father was part of this organization. It was his life, and it was what he wanted for me. So it couldn't be wrong.

When I arrived home that night, I kissed Maria and then sat down on the couch. A little later, the doorbell rang. I called for her to get it, but she had gone upstairs. So I went to the door myself.

The machine gun was the first thing I saw. Then the fedora and pinstriped suit.

"Gimme all da candy, or I'll blow ya away," a small voice said. It was just a kid—a straggler making a last few grabs at stuffing his trick-or-treat bag before calling it a night. Relieved beyond words, I looked around the room and spotted the bowl of candy Maria had provided for the stream of masqueraders.

"Hold on, tough guy," I said.

I grabbed two big handfuls of candy and dropped them into the kid's bulging shopping bag. His eyes became as big as silver dollars.

"Thanks, mister!"

"Were you really going to shoot me?" I asked.

The kid looked up, waved the toy machine gun, and affected his meanest snarl.

"Trick or treat. That's the rules, mister."

— 55 —

I went to work the next day as usual, and I didn't feel any different. Nothing had changed for me. Some of the other recruits changed drastically. They put on sleek suits, flashed diamond-and-gold pinky rings, and began walking with a swagger. But that wasn't for me, and it also wasn't the way of the family. The rule was, you never tell anyone who you are. You don't wear you credentials on your sleeve. You don't hand out business cards saying "Michael Franzese, Cosa Nostra Soldier." The people who need to know will know, or they will be told.

The key was in the introductions. "This is Tony. He's a friend of ours." That meant that Tony was in.

"This is Joey. He's a friend of mine." This meant that Joey was not in. Joey was merely an associate.

But after a few months, even that much identification was no longer necessary. Everybody knew—somehow. I was suddenly treated with awe and respect. The mantle was there. I couldn't see it or feel it, but everyone around me felt its weight.

For several months my activities were limited to attending weddings and funerals, the two big mob social events. Among the funerals I attended was that of Joe Colombo. The former boss had vegetated for seven years after being gunned down in his most glorious moment. As they lowered Colombo's casket into the ground that day, I thought back to the day he had been shot. I had been only a few feet away from him, a college kid then, a future doctor, caught in the middle of a major mob hit.

So much of my life had been like that. Cops hanging around the house and harassing my family. Assassinations right in front of my eyes, the sound of the gunshots ringing in my ears. My father's frame-up and fifty-year "death sentence" jail term. My own grand jury indictments and trials, all based on false accusations and police harassment. The mob had shaped every part of my life. And most of it was bad. Would I end up like Joe Colombo?

My first payoff for joining the mob came when an associate introduced me to Gerard Nocera, a vice-president at Beneficial Leasing Corporation. I wanted to get the Mazda dealership out from under the strangling floor plan financing arrangement I had with Lloyd Capital. Nocera was the first example in a long line of what the prosecutors would later claim to be my greatest talent—finding legitimate businessmen who liked to play on the edge. The Beneficial man, who had relatives associated with the mob, came through with a $600,000 floor plan. And instead of having to pay Tom Scharf $75 to $150 a car, I only had to pay Nocera $25 to $50. With Nocera, however, there wasn't even a thin veil of "consulting" involved. His payments were all slid directly under the table.

My best friend, a high-living embalmer and mob associate named Larry "Champagne Larry" Carrozza, unearthed another nine-to-fiver looking to increase his profits. Louis Fenza had worked his way up to vice-president of Japan Lines, an international marine cargo company. I formed a shipping-container repair firm, and Louie Fenza began writing work orders for me. It started at five to one, meaning for every container my firm repaired, Fenza would bill Japan Lines for five. Eventually, the ratio grew to ten to one, fifteen to one, and finally twenty to one, as the scam went unnoticed. We were pocketing $2,000 a week for phantom work. I rolled the Japan Lines money in with my Mazda profits and put $100,000 on the streets, an investment that produced two to three shylock points ($2,000 to $3,000) every week.

— 56 —

As time passed, I developed a three-point strategy to guide my new life. Points two and three were to succeed in business and to be a good mob soldier. Point one was the same as always—to get Dad out of jail. My passion in that area became my weakness. Anyone wanting to get close to me, set me up, or shake me down used my love for Dad to his advantage.

In 1978, Dad had a critical parole hearing scheduled. He had served nine years, enough time to earn a legitimate parole. Still, he was Sonny Franzese, and his chances appeared slim. That's when a rival car dealer suddenly appeared claiming to have connections with the parole board. For $150,000, he said, he could ensure that my father would be freed. But he wanted the money up front.

He told me they had to work through a specific attorney, Harold Borg. I knew Borg from the "West Hempstead Seven" trial because he had represented one of the Chubby Brothers. I was willing to hire Borg, but I balked at paying the bribe money to the dealer. Instead, I offered to pay $75,000 when my father was granted parole and the second $75,000 when he walked free. This split was necessary because the actual release of a prisoner can be as long as six months after a parole hearing. And that lag time can be filled with snags. To make my point, I filled a suitcase with $150,000 in shylock cash borrowed from the Colombo family, sat in the corner of my office, and invited the car dealer over to take a look.

In September 1978, although I hadn't paid out any bribe money, Dad's parole was granted. From my own intelligence gathering, I determined that Borg was totally legitimate and knew nothing of the hustle. The parole was gained by the attorney's efforts and my father's good behavior, not through any connections. In fact, when Borg later learned of the bribe agreement, he advised strongly against paying the money.

The car dealer and his secret partner, if there ever had been one, were apparently gambling on a good attorney and the timing of the hearing. If my father made it, they could claim credit, and if he didn't, they could claim "a last-minute foul-up."

The dealer was furious when I refused to pay and threatened, "You don't know what they'll do. These people can have you killed."

"I'll take the chance," I shot back.

"They'll have *me* killed," he protested.

"Well then, you'd better buy a bulletproof vest," I advised.

Dad came home five months later, in February 1979, and we threw another big welcome-home party to celebrate. The very next day, he and I resumed our 6:00 A.M. breakfast meetings from a decade earlier. I set my alarm for 5:00 A.M. so I could shower, shave, dress, and make the ten-minute drive from my home in Jericho to my parents' house in time to operate the drip coffee machine. Now, however, intermingled with conversations about sports and entertainment, we talked shop. It was then that Dad began educating me about the ways of La Cosa Nostra.

— 57 —

Dad taught me which family members could be trusted, whom to be wary of, and whom not to trust. He advised me never to say anything of consequence on the telephone or in an enclosed room, and to treat all strangers as if they were undercover FBI agents.

"Don't let your tongue be your worst enemy," he said.

I gave him an office and a job as a Mazda salesman, one of the conditions of his parole. I then held my breath, expecting the earth to shake under his feet as it had done before.

Dad requested that I transfer to his army, but Andy Russo, my capo, vehemently protested. The Colombo ruling council decided that I belonged with my father.

Although my immediate family was elated to have Dad home, things didn't work out as I had imagined. For one thing, the strict parole conditions imposed on him severely hampered his activities. For another, his once loyal and feared army had dissolved during his decade-long incarceration. Among those still alive or free, the only one who asked to transfer back to him was Jo Jo Vitacco, and he was refused permission. Officially, the Colombo family still viewed Sonny Franzese as being either too hot or too dangerous, and they did nothing to help return him to power.

Dad knew the score, so he remained low-key, explaining to me, "There's no rush." Because of this, I never got to see the legendary Sonny Franzese of the 1960s whom Phil Steinberg knew. I understood the reasons, but still it was disappointing. I had always idolized Dad, and now, for the first time, I realized that he was just a man.

I was once again angered by the Colombo family's refusal to give my father his due. It no longer surprised me, after the way they'd treated him while he was in prison, but I'd always believed that things would be different once he was back on the streets. Besides, I was now part of the family. Where was the brotherhood? Where was the respect my father had earned by keeping his mouth shut and giving up a decade of his life rather than implicate someone else?

Complicating matters was the success of Carmine "the Snake" Persico Jr. He was paroled around the same time as my father and promptly took over the family. He had also served ten years in prison, but his fall, from a much lower perch, had been softer. He was able to keep his army together during his incarceration, install the aging DiBella in his place when Colombo was shot, and power his way to the top.

The Snake was a throwback, a don right out of Central Casting. He was a tough, gritty man who stood five-foot-seven and ate, drank, and slept the mob. He was a veteran of the street-war days and was comfortable with the violence so often associated with organized crime. To the Snake, murder was a vital cog in the business machinery of the family. A forceful, aggressive leader, Persico brought an ironfisted rule back to the Colombo family. Dad's fortunes would never return, but with Persico in power, mine were about to soar.

— 58 —

Carmine "the Snake" Persico wasted little time flexing his muscles. A parole board's worst nightmare, he left prison determined to settle a list of old scores. By chance, there had been a breakthrough in one of the oldest and most painful. In the early 1960s, an insanely courageous band of young toughs hit upon a wild scheme of making quick cash by kidnapping mob soldiers and holding them for ransom. The families paid off, more to silence the insult to their image than to protect the lives of their men. They ground their teeth and handed over the money, vowing never to rest until all the kidnappers were identified, hunted down, and killed.

Nearly two decades had passed now, and only a few remembered about the kidnappings, and even fewer cared. Among those who did remember, some held a grudging admiration for the accomplishment of the reckless band. Plus, it was widely believed that some, if not all, of the kidnappers had eventually joined the various mob families.

Shortly after Persico took over, someone erased a heavy shylock debt by playing an ace carried for twenty years and fingering some of the kidnappers. An investigation was launched, and the information was confirmed. Not surprisingly, one of the former kidnappers had become a trusted Colombo family associate. He was a tough, fiercely loyal man who was part of my growing crew. Both my father and I respected him, knew his wife and children, and considered him to be one of our most valued and dependable men. In late 1978, I received a call from Persico that unsettled my world. The family boss explained that he had ordered the death of this man.

It was the first time I'd had to face anything like this. I didn't know what to do, so I did what came naturally: I protested. My strong feelings for the man prompted me to tread on dangerous ground. I challenged the order and questioned the accuracy of the information. Persico tolerated my insolence and took the trouble of outlining the case against the man. There was no doubt. The associate had unquestionably been part of the gang of renegade kidnappers.

I tried another tack. The offender had been a raw and ignorant kid back then. He had since matured into a faithful associate. I argued that his value to the family was worth more than the value of revenge. Persico took it all in but was unmoved.

"We respect your efforts on his behalf," he said. "However, the crime he committed is unforgivable. The guy's gotta go, and that's the end of it."

This last statement indicated to me that Persico would not allow any more second-guessing on my part, so I left it there. What more could I do? Two weeks later, I heard that the hit had been successfully carried out.

— 59 —

One day in January 1979, I found myself on the other end of things. Champagne Larry Carrozza rushed into my Mazda office with some disturbing news. One of the middlemen in the

Japan Lines scam, a short, thin, dark-haired Italian named Joey Laezza, had been nabbed by the police and was about to sing. I called a meeting of my men and had Larry repeat the information. Before I finished, five different associates volunteered to kill Laezza that same day.

"Just give the word, Michael," Larry said.

I knew why my friend was so concerned. He had made the introduction, so Joey was his responsibility. If Joey rolled over, Larry would have to pay with his life. That was the rule of the mob.

I weighed my words carefully. "Let's get some more information. Let's be absolutely certain."

The men appeared to be upset. They were distressingly eager to kill. I could see that they were also fiercely loyal and totally dependent upon me. They would do anything, kill anyone, to protect the income and lifestyle I was providing them. A strange and disquieting sense of power swept over me. It was wrong, and it was evil, but it was oh so intoxicating.

As the newspapers reported, at 10:30 A.M. the following day, January 16, the body of Joseph Anthony Laezza, thirty-six, was discovered slumped in the front seat of his car at 18 Gravesend Neck Road in Brooklyn. He had been stabbed eleven times, six times in the face and head. The placement of the wounds made the medical examiner marvel at the murderer's skill and knowledge of anatomy. The wounds were so deadly and so exact, it was reported, that it appeared as if the knife had been wielded by a surgeon. My friend Champagne Larry Carrozza owned a funeral parlor and was a mortician and embalmer.

"We had to do it," he reported later that day. "It was too close to home. We followed him and saw him talking with the cops. He was gonna take Michael down."

In the end, it had not been necessary for me to order the killing. It was taken care of for me.

Nevertheless, as I drove home that evening, my conscience was tormenting me. I had vowed to myself that I would stay away from the bloody side of the mob, thinking that I could do my business bit and leave the messy stuff for the Brooklyn soldiers. But in the mob, apparently no one could remain clean. I had viewed myself as a white-collar criminal, but the bodies were already starting to pile up around me.

— 60 —

Not long after that, I was summoned to a dinner in Brooklyn. As I was leaving to make the long, hated drive into the city, an associate entered my office.

"Michael," he said, "Tommy was hit last night."

"What? Tommy! What for?"

"I don't know. Something he did long ago. He was probably one of the kidnappers. Someone's ratting them all out."

Tommy was another one of my men. He had recently gotten out of jail after a long stint, and I felt sorry for him. I knew from my father how hard it was for the long-termers to readjust. Tommy's wife had waited for him faithfully for nearly a decade. My father and I had personally befriended both Tommy and his wife. Now, after she had waited so long for her husband to come home, he had been shot through the brain and stuffed into the trunk of a car. It just didn't seem right.

The wasted lives and constant killing gnawed at me as I drove into Brooklyn. At the gathering, held in an associate's house, I was introduced to four new recruits. They were young, hard-looking toughs from the streets of Brooklyn. They were pumped so high that I suspected they were on something. In fact, they were—they were flying on adrenaline. It was a party to celebrate the recruits having "made their bones." They had apparently accomplished it by killing my friend Tommy the night before. I surmised that they had invited me as a way of informing me, without ever saying a word, that the hit was "in family" and there was no need for retaliation.

"To a job well-done," said Johnny Irish Matera, the recruits' sponsor, raising a glass in a toast. I was lost in thought when Jimmy Angellino nudged me. I saw the glasses raised, and so I raised mine too.

"To a job well-done," I said, clinking my glass with those of the recruits.

As I drank the blood toast, the words of another friend, also a made man, echoed in my mind—"You know, Michael, we're all sick. The lives we lead...we're all sick."

I was beginning to believe that he had been right.

— 61 —

Being part of the mob definitely had its advantages when it came to doing business. One day, I received a call from the brother of a girl who had sung in a band I managed in the 1970s. He was Rafael "Big Red" Celli, a six-two, two-hundred-thirty-pound bear of a man. The nickname derived from Rafael's scarlet hair and beard. Big Red was in the construction business and found himself in a quandary over a massive apartment-house renovation project. The three-thousand-unit Glen Oaks Apartments in Glen Oaks, Queens, was going co-op. The owners, Gerald and Reuben Guterman of Guterman Homes, wanted to keep costs down and profits high. The problem was that the powerful New York labor unions had swooped in, pressuring the owners to sign an expensive union contract. If they succeeded, the influx of three hundred union tradesmen and laborers would triple the costs of the renovation, decrease the quality of the work, and postpone the completion date.

Big Red asked if I could do anything to help, warning that the union representative was a "heavy guy."

"I don't know if you can handle it," Big Red said.

I asked who the union rep was.

"Bob Cervone," he said.

I smiled. Basil Robert Cervone was a big, fat man in his six-
ties who sported a cigar, wore a fedora over a shaved head, loved
flashy clothes in loud colors, and drove a shiny Eldorado convertible. He always traveled with a wiry little dude who was his man
Friday. Cervone had been an AFL/CIO and Laborers' International Union official for nearly forty years. He knew every psychological pressure tactic ever invented, and builders trembled at
the sight of him.

I told Big Red I'd give it a shot, but I would need to speak
with the Gutermans first. An introduction was arranged. Reuben
Guterman confirmed that they wanted my intervention. Ideally,
the goal was to keep the union out. Second-best would be a sweetheart contract. I explained that I would negotiate an arrangement and then get back to them with the terms.

Bob Cervone agreed to meet me at the Silver Moon Diner,
a popular eatery off Union Turnpike in Long Island. He arrived
complete with shiny head, hat, cigar, and man Friday, and I got
right down to business. "Glen Oaks. Reuben Guterman. Gerry
Guterman. They're with me."

A big smile appeared on Cervone's face. "That's terrific.
Whatta you want?"

"No union," I said.

"Okay," he responded.

It had to be harder than that, I figured.

"You're going to do this out of friendship?" I asked.

Cervone smiled again. "Come on. The Jews are loaded."

The man had done his homework. Among other things, Gerald
Guterman owned a fine art collection valued at $40 million.

"We've been contacted by the plumbers, carpenters, painters, and you," I explained. "We'll make a deal, but I want you to
handle everybody. Can that be done?"

"Certainly," he said.

"Talk to your people, and get back to me," I offered, and our
meeting came to an end.

We spent the next week trading offers. Cervone demanded $200,000 paid up-front in cash, just for starters. That would be on top of a per-apartment fee. I told Basil Bob he was dreaming. After a week of haggling, we eventually settled on a price of $50 per room, which came to $150 to $250 per apartment, depending upon the number of rooms each apartment had.

The numbers were impressive. The renovations using non-union labor were expected to cost about $2,000 per unit. With union labor, the cost would have risen to $6,000. So for $250, I saved the Gutermans $4,000 per unit. About two thousand of the three thousand apartments were eventually renovated, and the remainder were bought by residents wanting to stay on. When the project was completed, I had saved the builders $6 million to $8 million, and the union ended up with a long-term payout of about $400,000 for doing absolutely nothing.

To put some frosting on the deal, Cervone reserved the right to provide the bricklayers. He did so from a company he partly owned with a man named Ralph Perry. (Perry later testified against Cervone when Cervone was convicted of receiving union payoffs for an unrelated project.)

In return for my services, I became Glen Oaks' general contractor. To handle the duties there, I formed four companies: Flexo Contracting, Close-Rite Windows, Bentwood Carpentry, and M.R.C. Business Relations. Among my functions was to facilitate the cash payments to the unions. Union bosses didn't want to accept traceable checks for work never performed.

The Glen Oaks renovation went so well that I worked with Guterman Homes on a half-dozen other projects. These included Cryder Point in Queens, Hamilton House in New Jersey, the Parc Vendome and Colonade co-op conversion in Manhattan, and the Water's Edge in Patchogue, Long Island. I was able to keep all the unions out of these projects except for the painters' union on two high-profile Manhattan projects. And even with them, I arranged a "sweetheart" deal. In return, I put $2 million in my pocket from my general contracting services.

— 62 —

Things continued to get bigger and better for me in the business world. The owner of Rumplik Chevrolet in Suffolk County, Thomas O'Donnell, enlisted my financial help in making a run at buying the Twentieth Century Hotel and casino on Tropicana Avenue in Las Vegas, a former Howard Johnson's, later renamed the San Remo Hotel. I lent O'Donnell $70,000 at two points per week. O'Donnell said he needed the money to clear some debts at his dealership so he could pass the Las Vegas Gaming Commission's licensing investigation.

O'Donnell, who loved to gamble, promptly defaulted on the $1,400 weekly interest payments and offered his seventy-five percent share of the dealership to cover his debt. Another reason he was anxious to divest himself of the dealership's problems was to stave off the Vegas investigators. Although the price of the fifty-year-old dealership was dirt cheap, included in the deal was the burden of taking on $320,000 in long- and short-term loans. I went to my financing buddy Gerard Nocera and brought in a new, $1 million floor plan.

O'Donnell and I then became partners on the Las Vegas venture. I arranged for a $5 million financing package to help the Irishman swing the deal. Everything was set, but it all hinged on O'Donnell's receiving a critical casino license.

As it turned out, it wasn't even close. The commission blew O'Donnell's application away, collapsing the deal. He turned out to be quite a character. He had left the Chevy dealership with such a maze of shady paperwork that it eventually strangled the operation. Included among O'Donnell's tricks was financing cars twice from different banks or selling them for cash and then sending through paperwork claiming that they were purchased on credit. A Mercedes-Benz sold to New York Jets' quarterback Richard Todd had been financed twice, complete with Todd's forged signature on a second set of papers. The former University of Alabama star was unaware of the chicanery until the second bank came after him for back payments. O'Donnell was later convicted of grand larceny and fraud, made a deal, and vanished into the Witness Protection Program.

The former owner's problems resulted in some unpleasant déjà vu. Shortly after I took over the dealership, a squad of twenty-five Suffolk County police officers charged into my office one day, breaking down the door with an axe. They were attempting to confirm my position as Rumplik's new owner and dig up records of illegal financing activities. Fortunately, I was tipped about the raid by an informant inside the Suffolk County Police Department, and I made sure that neither I nor any worthwhile records were present when the police squad paid its visit.

— 63 —

Another lucrative business opportunity found its way to me when I was contacted by Daniel Cunningham, president of the Allied International Union, a lucrative Great Neck, Long Island security guard union. Cunningham needed help. He wanted to align himself and his growing union with a connected guardian angel before someone tried to squeeze him.

Although I found the sloppy, freckle-faced Cunningham to be personally repulsive, I did like the man's cash-heavy union operation. I explained that I would be happy to give him protection.

I installed one of my men, Japan Lines executive Louis Fenza, as vice-president of the security guard union, and together we received an education in union-skimming. Among the scams, Cunningham was paying about $6,000 a month for a health and dental insurance plan for his members, then turning around and billing the union $20,000. The extra $14,000 went into his pocket.

Cunningham's big plan was to expand his union into the hotel and casino hotbed of Atlantic City. He enlisted my help in convincing the security guards to sign the cards needed to push the union issue to a vote. First, I arranged a meet with Philadelphia boss Nicky Scarfo. Atlantic City's bartenders and waitresses were already unionized under the protection of the Scarfo and Gambino families, and I had to go through the proper channels. Scarfo gave his approval, and Cunningham opened an office in Atlantic City.

The unionization drive blew up much the same way the Vegas casino hotel project had crumbled, and Cunningham was eventually indicted on fifty-two counts of union fraud. When the New Jersey press got wind of the indictment, the stories effectively choked the union drive. Cunningham was subsequently convicted of forty of the fifty-two counts and was sent to prison.

Once again, I was having a difficult time selecting the reputable front men I needed to shield my operations from government investigators. The legitimate business world seemed to be overflowing with thieves.

This is not to imply that the union operation died with Cunningham's conviction. Anthony Tomasso, Cunningham's underling, took over. Not long afterward, Tomasso had a heart attack. That left my man Louie Fenza as the new union boss. Several dominoes had fallen, and I suddenly found myself in control of a million-dollar security guard union operation.

About this same time, I was contacted by a man with mob connections who wanted me to arrange the killing of his father-in-law, who he believed was going to testify against him before a grand jury. I reported this request to Persico, and the boss affirmed what I already knew: La Cosa Nostra did not kill people for associates. Contrary to popular belief, it didn't even kill for hire (although some soldiers would quietly hire themselves out on the side). The mob killed for mob business only. In those instances, the hit men or hit squads were never paid for their services. The idea of a "contract" being put on someone's life, while it existed in other areas of society, was merely figurative when it related to the mob. All Cosa Nostra soldiers were expected to be killers. I explained to the man that I couldn't help him with his father-in-law, but I did use the opportunity to get involved in his business.

— 64 —

During this period, I also found myself back in the flea market game. The part-owner of a flea market in the Bay Ridge section of Brooklyn was having problems with his partner. The man had become addicted to drugs and was dealing on the grounds to support his habit.

"I'll get him out," I assured the owner. "And then I'm your new partner."

I dispatched two of my men to scare off the unwanted partner. One of the enforcers was a jumpy Vietnam vet named Anthony Sarivola, better known as "Tony Limo" for his job of driving a hearse for Larry Carrozza's funeral parlor. Tony Limo bullied the flea market junkie and told him to hit the road. Three days later, I received a call from Jimmy Angellino, later a Colombo captain and fast-rising star in the family. Angellino told me that John Gotti, then a soldier in the Gambino family, wanted a meet.

Gotti and I met the next day at a restaurant in Queens. John, later the much-publicized Gambino family boss, arrived with a soldier named Angelo Ruggiero, and I took a Colombo soldier with me.

The meeting turned into a classic example of a high-stakes Cosa Nostra sit-down. Contrary to previously published reports— including the version that was used as the basis of a scene in *The Godfather, Part III*—there were no heated arguments, cursing, or trading of insults in this meeting. We all spoke calmly and treated each other with respect, as decreed by family policy. It was the subtlety of the verbal sparring that provided the fascination.

After we'd politely introduced ourselves, Gotti took the lead. "This kid at the flea market, he's with me."

"How can that be, John?" I countered. "He's a drug addict and a dealer. You know the rules."

"You don't know that," Gotti said, feigning surprise.

"It's been confirmed. He's using and selling. How can a man like that be with you?"

"If he's doing drugs, we'll make him stop," Gotti said, being careful not to admit any prior knowledge of his alleged associate's drug use. "Even so, his interest in the market is still mine."

"If he's into drugs, then you can't be associated with him. And if you can't be associated with him, then you have no interest in the market," I said.

"That's not the way it goes," Gotti countered.

"You know the rules, John."

Sensing that I had Gotti cornered, I decided to take the offensive. "Who you kidding, anyway? He's not with you. He ran to you after we threw him out."

"No, no," Gotti insisted, shaking his head. "He's been with me a long time. A long time."

"If he's been with you a long time, then how come you aren't aware that he's using and selling drugs?" I countered, sensing that I had him pinned.

We each repeated our positions. Gotti promised to make the guy kick his addiction and clean up his act. I repeated that the man's long-term drug use severed any tie Gotti had to the rich, unpoliced market. Then I added that, no matter what they decided, the guy was out.

"We can't have a junkie around the market," I insisted. "It's no good. You can't argue that. And since when are we in the drug-rehabilitation business?"

"I'll install somebody in his place," Gotti offered.

"I'm not convinced you have claim to begin with," I insisted.

Although Gotti's position was weak, his towering ego wouldn't let him lose the argument. We decided to take it up with our captains and meet again. I went to Persico and told him what had happened, and he gave me the okay to press the issue.

The day before the next meet, I received a call informing me that there was a third partner in the flea market, and that partner was aligned with Collie Dipietro, a soldier in the Genovese family. This further muddied the waters. It also confirmed to me that Gotti was lying. If he had been with the flea market for as long as he claimed, he would have known about the Genovese connection.

I knew Collie. He had served time at Leavenworth with my father. He was in his mid-forties, dressed sharply, chewed a fat cigar, and possessed an ego that rivaled Gotti's. We met at the Bergin Hunt and Fish Club in Ozone Park. I suspected that Collie and Gotti would join forces against me, which is exactly what happened. Without hesitation, Collie showed his cards by acknowledging Gotti's claim on the market. That negated my assault on that front. I also knew I couldn't coexist with these two ego-guys. My only remaining tactic could be to have them buy me out.

Collie had a different plan.

"Look, we know that each of our guys is a thief," he said, slandering our associates. "I have a solution. There's this Jew I know, a real business whiz. We'll have him run the market and look out for all our interests."

I stifled a laugh. Collie's Jew would not be looking out for anyone's interest but Collie's. I countered that my man had founded the market and was its backbone. There was no way I could justify giving anyone say over him. We ran this around for a while and finally decided to kick out the junkie, replace him with Gotti's representative, and bring in Collie's Jew on a trial basis. If it didn't work, then one party would have to buy out the other.

As I expected, the arrangement didn't work. By the third weekend, the new flea market partners were at each other's throats. Another meeting was set. This time I convinced Collie and Gotti to put up $70,000 to buy out my man's interest.

I came out of the flea market meetings $20,000 richer—my share of the $70,000—and, more importantly, with valuable experience and knowledge. The negotiations had been mob business as usual, infused with deceit, lying, and twisted gamesmanship. Yet, I had not only held my own under those circumstances, I felt I had won as well.

I was also left with a grudging admiration for John Gotti. I found the future Gambino boss to be a true mobster who loved the life and everything about it. He was sharp and tenacious, and it was obvious that he would reach the top—or die trying. I wasn't overwhelmed, however, by Gotti's show of toughness. He was tough, but I knew that I had come from the toughest of all— Sonny Franzese.

"Who's John Gotti?" I remarked to an associate prior to the third meeting. "Remember, I came from the best."

It was a psychological edge I carried throughout my mob tenure. By comparing every opponent to my father, I could never be intimidated.

Within a year, the flea market wheezed, sickened, and eventually died, and the business whiz Collie had installed to run the market was convicted of an assortment of felonies relating to his handling of the operation.

I had other encounters with Gotti and actually got to like him. As long as we weren't arguing over some mob business venture, he was cool.

— 65 —

While I was flying high, it was obvious to even the humblest mob associate that Dad was lying low and was no longer a factor in the organized crime hierarchy. Still, the government feared him, and in June of 1982, his unheralded return to freedom ended much the way he had originally lost it.

As part of his parole, Dad had been obligated to prove he could be a decent, civic-minded citizen. To show that he was moving in that direction, he joined the Brooklyn Kiwanis Club and dutifully attended the organization's Tuesday night meetings. A few times a year, the Kiwanis hosted joint meetings with brother chapters around the New York area. The gathering that summer was at the Georgetown Inn in Brooklyn.

Dad had often asked me to join him at these meetings, but I always begged off, considering them boring. This time, for whatever reason, he didn't mention it. Had he, I never would have allowed him to attend. The Georgetown Inn was a popular mob hangout, so popular that it was constantly under surveillance. The bartender was an FBI informant who regularly wore a wire.

As soon as Dad and a number of other felons were spotted entering the inn, the surveillance team outside perked up. A call went out to James Stein, Dad's parole officer, and the bartender was alerted to keep watch. In the course of the evening, my father bumped into two old friends, a Gambino capo named Carmine "the Doctor" Lombardozzi and an unidentified man he had met in prison. He spoke briefly to each, and no criminal activity was discussed. But both conversations were reported to have lasted longer than the three-minute limit set by Dad's parole guidelines. And one of the conversations occurred at the bar, right under the nose and hidden microphone of the bartender.

The following day, Dad received a call to meet with Stein. At the parole office, Stein informed him that he had violated his parole by "consorting with known criminals" and would have to surrender to authorities. Dad agreed to surrender and was taken back to the Metropolitan Correctional Center in New York.

"Dad, what happened?" I asked him over the phone when I heard the news.

"No good," he said.

My father's crime was a technical violation that should have netted him no more than six to nine months, but after the hearing, during which Stein testified about my father's activities at the Georgetown Inn, he was given a ten-year sentence.

"Ten years!" I was enraged, and I blamed Stein. I felt the duty of a probation officer was to help keep his subjects clean, not to sit on stakeouts to catch them in a violation. Outside the hearing, I found myself face-to-face with Stein.

"I'm sorry, Michael," he said. "That's how it goes."

"You know, Stein, you're a real scumbag," I said angrily.

"What?" he feigned surprise.

"You heard me," I said, my voice rising. "You were supposed to let him know if there was a problem. They said in there that he was under surveillance the past seven months, and you were obligated to warn him. You're a scumbag, and you helped set him up!"

A few days later, two FBI agents visited me at my Rumplik Chevrolet office. I ushered them out to the parking lot to talk in private.

"We understand that you threatened the life of James Stein," one of the agents sternly said. "We know about it, and if anything happens to him, we're coming after you."

"I didn't threaten his life!" I exploded. "I called him a scumbag, and he *is* a scumbag. I'll say it again right now. The guy's a scumbag! But I never threatened him in any way."

"That's not the way we heard it," they responded.

"Why don't you come inside and explain all this to my attorney," I encouraged, "I want it on the record."

But the agents declined the offer.

"I don't have time for this nonsense. Get off my lot!" I ordered.

— 66 —

It wouldn't be the last of the "scumbag" incident. My heat-of-the-moment hallway conversation with Stein was filed away to use against me. The FBI was now on my case and soon set up an undercover sting operation to seduce me into offering a bribe to free Dad.

An informer named Luigi Vizzini teamed up with undercover FBI agent Chris Mattiace, and the two men presented themselves to me as middlemen who had national parole board head Benjamin Malcolm in their pocket. Numerous meetings were arranged with them, most of them held at the Atrium Club in Manhattan, and during these meetings, the wired and highly trained undercover agent and his associate tried to cajole me into offering the bribe.

From my perspective, this was an excruciating balancing act. I didn't want to be suckered by an informant, but neither did I want to eliminate the chance that the men really had a connection that could free Dad. If they were legitimate, I'd have been more than willing to pay the money. Until I was positive, I took the precautions my father had taught me during all those 6:00 A.M. breakfast meetings: "Treat every stranger as if he were an undercover FBI agent." Along with that advice, some internal warning system now alerted me to be especially careful with these two. It turned out to be the first in a long line of instances in which my eerie sixth sense would kick in and save me.

Relying on verbal adroitness, I kept the doors open with these mysterious men while never saying anything on the tapes to clearly implicate myself. Assistant U.S. Attorney Charles Rose deemed all the recordings useless and killed the investigation. I didn't learn until four years later, at a bond hearing, that Mattiace was an agent and that the conversations had been recorded.

Despite this failure, the FBI tried to trap me again. In 1983, the agency launched a heavily financed sting operation aimed at bringing down famed boxing promoter Don King by linking him to the mob. A former member of Muhammad Ali's entourage, Reggie Barrett, had been turned by the FBI and was being used as its entry into big-time boxing. Barrett was paired with a Latin undercover agent named Victor Guerrero. Guerrero, operating under the pseudonym Victor Quintana, proclaimed himself to be a mega-rich South American trying to buy his way into boxing.

This duo had been introduced first to my father by fight manager Chet Cummings shortly before Dad's parole was revoked. Cummings made the introduction at a boxing match in Atlantic City. Guerrero and Dad became fast friends, dining together and frequently playing each other at racquetball. At some point, Dad advised his new buddy that I was the man to see to get to King. Although I didn't know King, Dad figured that I could do anything.

Right about then, Guerrero and Barrett must have thought they had struck gold. The operation had barely started, and they already had met both Michael and Sonny Franzese. The mob/boxing link was all but established.

I met with Guerrero and Barrett more than fifty times during the next year, and the FBI put on a first-rate show. Guerrero opened an office in a high-rent district of Manhattan, drove a Rolls-Royce, wore $1,000 suits, and threw taxpayers' money around with abandon in other ways as well. He expressed an eagerness to get involved in all of my businesses. We traveled together to Florida and California, spending hours chatting. During the flights, he frequently adjusted his position and complained of a back problem. I later came to the conclusion that he was probably suffering the discomfort caused by a wrapping to secure his voice-activated microphone.

We talked and talked, and yet I gave up nothing. My sixth sense was on alert again. As usual, it wasn't strong enough to blow the deal away, just strong enough to make me cautious. Finally, unable to get a clear fix on the man known as Victor

Quintana, I agreed to arrange a meet with Don King. But first I wanted to see the $15 million Quintana claimed he had. The FBI set up a banker in Illinois to confirm the deposit, complete with official bank statements.

— 67 —

I was able to get to Don King through the Reverend Al Sharpton, the infamous New York rabble-rouser and preacher. Sharpton was a "player" who had friends in the Gambino family, and I had been introduced to him through his Gambino connections.

Sharpton and I had sometimes met at the offices of Spring Records in Manhattan to discuss our mutual interest in labor unions and entertainment. In public, he could be grating, especially to the white power structure, but in private, he was a gentleman and a good guy. He struck me as someone who believed strongly in his various causes.

During our meetings, Sharpton had offered to use the considerable black power forces he commanded to assist me in any way. I took him up on it during the drive to unionize the security guards in Atlantic City. Before that effort blew up, Sharpton was planning to organize his people to picket casino hotels.

I later read an article in which Sharpton claimed he had been associating with me merely to gather information for the FBI. I doubted that. I thought he was just covering himself when he found himself in a little hot water. Either way, he never did anything to hurt me, and he helped me get to Don King.

Before bringing Guerrero to Don King, I had a private meeting with the flamboyant, wild-haired boxing promoter. He turned out to be pretty much as advertised—boisterous, verbose, always smiling, always happy. I could believe his oft-repeated claim that his hair sticks up that way naturally. The man appears to be electrically charged.

I respected King because he came from the streets and climbed up the hard way. Personally, he struck me as a tough negotiator, but once you had a deal, he'd keep his word. Those who have cried foul in dealing with him weren't cheated. They were simply out-negotiated.

"Don, these guys say they have $15 million to invest," I said. "I confirmed the money, but I haven't been able to qualify them. I want you to play it straight. Play it as if you're talking to FBI agents."

King met Guerrero and Barrett and handled them as I had advised, and a promotion was set for Atlantic City—all above-board. When Guerrero failed to come through with the initial seed money, a few hundred thousand, both the deal and the connection collapsed. Apparently, an FBI budget cruncher had decided that the agency wasn't in the fight business and pulled the plug on the whole operation. Had the FBI put up the money to promote a few fights, both King and I might have softened.

Guerrero was left with fifty-two taped conversations with me, but none amounted to anything. In fact, the operation backfired. When King was later indicted for tax evasion, I had my attorney send him the tapes that pertained to him. King's lawyers used the recordings to show the lengths the government had gone to in order to sting the colorful promoter. The jury frowned upon the tactic and found King innocent.

Following the trial, King sent me a note: "Thanks. I owe you one. —Don King."

— 68 —

In 1981, things definitely took an upward turn. I was about to land my biggest scam of all. It all began when Sebastian "Buddy" Lombardo went to my father with a problem. His boss, Lawrence Iorizzo, was being shaken down by a gang of thugs attempting to move in on Vantage Petroleum, his multi-million-dollar wholesale gasoline business. Dad referred Lombardo to me. I checked out Iorizzo, and the information I received on the gas man raised my eyebrows.

Larry Iorizzo was the son of a jazz saxophone player who had worked on Broadway and in Brooklyn burlesque houses. The younger Iorizzo grew into a mammoth, six-four, four-hundred-fifty-pound businessman who ate pizzas the way most people eat Ritz crackers. Since he was the size of two men, he apparently decided that he needed two wives. Interestingly enough, it was not a "then" and a "now," as frequently happens in our society, but two wives at the same time. Only one of these was a legal wife, of course. The other was just a girlfriend.

Iorizzo would spend half the night with one wife, usually from dinner until 3:00 or 4:00 A.M. Then he'd wake up, tell her he needed to check his gasoline stations along Long Island's highways, and then bed down the rest of the night with his other wife. He followed this schedule for more than ten years, routinely having dinner with Wife I and breakfast with Wife II. Between the two women, he had seven children.

In addition to his bizarre domestic life, Iorizzo had gone through a much-publicized spat with Martin Carey, the brother of then New York Governor Hugh Carey. The squabble over Carey's cut-rate gasoline business led to a lawsuit. Iorizzo later testified before a congressional subcommittee that Carey was blending gasoline with cheap, hazardous waste to jump his profits and provide funds for his brother's successful reelection campaign for governor in 1978.

I could accept the girth, the wives, and the mixed brood of offspring, but the lawsuit and rumors that Iorizzo had cooperated with the government were something else. Although his gasoline business was a plum, I decided to pass on it. But Lombardo refused to give up, pushing me just to meet with Iorizzo, and after seven months of his insistence, I relented.

Iorizzo and I met at Peter Raneri's restaurant in Smithtown, Long Island. He was already seated when I arrived, and although

I could tell that there was a mountain of flesh bubbling under the table, I was surprised that from the neck up Iorizzo looked like a normal person. Even below the neck, he wasn't sloppily fat. There were no rolls of lard flopping around his body or hanging down like melting wax from his arms. He was definitely an obese man, but he was also solidly packed.

As he picked at his food, Iorizzo outlined his impressive operation. He owned or supplied three hundred gasoline stations in and around Long Island, an operation that grossed millions of dollars a month. His problem was that despite being rich and successful, he lacked power. He was having trouble with a group of men who were trying to extort him and muscle in on his supply stops.

"I'd be very appreciative if you could help me with this problem," Iorizzo said.

I asked who was shaking him down, and it turned out to be a band of small-fry associates of another family. Eliminating them wouldn't be a problem I was sure. I was more concerned with learning about the Martin Carey incident. The fat man explained that it was a civil suit, meaning it was a personal battle between businessmen that didn't involve anyone "ratting out" to police or prosecutors. That made a difference with me. What Iorizzo didn't admit to me that day was that he had previously reported Carey to both the police and the FBI.

As I listened and observed, I noticed that Iorizzo ate very little. This was notable because I had been told that the man had once eaten fifty hamburgers at a sitting and then consumed two large pizzas for dessert. During our entire relationship, I would never witness such a display. From the beginning, Iorizzo maintained a policy of hiding his gluttony from me, and I took this as a sign of respect.

— 69 —

Fixing Iorizzo's problem proved to be easy. I sent out a squad headed by Vincent Aspromonte, a menacing figure who sported an ugly scar across his forehead. A butcher by trade, Aspromonte had acquired his image-enhancing scar in a knife fight (or an auto accident, depending upon which story one believed). Either way, the result was effective. The shakedown artists took one look at the scar and were never seen again.

"Larry, your problem is solved," I announced, visiting Iorizzo at his Vantage office. The moment the words left my lips, I sensed a change in him. He could feel the power I commanded and felt that he had tapped into the flow of it.

"Here's how I'll repay you," Iorizzo said, and for the next hour, he proceeded to outline how we could milk hundreds of millions of dollars in illegal profits from his gasoline operation. The key was the incompetence of the federal, state, and county governments in collecting gasoline taxes. Together, the three governing bodies demanded a twenty-seven-cent bite out of every gallon of gasoline sold. But demanding it and getting it were two different things. The slack collection of the tax enabled Iorizzo to stall having his owned or leased stations pay the gasoline taxes for as long as a year. By that time, they would close the station, the owners would vanish, and then, a month or so later, the station would reopen under new management and start again.

Iorizzo further snarled the works by having all his companies registered in Panama. Under Panama's bearer stock law, the owner of a company was the person who had his hands on the stock. That meant the "official" owners of the gasoline stations—and of Iorizzo's umbrella operation—could be (and often were) two guys with machetes out in a Panamanian sugarcane field. When the government agencies went looking for their tax money, that's where they'd have to look.

We opened a new Panama company, Galion Holdings, to oversee our joint operations. Vantage, which was mired in Iorizzo's past shady tactics, supplied Galion Holdings with the gasoline, and Galion supplied the stations. I installed John Gargarino, a retired union official, as Galion's president. Aspromonte was made vice president. I then "bounced" most of the existing station managers and lessees and began inserting my growing team of men in their place. Each of my associates was given three to six stations and paid a salary of $500 per week per station. All the remaining money would come back to Galion.

My deal with Iorizzo was that twenty percent of the profits (off the top) would go to the Colombo family. The remaining money would be split fifty-fifty between us. Iorizzo handled the paperwork while I protected the stations and dealt with other suppliers. The operation soon began producing millions of dollars in skimmed tax money, a good percentage of it delivered as grocery bags full of cash that reeked of gasoline.

That same year, officials in the state of New York figured out how they were being beaten for tens of millions in gasoline tax dollars and decided to change the law. Instead of the stations being responsible for the taxes, the burden would be shifted to the wholesalers. This change couldn't happen overnight, so the state alerted the operators and gave them a year to make the switch. This grace period gave Iorizzo ample time to figure out how to play the shell game on the wholesale level. What he discovered thrilled him: the state had made it easier and far more profitable to steal the tax money than before. We would no longer have to rely upon collecting bags of money reeking of gasoline from the service stations. We could rake it off the top of huge wholesale shipments.

The method Iorizzo developed to do this was known as a "daisy chain." Under the new law, the gasoline could be sold tax-free from one wholesale company to the next. The last company to handle the transaction, the company that sold directly to the retailers, was responsible for the tax. Iorizzo would take a shipment of, say, a million gallons into Company A and sell it to his stations and those on his growing supply route. On paper, however, instead of the gasoline going to the stations, it would go to Company B, then to Company C, and finally to Company D. On paper, it would show that Company D had sold to the stations, but companies B through D were just shell firms that consisted of nothing more than a phone number and some stationery.

Company D, the one responsible for paying the taxes, would be owned by those same guys down in the Panama sugarcane fields. After a few hundred million gallons of invisible gasoline passed through Company D, it would then declare bankruptcy. When the state and federal governments tried to collect their tens of millions of dollars in tax money, they'd have to go on the mind-numbing paper trail from Company A through Company D. At the end of this grim rainbow was no pot of tax gold but the "burnout" firm, owned by some guy named Juan in Panama, current address unknown.

Since Company A was selling tax-free gasoline to the stations, Galion Holdings could undersell everyone in the area—except those who were also stealing. Station owners, who could in turn sell the fuel tax-free to their customers, began begging to get on Galion's supply route—a direct contradiction to charges later leveled by prosecutors that the station owners had been forced into buying Iorizzo's gasoline by my "goons." Galion never had to force anybody to purchase gasoline at ten cents a gallon less than they could anywhere else. Even the stations supplied by Mobil, Shell, Exxon, Texaco, and other major oil companies shuffled their papers so that they could illegally purchase fuel from Galion or one of its subsidiaries. When they called, they asked Iorizzo to make deliveries at very early morning hours to avoid company spotters.

Of course, we were ripping off the public, but we didn't see it that way. Instead of being ripped off, we reasoned, the New York public was actually benefiting from the Robin Hood-like operation. Gasoline prices dropped in New York City and Long Island, as station owners had an extra profit margin to work with. Since the wholesalers were responsible for paying the taxes, the gasoline stations were in the clear. Thus, station owners and managers buying Galion gasoline could undercut everyone else in the area and still make a larger profit. This fact helped salve our consciences.

– 70 –

As our operation grew, Galion swallowed up large and small independent suppliers all across New York and Long Island and into New Jersey, Connecticut, and Pennsylvania. Galion also purchased the valuable wholesale distributors' licenses from those companies to keep the daisy chains going.

We created so many shell companies that finding names for them got to be a chore. We alleviated the monotony by giving them humorous names, as I had done earlier in the construction business. Among the multitude of companies we created were S.O.S. Oil; Southern Belle Petroleum; Dine, Dance, and Drink, Inc.; and Down to Earth Management.

With the money came the toys. Galion Holdings was able to purchase a Learjet and a Bell jet helicopter, as well as a twenty-five-foot Chris Craft speedboat and a forty-foot Trojan yacht named *John-John*, both docked at my half-million dollar home in Delray Beach, Florida. Galion also custom-ordered the *Trump Princess* of Winnebagos, a $370,000 mansion on wheels furnished better than most doctors' homes. I purchased an assortment of condominiums and settled Maria and our three small children in a multimillion-dollar Brookville, Long Island, mansion, complete with its own racquetball court and satellite television system.

Whatever guilt I had about thievery on this level was also erased because there was no real perceived victim. I wasn't stealing from people but from institutions, I reasoned, and the institution I was stealing from in the gasoline business was the government—the same government that had sent my father to prison for fifty years on the testimony of a few lowlifes.

To celebrate the gas gang's continuing good fortune, I began hosting a dinner-and-dancing party every Monday night at the Casablanca nightclub on the Jericho Turnpike in Huntington, Long Island. I owned a share of the club and closed it for these nights of private frivolity. Between fifty and a hundred guys and dolls showed up each week for the occasion. Over the several hours these spirited Monday night parties lasted, I would meet with various associates or prospective associates in back rooms. They entered, paid their respects to me like I was Don Corleone, then stated their business. I did what I could for them. The feeling of power that this routine produced was absolutely intoxicating.

Iorizzo was so fond of these weekly galas that he rarely missed one. Quick to become intoxicated despite his great girth, he once became so giddily drunk that he picked up a flower pot, put it on his head, and danced around the room. By then he was pushing five hundred pounds. His surrealistic Carmen Miranda imitation made for an unforgettable sight. Later that evening, I drove the big man home in his brand-new Cadillac.

"With the money we're making, we don't need anything," Iorizzo said, inebriated as much by cash and power as by alcohol. "We don't need this car."

With that, he ripped the door off the glove compartment and threw it out the window, howling with laughter.

"We don't need this arm rest!" He railed as he ripped that off and tossed it out.

"We don't need this sun visor!" And that went next.

Iorizzo proceeded to strip the inside of the car, piece by piece, bouncing parts of the lavish interior down the highway.

"We don't need nothing, Michael!" he concluded. "I can just buy another new Cadillac tomorrow!"

And it seemed that he was right. In some ways, it was the best of times.

– 71 –

There were a few problems. One major one was that Iorizzo went on a power trip that knew no bounds. During the next three years, he asked me to kill at least fifty people who had offended him in various ways. I refused every request, telling him that murder was bad business. On the streets, my men were also becoming drunk with money and power. They made their own requests to hit this person or that, or raze rival stations and trucks. I always turned them down, saying that it was unnecessary.

The men didn't limit their bullying to outsiders. Frank "Frankie Gangster" Castagnaro walked into Galion's office one afternoon, pulled out a .45, and stuck it in Iorizzo's face.

"If you ever sell Michael out, I'll kill you," he warned.

Things became so unruly that I was forced to call a meeting of the troops. I summoned everyone to a large basement assembly room in one of Galion's offices in Commack, Long Island. When everyone was seated and accounted for, there were more than fifty in attendance. I stood before them at a podium like Lee Iacocca addressing his top executives at Chrysler. My topic that evening was violence and the new mob.

"Violence is bad business," I said. "It will bring too much heat on this operation. This isn't the 1930s, and they're not the days of Al Capone. Those days are gone. We are in a new era. We are not shylocks and pimps. We are businessmen. We have a good thing going here, and we can all make a ton of money, but only if we're smart.

"We want to be friends with our competitors so we can win them over and bring them into our operation. Whenever possible, we don't want to extort them or bully them or beat them up. The age of the bent-nose enforcer is nearly over. We can offer our competitors a service they can't get anywhere else, and we can offer them profits they can't make anywhere else. We don't need to force them. They'll join us willingly. Play it my way, and they'll have no choice.

"From this point on, there will be no violence of any kind unless I personally approve it. There are no exceptions. If you have a problem, bring it to me and I'll solve it. If I can't, we'll use our muscle as a last resort—but only as a last resort."

At the end of my speech, I ordered an associate to pass out beepers, and I instructed all my men to wear them twenty-four hours a day. Prosecutors would later dub us "the Beeper Gang."

Not long after that meeting, Iorizzo broke the rule and proved me prophetic. The fat man and a Long Island wholesaler named Shelly Levine had a difference of opinion over $270,000 Iorizzo claimed Levine owed him. The sum was a pittance considering the money we were raking in, but Iorizzo was a power junkie and needed to throw around his considerable weight. He called the frizzy-haired Jewish man into his office and slapped him around. When I heard about it, I was livid. Levine had a big operation that I was looking to sweep into Galion. I came down hard on Iorizzo, a process amplified by the fact that he had always been terrified of me.

Shelly Levine did exactly what I feared he would do: he ran and got his own muscle. The man Shelly turned to was stubby, cigar-chewing Joe "Joe Glitz" Galizia, a soldier in the Genovese family. Iorizzo and I were basking in the Florida sun when the call came. Joe Glitz was so eager to settle things that he told me he was flying to Florida for the meet.

"See what you did?" I scolded Iorizzo. "We could have had Shelly with us. Instead, you smacked that guy, and now I've got to deal with Joe Glitz."

Glitz arrived the following afternoon with Shelly Levine in tow. I met them on the outdoor patio of the Marina Bay Club in Fort Lauderdale. The first thing I did was order Glitz to bounce Levine from the meet. I didn't want to talk interfamily business with an outsider.

"Shelly's with me," Glitz said, chomping on his cigar, thumping his chest and offering the traditional Cosa Nostra opening. "He's been with me for a long time."

"Don't lie to me," I growled. "Larry smacked him, so he ran to you. Don't hand me that 'long time' line. And if Shelly's with you now, then you're responsible for the $270,000 he owes us. That's the first matter of business. Without that, we have nothing to talk about."

Glitz didn't argue. The Genovese soldier agreed to pay the debt and put it on record with his family. It wasn't hard to figure Glitz's angle.

"I want to get into the gasoline business with this guy," he said. "We need your help. Give us a line of credit so we can get rolling."

I had no alternative but to agree. It was a courtesy one made man expected of another. In the end, I got what I wanted: Shelly's extensive operation would be swept under Galion Holdings along with everyone else. The only trouble was that there was now another gangster fly in the ointment.

After a satisfied Joe Glitz departed, I confronted Iorizzo.

"Slapping Shelly was the stupidest thing you've ever done. You just introduced another family into the business," I lectured. "Don't ever chase anyone away from us again."

— 72 —

After that bit of unpleasantness, we shifted our attention to one of our reasons for being in Florida in the first place. We had expanded our operation to the Sunshine State through a Fort Lauderdale company called Houston Holdings. Within months, we were moving forty million gallons of tax-free gasoline a month, taking in another half-million per week each.

Iorizzo quickly got back into my good graces by updating me on a side operation he had going. In the Learjet on the way to

New York, while we feasted on shrimp and steak, Iorizzo laid it out.

"We're going to make a bundle this weekend," he announced.

Iorizzo had bought off the dispatcher at a New York gasoline loading dock. From Friday night to early Monday morning, he sent a succession of tanker trucks to the station to fill up. As we worked on our tans, Iorizzo kept a running tab of how much gasoline he was stealing. With each report, he sang, danced a Jackie Gleason jig, and toasted another successful hour of thievery. By Monday morning, he had emptied the tanks of three million gallons of gasoline, which we immediately sold for a pure profit of $2.5 million.

The fat man already had all the money he could ever spend, but that didn't matter. He was totally hooked on the thrill of stealing and the vicarious power he wielded through me.

My "success" wasn't going unnoticed in Brooklyn. Although Persico was back in prison, he issued an order that was quickly relayed down the pipeline, and I received a call requesting my presence at a designated house in Brooklyn. When I arrived, I was greeted by Jimmy Angellino and other family members.

"The boss says he wants to make it official," Angellino said. "You are now a captain in La Cosa Nostra. Congratulations, Michael."

I thanked them and returned to Long Island. Becoming a caporegime meant I could officially be the leader of a band of soldiers and associates. I was already doing that and had been for years, so as far as my day-to-day activity went, this didn't change anything. But the new title gave me increased authority, more recognition among the made men and mob associates on the street, and more power in dealing with members of other families. It also meant that, along with recruiting my own crew, made men soldiers would also be assigned to my command.

There was a downside. Being a captain gave me more responsibility and tied me in closer to the central command in Brooklyn.

— 73 —

At the same time Iorizzo and I were running our gasoline scam on Long Island, a flamboyant mobster named Michael Markowitz was running his own billion-dollar gasoline scheme in and around New York City. For most of the 1980s, Markowitz, a jowly man with thinning, curly brown hair, reigned as the king of the mysterious wave of Russian and Eastern European immigrant gangsters who settled into areas like Brighton Beach in Brooklyn. While my army of kinder and gentler mobsters and I were ushering organized crime into the 1990s, Markowitz and his fellow Eastern Europeans were dragging it back to the violent 1930s. A similar invasion of Cuban immigrant thugs, dumped ashore during the 1980 Freedom Flotilla, was ravaging Miami.

Markowitz, alternately referred to as a Russian or as a Rumanian (I always thought he was the latter), extended his ethnicity to a third area when he was dubbed "the Jewish Scarface." Actually, it was a fourth description of Markowitz that was more memorable. Once the money started pouring in, the heavyset Markowitz began enveloping himself in what he obviously felt was the chic clothing of a successful young American. His version consisted of screaming sport shirts open to the chest, shiny John Travolta disco suits, thick gold chains, and a fistful of gaudy diamond rings. In these getups, he reminded many who met him of the shoulder-shimmying, pseudo-hip Czech brothers created by comedians Steve Martin and Dan Aykroyd on *Saturday Night Live.*

As Markowitz's operation grew and his bankroll increased, he glittered around town in his tasteful Rolls and tasteless wardrobe. This high-profile life led to another lesson in Americana. He quickly made himself a target for both the state regulatory office and for various shakedown artists trying to cut into his operation. His problem was the same one that previously faced Larry Iorizzo: he had immense wealth but no power, and so he needed a protector.

At the end of 1982, Markowitz's empire was about to come crashing down. The state had pulled his wholesale license just as the shakedown vultures were closing in on him. Desperate to keep his massive business alive, he began to put out feelers for someone to help him. He came in contact with Vinnie Carrozza, the brother of my close friend Champagne Larry, and Vinnie asked me if I could collect a $7,500 debt for Markowitz from a gasoline station operator. The insignificant amount dramatized the Rumanian's lack of influence. I got the money that same afternoon. Vinnie then scheduled a meet at an oversized Mobil station in Brooklyn that Markowitz owned and used as his headquarters. With Markowitz that day were his Russian-born partners, David Bogatin and Leo Persits.

I stifled a laugh when the gaudy Rumanian walked in looking like a rug salesman who had just hit the lottery. Yet, as we talked, I could see that we had a lot in common. We were both more educated than those around us, we both idolized our fathers, we both had a knack for business, and we both liked high-risk operations that produced big numbers. I also liked Markowitz's partners. They were tough Russians who had clawed their ways out of that country, come to America, and made a fortune. Bogatin had an especially rough background, having served three years of hard time in a Russian prison.

Putting aside my warm feelings for the men, I cut a deal with them that was ice cold. I would take over their billion-dollar operation for seventy-five percent of the pie. They would get the remaining twenty-five percent. They were so desperate that they agreed.

– 74 –

The deal with Markowitz and associates greatly increased my authority and expanded my influence. My inner circle of soldiers and top-level associates grew to about forty men. Beyond them, there were hundreds of men who were under our command and many more clamoring to come aboard.

The size of my "army" was somewhat ironic because I had never actively recruited anyone. Men were just drawn to the success of the operation. They came to me, and I was then able to pick and choose those I wanted.

Personally, the success, the money, and the level of power I had now achieved were both exhilarating and tiring. There were people around me catering to my every wish, and I could issue any order pertaining to anything, from business to matters of life and death, and it would be carried out without question. I was happy that I had a strong, wealthy crew that everyone wanted to join, but with it all came a tremendous amount of work and responsibility. The mob was not a business—it was a life. And that life consumed all of my time and energy.

As my profile increased, I also became a more inviting target. I knew that law enforcement and prosecutors—or even one of my own men—would one day be coming after me.

At this point, it was said that the money pouring into our operation resembled the gross national product of a mid-sized country. Estimates had Iorizzo and me earning anywhere between $5 million and $8 million a week, and this went on every week for nearly three years. Still, despite the enormity of those numbers, some prosecutors have privately admitted that the government underestimated the take to stave off embarrassment. At the height of the operation, Houston Holdings, which swallowed up Galion Holdings and its fifty different paper subsidiaries, was moving three hundred million to five hundred million gallons of gasoline a month in five states. Figuring that we offered discounts of five to ten cents a gallon to monopolize the market, a ballpark estimate was that we were stealing twenty cents a gallon. That was $60 million to $100 million a month in stolen taxes alone, not counting legitimate profits. How much of this money found its way into my pockets and exactly what I did with it were matters for speculation. In comparison, John Gotti, at one time the head of the largest of the five New York Mafia families, was said to have made "only" between $5 million and $10 million a year.

With Markowitz and his crew aboard, the Monday night parties at the Casablanca reached new levels of intoxication. Iorizzo would lug his four hundred fifty pounds to the club, do his Carmen Miranda imitation, and rip apart a luxury automobile. Markowitz would follow, proudly displaying twenty pounds of gold jewelry splashed over his latest hideous suit. Both men would arrive with their swelling entourages, including Markowitz's quizzical band of Russian-speaking criminals.

On occasion, Markowitz returned the favor by hosting a gala event of his own at a favored Russian bar in Brooklyn. The Soviet-styled parties included an endless procession of trays piled a foot high with steamed lobsters. There were oceans of wine and vodka to wash it all down, and there were dancing girls to entertain everyone during dessert.

Regardless of where the parties took place, I was always in some inner office overlooking the proceedings and taking requests. My power inside the New York Mafia families had grown with every dollar, and my profile outside the mob had more than kept pace. A deputy attorney general in the United States Department of Justice reported to a congressional subcommittee that my operation had grown so large that I had been awarded my own Long Island-based family and had jumped from being a Colombo captain to a full-fledged, Marlon Brando-like Mafia don. That was an exaggeration. The Colombo family wasn't about to allow that to happen. Still, it's not hard to see how the feds got that impression. Counting all my subordinates in the wide-reaching gasoline industry, along with the savage Eastern Europeans I had organized under my ever-expanding wing, I now commanded an army that was large and financially powerful and capable enough of operating as an independent family. And I was only thirty-two years old. What was next?

— 75 —

In the spring of 1983, something began stirring that would change the course of my life forever. On April 21 of that year, representatives from eleven separate state, county, and federal law enforcement agencies marched like suited soldiers into the basement of the federal courthouse in Uniondale, Long Island, to hold what would be the first of three dozen intensive, day-long meetings convened over the next twelve months. These guys were serious.

Seated around a large U-shaped table was an impressive array of government muscle. Assigned to the massive interagency crime-fighting squad were Ray Jermyn, special assistant U.S. attorney and the driving force behind the Long Island Organized Crime Oil Industry Task Force; Edward McDonald, attorney-in-charge of the powerful, Brooklyn-based Organized Crime Strike Force of the Eastern District of New York; Jerry Bernstein, McDonald's tenacious assistant and a special attorney with the U.S. Department of Justice; Bill Tamparo and Kevin Craddock, special agents with the IRS; Danny Lyons, head of the Long Island FBI office; Dick Guttler, special agent, FBI; John LaPerla, United States postal inspector; Jack Ryan and Vincent O'Reilly, special assistant U.S. attorneys representing the New York State Attorney General's Office; Jim Wrightson, special investigator, New York State Attorney General's Office; Joel Weiss, Rackets Bureau chief, Nassau County District Attorney's Office; detectives Frank Morro and Al Watterson, Rackets Bureau, Suffolk County Police Department; and detective Bob Gately, Rackets Bureau, Nassau County Police Department.

After a few organizational meetings, the scope of the investigation was broadened even further. Joining the task force were Sam Badillo, special agent, U.S. Department of Labor, Office of Labor Racketeering; Tom Sullivan, special agent, Florida Department of Law Enforcement; and Fred Damski, assistant state attorney for Broward County (Fort Lauderdale) Florida.

This massive, fourteen-agency government task force had one assignment—to bring me down. The reason, I was later told, was that they considered me to be the Mafia's most financially powerful new superstar. Their basement meetings were just the opposite of our Casablanca disco celebrations. Instead of dancing to pulsating music and feasting on lasagna, veal, pasta, wine, scotch, vodka, and beautiful women, the law enforcement agents rolled up their sleeves and went to work. They paused only to dash across the street to a Roy Rogers fast-food outlet and bring back sacks of cold hamburgers and greasy french fries, which they ate while they worked through lunch.

Under the direction of McDonald and Bernstein, members of the group, known officially as the Michael Franzese Task Force, pooled their resources, shared information, plotted strategy, and struggled to keep up with my rapidly expanding criminal empire. When conflicts arose over jurisdiction and assignments, the FBI's Lyons settled the disputes and acted as sergeant at arms. That wasn't a difficult assignment. Egos were suppressed as the prosecutors, government representatives, special agents, and police were united behind the single-minded cause of bagging the man they had come to call "the Yuppie Don."

It took months just to untangle the maze of my far-reaching criminal domain. The squadron of government agents shook their heads in amazement when Lyons displayed a large, colored chart that outlined my interests. Jermyn counted twenty different Magic Marker colors on the chart, each representing a rich vein of illegal income.

Although the colorful lines on the FBI's chart led to me like streamers to a maypole, the chain of evidence needed to build a court case usually broke down before it reached that far. This was by design. I had taken mental notes during those 6:00 A.M. breakfast meetings when my father sipped freshly brewed coffee and explained the art of insulating oneself from everything except the flow of cash.

I was unaware of the force gathered in Uniondale, but my antennae began alerting me like never before. I could almost feel the weight of the mysterious army that was now shadowing my every move. The cars that followed me to restaurants and nightclubs and parked outside my home and offices no longer were easily identified as pesky Nassau and Suffolk County police units. They didn't even appear to be vehicles operated by FBI agents. These were cars and tags of men that gave off an eerie aura that I had never felt before, not even in my father's heyday.

It was time, my senses warned me, to relocate my base of operations as far from New York as possible. Time to laugh, have fun, and escape to a place where the air was warm, the sun was bright, and people played in the sand. I needed a sensory diversion strong enough to blunt the increasing realization that I was a fox who had stolen once too often from the hen house, and that the cloud of dust hovering over the horizon was being kicked up by a charging herd of snarling bloodhounds and furious farmers. It was time to seek out the mental distraction of the man who had become my court jester, Jerry Zimmerman.

— 76 —

Jerome Zimmerman had met my father long before he knew me. Dad had traveled to a Long Island car dealership in the mid-1960s to visit a friend named Charlie Gerraci. Dad was at the top of his form then and was widely regarded as the most feared mob enforcer in New York. Gerraci took him for a walk around the lot.

The dealership owner spotted the gregarious Zimmerman up on a ladder, fixing the dealership's promotional sign. Gerraci signaled for his partner to climb down.

"Hey, Spaghetti, what's doin', man?" Zimmerman asked.

"What did he say?" my father asked, the muscles in his bull neck tightening.

"What's happening, Spaghetti, my man?" Zimmerman repeated as he descended.

"Hey, what's this guy talkin' 'spaghetti' ?" my father inquired of Gerraci.

By then, Zimmerman had reached them. "Jerry, I'd like you to meet a friend of mine, Sonny Franzese."

My father gave Jerry a look that nearly brought him to his knees.

"Ah...uh...glad to meet you. I'm...I'm...you know...just a kidder. Me and Charlie, we're tight. We kid around all the time...you know?"

My father understood, and what he understood he didn't like. He apparently wasn't too upset, though, for Zimmerman survived.

I met Zimmerman during my Italian-American Civil Rights League days. He was friends with various mob guys and supported Joe Colombo's misguided organization. After Colombo was hit, Jerry and I stayed in touch. When my auto-leasing business began to prosper, I made him one of my managers. When I was inducted into La Cosa Nostra, Zimmerman held his ground and worked himself into my inner circle.

I never trusted Jerry and suspected him of pocketing payoffs and ripping me off for petty sums in countless ways. Regardless, the big Jewish man was a world-class con artist whose crazy schemes were wildly amusing. Despite his flaws, I allowed him to get close to me.

Zimmerman moved to California in late 1979 and acted as an advance scout for me there. He started a used-car dealership, and I frequently shipped him cars that had a higher value on the West Coast than on Long Island. More importantly, Zimmerman's operation gave me an excuse to travel to Los Angeles. I loved the sunny skies and casual lifestyle there. I especially loved the fact that California was three thousand miles away from Brooklyn.

— 77 —

Zimmerman also frequented Las Vegas, where he would run various scams on the big casino-hotels. If a scam was going particularly well, he'd call and ask me to catch a plane to join him.

On one memorable occasion, Zimmerman conned the management of the Sands into believing that fat, dumpy Peter "Apollo" Frappolo, one of my underlings, was the don of the "powerful Franzese crime family in Long Island." He told the Sands that the family was moving its operation to Vegas and was going to dump millions into a hotel. The Sands responded by giving Frappolo and Zimmerman the hotel's best suite and surrounding them with all the trappings of luxury.

When I arrived, I couldn't believe my eyes. Frappolo was perched in a thronelike chair and had two beautiful women attending him hand and foot. When I approached, Frappolo waved me off and picked up the telephone receiver. "Excuse me, Michael, I need to make a call."

"Excuse me?" I said, burning a hole through my underling.

Zimmerman swept me into a nearby room.

"He believes it!" Zimmerman said, rolling on the bed laughing. "The guy really thinks he's Don Corleone."

When we returned to the room, the two women were feeding Frappolo strawberries. Zimmerman and I had to duck back into the bedroom to hide our laughter.

By the time we had composed ourselves enough to make a third pass at the "don," he was being feted by the hotel's manager.

"Mr. Appolo, I want to remind you that you have an appointment for a haircut and manicure in fifteen minutes, if that's okay?" the manager asked. Frappolo indicated that it was.

When I tried to talk to him a few moments later, Frappolo interrupted. "Michael, I have a haircut and manicure scheduled."

I calmly asked the manager and the strawberry twins to leave the suite and give us some privacy.

"Pete, snap out of it!" I ordered. "Get your rear end out of that chair. I've got to figure out how to bail you two out of this mess once they catch on."

Zimmerman explained that they were being "comped" on everything and had a $70,000 line of credit at the casino, which they planned to cash in. I advised them not to play the scam out too long. We hung around a few more days, then left with the money.

— 78 —

Aside from his amusement value, Jerry Zimmerman performed another valuable function in my life. He was the one who introduced me to the movie business.

During one of my Los Angeles visits in early 1980, I found my con-man friend especially upbeat.

"Michael," he said, "I want to do a movie!"

"What do you know about doing movies?" I asked.

"It's easy. Listen...."

And he laid it out. He had gotten his hands on a script for a horror movie called *Mausoleum*. He said the total budget would be a mere $250,000, and he already had two people willing to put up a third each. If I kicked in the final third, about $83,000, Zimmerman promised me a third of the action and the title of executive producer. It sounded good to me and, at that point, eighty-three grand was pocket change, so I agreed, and Zimmerman set the deal in motion.

From the start, the project was beset with the woes of amateurs. What's worse, the two other financiers never materialized, leaving me with the entire $250,000 initial budget. That sum was swallowed up before we were half finished. About $1.2 million later—$900,000 of which was my money—we had two film cans full of a hodgepodge of a movie ready to distribute. *Mausoleum* promptly bombed. The only people the movie terrified were the financiers.

During the filming, Zimmerman had his hooks into an older man from the Midwest named Jim Kimball, a legitimate businessman, who was interested in getting into the motion picture business. After being drained for a few hundred thousand, the guy shut off the tap. Kimball was in Zimmerman's office on Ventura Boulevard one afternoon checking out his investment when in walked Lenny Montana, the burly actor who played Corleone family enforcer Lucca Brazzi in *The Godfather*. (For those who have seen the movie, he was the guy who got the knife through his hand at the bar.) Zimmerman and Montana were about to put on a well-thought-out dramatization that would cause Kimball to cough up some more money.

Montana, a real-life crook, screamed at Zimmerman, claiming he was owed a considerable sum of money. Zimmerman pleaded for time. Then the argument grew nasty. Suddenly, Montana pulled out a gun and shot Zimmerman in the upper body. Blood splattered everywhere as the big man dropped to the floor, gasping for breath.

Kimball, scared out of his wits, pleaded with Montana not to finish Zimmerman off. He promised to pay the $50,000 debt. Montana, apparently satisfied, put away the gun. Some of Zimmerman's associates dragged their bleeding boss to a car and rushed him to a hospital.

Left alone in the office, the shaken investor called me.

"Lenny shot Jerry!" he screamed. "Michael, Lenny shot Jerry!"

I put my hand over the phone and laughed. It never even occurred to me that the shooting might have been for real. I composed myself and continued the conversation.

"I'm going to pay!" Kimball reiterated. "I'm going to give him the money, okay? I'll make it good! You don't have to kill Jerry!"

I said that would be satisfactory. When I hung up, I dialed Zimmerman's home. He answered.

"I just received an interesting call," I said. "I understand you've been shot?"

"You should have seen the guy's face!" Zimmerman howled. "You should have been there!"

"You guys are insane," I told him.

Kimball coughed up the $50,000, which Zimmerman and Montana pocketed. Kimball then pushed to visit Zimmerman in the hospital to make sure he was okay. They held him off as long as they could, then went to a local hospital and rented a room under the guise of needing it for a scene in the movie. They bandaged Zimmerman and laid him in the hospital bed. Kimball visited him for an entire half hour, and all that time, Zimmerman moaned and groaned and never once cracked a smile.

The final coup came a few weeks later after Zimmerman had "recovered." I called Zimmerman, Montana, and Kimball into my office. I reamed out Zimmerman and Montana for the shooting and told them they'd better toe the line or they'd both be whacked. Kimball's hands trembled as he witnessed a real-life gangster laying down the law. After Kimball left, the three of us rolled with laughter.

That was the highlight of *Mausoleum.* I never recovered a dime of my $900,000 investment. Not only that, but Zimmerman had raised some of the budget by banking on my name and reputation, promoting me as a rich New York mobster with a bottomless pit of cash. That resulted in a grand jury investigation headed by a California Organized Crime Strike Force attorney named Bruce Kelton. Kimball was called as a witness and made no mention of the shooting incident. Despite losing his money, he testified that everything had been on the up-and-up. The grand jury investigation came up as empty as the *Mausoleum* box office cash drawers.

– 79 –

Despite the financial horror of this experience and the close call with the feds, I was bitten by the movie bug. I quickly saw, however, that the money to be made in movies wasn't in production, but in the distribution end. I invested another half-million in a legitimate distribution firm headed by a man named John Chambliss. The company distributed B- and C-grade movies regionally and made a solid profit. I leased a condominium in exclusive Marina Del Rey and looked forward to spending time in the California sun.

As always, I registered my dealings with the Colombo family. They approved of my efforts, pleased to get a foothold in Hollywood. However, instead of extolling the wonders of Los Angeles, I made sure I always bad-mouthed the city and the surrounding area to them. I didn't want any of my mob associates moving in on my territory.

"The place is horrible," I'd report to the bosses in Brooklyn after a long West Coast visit. "The pollution is so bad you can hardly breathe. The city is dirty, and it stinks. You guys are so lucky to be able to stay here in beautiful Brooklyn."

It was absurd, but the old-time mob bosses were so infatuated with Brooklyn that they reveled in the comparisons. I played the same game with Florida, describing it as a steamy swamp infested with bloodsucking insects and assaulted by staggering heat and humidity.

"Florida's not fit for human habitation," I warned.

Meanwhile, I started shifting my operations to those two "dreaded" locations.

In 1982, I took a stab at producing another film. This one was entitled *Savage Streets*. It boasted a semi-star, Linda Blair, from the horror blockbuster *The Exorcist*. *Savage Streets* was a vigilante movie in the *Death Wish* tradition. Blair was shown exacting her revenge on a gang of street criminals who had raped her sister. Smartening up on the ways of motion picture financing, I financed nearly all of the $2.3 million budget for the film through a loan from Michigan National Bank and a bond from Union Indemnity Insurance of New York. Although considerably better than *Mausoleum, Savage Streets* suffered from poor distribution, and it also bombed. Whatever money the film made went back to the Michigan bank. By then, the insurance company had far bigger problems: it never recovered from the staggering loss it suffered in November 1980 when one of its clients, the MGM Grand Hotel in Las Vegas, burned down.

My third foray into the movie business was picking up an Italian horror film, reediting it, changing its name to *Gates of Hell*, and sending it to the masses. The masses didn't like that one any better than the others, but the costs were so low the film actually turned a profit.

A better investment once again came from the distribution end. I worked a $3 million, eight-picture deal with Vestron Video, an aggressive company that delved into all aspects of the movie business, including the new trade of supplying video cassettes to the rapidly expanding home VCR market. I made money by picking up various foreign and domestic films for about $70,000, reediting them and changing their titles if needed, then reselling the video, domestic, and foreign rights for $350,000. I was on my way in the movie industry.

— 80 —

As the action picked up in California, the agony continued in New York. In early May 1983, I returned from Los Angeles, tan and refreshed, only to be informed that Carmine Persico's son Alphonse and Anthony "Tony the Gawk" Augello had been indicted on a narcotics charge. That caught everyone's attention. Persico was young and from another generation, so the drug charge against him wasn't that surprising. The Gawk's role was mystifying. A big, bearish man with huge hands, he was an old-timer who had come up with my father and the elder Persico and was schooled in the traditional ways of the mob. For him to get involved in drugs was a direct breach of his oath.

I knew the Gawk well. Like many of the Colombo soldiers, he had spent so much time at our house that he was like an uncle. Among my "uncles," I held a special feeling for the affable, smartly dressed Gawk. The big man had often attended my junior high and high school football games with my father, loudly cheering from the sidelines every time I ran the ball.

Following his release on bail, the Gawk paid me a visit at Rumplik Chevrolet. He pulled up in his trademark bright green Eldorardo.

"I've got a good shot at beating this," the Gawk said, as much to convince himself as me. "These charges are all phony. Man, I hope the guys don't think I'm involved in drugs."

"If it ain't true, it ain't true," I said.

Although the Gawk's words were confident, his body language was screaming something else. He was fidgeting and trembling as he talked. His hands were shaking so much that his diamond pinky ring sparkled like a mirrored disco ball in the sunlight. I had never seen the big man act like that before.

"It'll be all right," I assured him. "No one blames you."

"Yeah, yeah. How can anybody blame me? I mean, it's the boss's son, right? The boss's son. Right, Michael?"

"I don't think you have anything to worry about."

After the Gawk left, a chill washed over me. He wasn't handling this at all well.

Two days later, I received a call from one of my men. "The Gawk just blew his brains out in a phone booth on Broadway. He called his wife, told her he loved her, then ate his gun. Can you believe that? Blew his teeth clean outta his head!"

I shut the door of my office, turned off the light, and sat quietly in the dark for more than an hour. The trouble was, I *could* believe it. That was what was so unnerving. The Gawk had been one of the few real tough guys I had known. He would have confronted ten armed men and bravely fought to his death for the family. He would have walked fearlessly through a wall of cops. But the Gawk couldn't live with his own fear. He couldn't live with the wait, not knowing which one of his thirty-year blood brothers was going to take him for a ride and put a bullet in his head. He couldn't live waiting to be called into that final meeting where you never come out. The Gawk had done it to others, so he knew how it went.

I thought of how the previous week must have gone for the man. The tension, no doubt, had been unbearable, tearing at his mind and body. Whom could he trust? Who would his killer be? When would the call come? Why don't they just get it over with?

To relieve the paralyzing agony, the Gawk had become his own assassin, having determined that death was better than living with the torment he had created.

The drug case against the younger Persico lingered, was transferred to another district, and then it was dropped.

Sadly, the Gawk had hit himself for nothing.

— 81 —

May 1983 turned out to be, quite literally, a deadly month. First was the Gawk's suicide. Then my best friend Larry Carozza was found dead in his car along a Brooklyn highway, the circumstances of which weigh heavy on my heart even to this day. Later, on May 27, my thirty-second birthday, another tragedy occurred that set into motion a series of events that would change my life forever. Jerry Zimmerman's nineteen-year-old son Ira died of leukemia.

Ira's passing threw Jerry into a deep depression. He had always experienced huge mood swings, but this time it looked like he was down for the count.

I wasn't in great shape myself. I was haunted by the specter of the still-undisclosed joint task force and was emotionally rocked by the Gawk's suicide and the murder of my good friend (mob business as usual). To deal with all of this, I focused my energy on trying to cheer up Zimmerman. When nothing worked, I decided to make another movie—just to snap him out of his depression.

Although Jerry had introduced me to the movie business, albeit with the terrible *Mausoleum*, he wasn't able to mesh with John Chambliss, so he had withdrawn from subsequent movies. I called Zimmerman now from my home in Delray Beach and told him I needed to see him in Florida immediately. I didn't say why.

When Zimmerman arrived the next day, he was still depressed.

"What's up?" he asked.

"I want to make a movie here in Florida," I told him, "and I want you to produce it with me."

His face lit up as his depression lifted.

"What kind of movie?" he asked.

"I don't know," I said. "I like music. Why don't we do a musical this time."

"Sounds great!" Zimmerman gushed.

We had no cast, crew, director, or even a script, just a vague idea and my desire to help a friend shake the blues. I solved these problems with a few phone calls. The first was to a Hollywood agent named David Wilder. I instructed Wilder to put out an order around town for a musical script. Wilder responded a few months later with a screenplay entitled *Never Say Die*, written by Leon Isaac Kennedy, a suavely handsome black actor known for the *Penitentiary* boxing films and the Chuck Norris hit *Lone Wolf McQuade*. He was also known as the former husband of Jayne Kennedy, the onetime NFL football announcer. Leon Kennedy had woven an energetic, interracial love story around a street gang, a rock band, and the fad of break dancing.

The project presented an intriguing casting dilemma. Instead of searching Beverly Hills for Hollywood's A-list, we'd have to cull the cast of such a movie from the squalid black ghettos of Miami and the gang-infested Latin barrios of Southern California. This could be interesting!

— 82 —

Through this film, another influence came into my life in the person of a beautiful nineteen-year-old Mexican-American woman. I first caught sight of her as she was lifting herself from the Marina Bay Club's pool in Fort Lauderdale. Her long, coffee-colored hair was wet and slicked back, accentuating her face and huge brown eyes. Her firm dancer's body impressed me. Her wet skin seemed to shimmer in the sunlight. In that moment, I felt a strange sensation in my chest that made me gulp for air. This woman had literally taken my breath away. And for good reason. She was, without a doubt, the most beautiful and exotic woman I had ever seen.

"Will you look at that!" Frankie Cestaro said, as struck by the dancer as I was.

"I noticed," I said. "That girl's young, innocent, and awesome. She could be a lot of trouble for me. I'm going to stay away from her."

"I think I'll give it a shot," Cestaro said.

"Be my guest," I told him. "I don't even want to get near her."

I had too much on my mind to be distracted by real romance. My whim to film a movie in South Florida had quickly grown into a master plan for building a major independent motion picture company there. I wanted to produce a series of big-budget, Hollywood-quality movies in Florida, and I had arranged with First American Bank in Fort Lauderdale to kick in $10 million to help with the initial financing.

Not that money was a problem for me. With the capital coming in from the gasoline business, I was capable of being my own financier. In the end, it happened just that way. The $2 million budget for Leon Kennedy's movie, renamed *Cry of the City* during the shooting and *Knights of the City* when it was released, came from my own pocket.

The movie, along with my grandiose plans, had made me, for the moment, the darling of the local media and of Florida's state, city, and county politicians—none of whom had apparently bothered to check out my background. The Florida Film Commission bent over backward, granting me permits to film at various locations. Miami Beach Mayor Malcolm Fromberg awarded me the key to the city and promised that the tourist town would donate prime land and help finance the building of an immense motion picture sound stage. Fort Lauderdale Mayor Bob Dressler tried to present me with a plaque but was unable to pin me down for the presentation. The Broward County Sheriff's Department even made me an honorary police commissioner.

A second reason for the open-arms welcome was the way we did the casting for *Knights of the City*. We held open auditions and encouraged disadvantaged youth to try out as dancers. The auditions were held in both Broward (Fort Lauderdale) and Dade (Miami) counties and attracted two thousand young people per session. From them, we selected 116 dancers and 250 extras, fed them, and paid them well. We also made it a condition of work on the film that those who were chosen would have to maintain good grades in school.

The glitter of the movies, the jobs for low-income youth, and the good-grades requirement further ingratiated me with the media and public. Despite my background and the danger of negative publicity, I opened the movie set to the press. This initially resulted in added waves of positive publicity.

In addition, I was able to avoid a problem that had frequently chased away potential filmmakers from South Florida. Although Florida was a right-to-work state with few unions, the Teamsters' South Florida branch was notoriously tough to deal with. The union specifically targeted movie companies and demanded that all the equipment trucks, including the trailers for the stars, be driven by Teamsters drivers. These drivers were paid $1,500 a week, even if they did nothing but stand by an idle truck or trailer for weeks at a time. This bled the limited budgets of independent films.

Shortly after *Knights of the City* opened a production office, a big, burly Teamsters representative paid Jerry Zimmerman a visit.

"This is a Teamsters film, or there won't *be* a film," he announced.

Zimmerman smiled. "You'll have to talk to my boss."

A meeting was set for the following day at the second-story office of Houston Holdings, the gasoline-company branch office in Fort Lauderdale. The union rep marched in and tried to bully his way around. "I told your partner, there will be no film without the Teamsters."

"Sounds like a threat," I said.

"No threat. Just a fact. No Teamsters, no film," he ventured.

"You see this window behind me," I said, pointing to the office's large picture window. "If I ever see your face in here again, you're going out that window."

"I don't think you understand what you're doing," he said, storming out.

Two days later, I received a call from the Teamsters representative.

"Mr. Franzese," he said meekly. "I'm sorry we got off on the wrong foot. Whatever you want, you got it. If there's anything we can do for you, just name it."

"Okay, here's what I'll do," I said. "I'll take one Teamsters driver so it doesn't get around that we busted you out. My guys will handle the rest of the trucks."

And that's what happened. We were on our way to producing low-cost films in South Florida.

— 83 —

As I stared at the young dancer by the pool that day in Ft. Lauderdale, all the hassles of making the movie and running the gasoline operation suddenly appeared insignificant. I fought with myself over whether to give in to my desire to woo her or to stay away and keep my mind fixed on business. There were plenty of available women around the set—uncomplicated women. I didn't need this Mexican beauty.

The only problem was that I couldn't keep my eyes off of her. When a cast member who was passing out T-shirts around the pool skipped her, I found myself doing what I had sworn I wouldn't do. I ordered one of my men to get a box of shirts out of the trunk of his car and bring them to me. Then I used the T-shirts as an excuse to meet the young woman personally.

Agent David Wilder was sitting near her by the pool and made the introduction. "Michael, this is Cammy Garcia, the girl we sent for in L.A."

"Hi! Nice to meet you," she said, briefly glancing up, then shyly diverting her eyes.

Up close, she was even more beautiful than she had appeared from across the pool. What struck me the most, however, was that she was both innocent and yet very exciting.

It was a troubling sensation. I had long made it a policy to never drink, take drugs, or fall in love—all for the simple reason that I always wanted to maintain control of every situation. As I walked away from the pool that day, I had to steel myself against the weakening effect of this woman.

There was something about the woman's name and something about the strange way Wilder had introduced her that nagged at me afterward. What was it?

It wasn't until I was back in my room that it came to me. Cammy Garcia. Cammy...Camille...Camille Garcia. It had to be the same girl. A week before, I had received a call from a man demanding to speak to the movie's producer. He said he was the father of one of the dancers and was worried about his daughter. He wanted to be assured that everything was on the up-and-up with her job in the film. His daughter, he said, was young, innocent, and inexperienced, and had never been far away from home.

In the world of movies and professional dancers, such a *faux pas* on the part of a parent could have doomed the young woman's chances. Movie sets can sometimes be the setting for wild and sinful happenings, and nosy parents are considered to be an unwelcome hindrance. But instead of being upset that day, I found the father's concern to be endearing. I promised him I would personally watch out for his daughter and make sure that she was safe.

After hanging up, I called choreographer Jeff Kutash and ordered him to give dancer Camille Garcia a private room, so that she wouldn't be bothered by some wild roommate, and also to boost her salary to $500 a week.

"Give her the $235 per diem expenses," I added (the top scale we were paying at the time).

Kutash didn't say anything. If I wanted to give special treatment to a particular dancer, he wasn't going to question it.

It turned out that Kutash was baffled by the whole thing. Although Camille was a member of his L.A. dance troupe, he hadn't selected her to be in the movie. She had lied to her parents and had come to Florida with a one-way ticket purchased with piggy bank savings and borrowed money, hoping to somehow crash her way onto the set and thus get her career going. When Kutash spotted her at the kickoff party, he was surprised.

"Blueberry Muffin!" he said, calling her by the nickname he had given her. "What are you doing here?"

She swallowed hard and tried to play it cool. "I heard something about a dance movie in Florida. Some of my friends have a part and invited me down."

"Don't worry," Kutash had said to her. "I'll get you in. I'll get you a part."

Then, in no time at all, the happy but confused young woman found herself with a top-scale dancer's contract and a private room at the Marina Bay Club with a view of the glittering bay. The weekly $235 per diem payment alone was more money than she had ever made in a week in any of her previous jobs.

Although Camille was confused by it all, and by how fast and how easy it had come, she was also smart enough not to say any of this to others.

I smiled as I thought about the weird set of circumstances that had enabled the dancer to crash the movie. When Wilder had introduced her as "the girl we sent for in L.A.," he was just putting his own spin on the fact of her unusual arrival. Once I knew all of this, it became clear to me why she had seemed so timid and afraid when we first met, glancing up and then quickly looking away. With her tenuous position, she certainly didn't want to attract the attention of the movie's producer. She must have thought I was staring at her because I couldn't figure out who she was and why she was on the set. A veteran performer would have jumped at the opportunity to get close to the producer, to try to snare a bigger part. This young woman just wanted to hold on to what she had.

The truth was that Camille Garcia almost hadn't been there. When she had tried out for his dance troupe in Los Angeles,

Kutash could tell that she was unschooled and probably came from an underprivileged family. He could also see that she possessed creativity and natural talent and made a striking appearance onstage. She had an ethereal quality some of the most professionally skilled dancers could never achieve. His group was big enough to embrace some dancers purely on potential, so he didn't dismiss her outright. In the end, it was a close call, but he decided to take a chance on the dark-haired teenager with the angelic face.

Camille Garcia had spunk, that was for sure, and that fact attracted me to her even more. A woman like that could crash her way into a man's heart the same way she had pushed her way into the movie. A woman like that, especially a woman as beautiful as Cammy, could be trouble. Yes, I definitely wanted to stay away from her.

— 84 —

The close, family-like atmosphere of a movie crew on location made my plan to avoid Cammy Garcia all but impossible. I kept bumping into her in the hotel lobby or around the set, and every time I caught a glimpse of her, it stopped me dead in my tracks. Each new sighting burned another image into my mind. The mere sight of this woman was enough to drive me crazy.

Late one afternoon the following week, I spotted her in the lobby. She looked incredible. I noticed that she was carrying an envelope in her hand and was heading toward the mail slot near the front desk. Just before she slipped it in, I grabbed her wrist.

"You don't want to mail that," I said.

She was doubly startled, first that someone had sneaked up on her, and second that it was the producer. The letter, as I had guessed, was to her boyfriend in California.

"Why not?"

"Who's it to?" I asked.

"A friend."

"What's his name?"

Her eyes flashed, and she smiled coyly. "How do you know it's a he?"

"You don't want to mail that," I repeated, affecting my best smile. "Why don't you throw it away?"

"Isn't that your girlfriend over there?" she said, pointing to a woman with long brown hair I'd been speaking with earlier.

"No, she's the girlfriend of a friend. He called and asked me to give her a part."

I looked at Camille intently. Then, just as quickly, I said, "I've got to go. See you around." And I left.

All that day, I tried to keep my mind on business, but the image of Cammy Garcia kept intruding. I remembered an Italian old wives' tale about men being "hit by a thunderbolt" because of the effect a particular woman had on them. There didn't seem to be any explanation, it was claimed. It just happened. I had laughed about that idea in the past, but now I wasn't so sure. My own personal "thunderbolt" seemed to have suddenly appeared out of nowhere.

When a group from the cast and crew got together to see the movie *Breakin'*, Cammy was among them. Although we didn't sit together, I spent more time watching the blue light from the movie screen dance over her face than I did looking at the movie itself.

The following evening, I saw her alone in the lobby. She appeared upset, so I approached her. "You don't look very happy. What's the matter?"

She looked up at me, and her eyes misted, and her lips trembled.

"I'm going home," she said. "These people are not my type. I was just trying to mind my own business."

"Why? What happened?" I asked.

"There's a rumor going around that I'm sleeping with you," she admitted.

I was so moved by her little girl reaction to the typical movie location gossip that I could hardly speak. What had started as purely a physical attraction at that moment turned into something far more terrifying. Michael Franzese was on the verge of falling in love.

"That's funny," I said. "This is just the second time we've spoken, and every time I try to talk to you, you're suddenly gone. Are you hiding from me?"

She brushed away a tear and briefly smiled. She must have been confused. I was the problem to begin with, and instead of combating the rumormongers, I was providing them with more ammunition.

"Meet me after the cast meeting, and we'll have a drink and talk," I said, trying to convince her to stay in Florida without revealing why it mattered so much to me.

"I don't drink," was her response.

"I don't either," I offered. "So, we'll have some milk."

She laughed and promised to wait for me.

I saw her come into the meeting and then exit a few minutes later, but when the meeting was over, she was nowhere to be found. I was disappointed—to say the least.

– 85 –

Although Camille had continually troubled my thoughts from the moment I first saw her, I had yet to realize that her room was diagonally across the hall from mine. Once I discovered this fact, I made no more pretense about keeping my distance from her. There was no fighting this thunderbolt, I had decided.

The trouble seemed to be that the proverbial thunderbolt had not yet struck her. Every time I bumped into her for the next week, I made her promise to drop by my room to visit me that evening. She'd say "Okay, okay," but then she'd never show up. Each time I was disappointed. At the same time, I also found this unusual conduct to be amusing. It didn't turn me off at all. In fact, Cammy's frequent no-shows only heightened my desire to see her.

I had to go to New York on business, and while I was there, I found myself agonizing over Camille the whole time. The pain of such intense desire, such intense *unrequited* desire, was new to me. I hardly knew this girl, but that didn't seem to matter. The separation did nothing to heal the strange malady that had overtaken me. I hated New York more than ever and wanted nothing but to return to Florida—to return to *her*.

Any chance of making another attempt at forgetting Cammy Garcia was dashed when, soon after arriving back in Florida, I paid a visit to the skating rink I had rented for the dancers, and she was there. The sight of her blew me away.

The following evening, I threw a pizza party in my suite and made arrangements to show the pay-per-view Thomas "The Hit Man" Hearns–Roberto Durán boxing match. A big, noisy crowd gathered, and the commotion attracted Cammy from across the hall. She wandered in, fresh out of the shower, with her hair still wet. I noticed what she was wearing—an oversized orange shirt buttoned up the front. She looked unbelievably beautiful. I wanted to rush over and welcome her to the party, but I was trapped. I was sitting in the center of the room with a sheet tied around my neck so that the movie's hairdresser could give me a haircut.

Before I could get free, Camille was gone. Fortunately, she returned twenty minutes later, just as Hearns was knocking Durán senseless with a thunderous combination.

"You came back," I said to her, not wanting to miss the second opportunity.

"I'm just looking for my friend Katie Lauren," she said. "I don't think she's here."

And she turned to leave.

I grabbed her hand, "Camille, before next Tuesday at midnight, you must come to my room and talk to me."

The deadline was arbitrary. It just popped into my head, but she promised to come.

Tuesday came and went, and Cammy never appeared. I was very baffled by this.

On Wednesday, Jeff Kutash invited me to watch the dancers practice in a local studio. I cleared my schedule to attend, and I wasn't going just to check out the progress of the movie's choreography. My interest in the dark-haired dancer was now apparent to everyone.

During the break, one of the other dancers rushed over to Cammy backstage.

"The producer is personally interested in you!" he gushed.

"Who?" she asked.

"Michael!" he replied. "Haven't you noticed? He's been burning a hole through you the whole time."

After the rehearsal, a group of the dancers and crew members were chatting about where they were going that evening. The consensus was Shooters, a popular Fort Lauderdale nightclub. Someone asked me to join the group, but I said that I was exhausted and needed sleep. I had been getting up at dawn each day in order to oversee my business interests in New York and keep the filming of the movie going.

"If you want, you can bring a date," a cast member piped in, figuring I had plans for a more private evening ahead of me.

"He doesn't need a date," Cammy said, edging in beside me and putting her arms around my waist. "He's with me."

The instant she touched me I felt like my body was on fire.

"That's...that's right," I stammered. "I'm with Camille."

"Looks like you have a date," Frankie Cestaro said, snapping me out of my fog.

"It does," I answered. "I'll go home to Delray Beach and get some rest. Call and wake me at about eleven, and if she's there, I'll go."

— 86 —

When Frankie called, I was in a deep sleep.

"Is she there?" I mumbled.

"She's here," Frankie confirmed, "and she looks sensational!"

His description of her popped my eyes open like a burst of caffeine, and I shot out of bed, quickly dressed and drove to Shooters. When I arrived, an associate from New York, Peter Napolitano, was sitting next to Cammy.

"Let me sit here," I whispered to him.

"Michael, I'm doing good here," he said, nodding Cammy's way.

"Pete, get outta there," I ordered, far firmer than he expected.

He got the message and bolted.

"Well, here we are," I said.

"We've finally gotten together." Cammy smiled.

"What made you put your arm around me today?" I asked.

"I don't know," she said.

"Well, it worked," I told her. "It got me out of bed."

We talked for the next couple of hours, and it was as if we were the only ones there. We chatted about the movie and her dancing and her life.

Cammy told me about growing up poor in the barrios of Norwalk, southeast of Los Angeles. She had known what it was like to go to bed without dinner, not because she was being punished, but because there was no food in the house. She also knew what it was like to walk barefoot through the grass, not because she wanted to feel the sensation, but because she had no choice.

Her father, Seferino Garcia, was a radical Chicano rights activist who had been arrested eight times during the turbulent 1970s, mostly during protests of one kind or another. Some of these arrests included violent confrontations with the Norwalk,

California police. He had been roughed up pretty badly a few times.

In a strange way, her upbringing seemed similar to mine. Cammy, too, had her doubts about law enforcement.

Cammy was the oldest of seven children and had seen pretty tough days most of her life. Despite that fact, she was determined to make something of herself, and this desire had often only increased her problems. For instance, when she tried out to be a cheerleader in the seventh grade and made the squad, her friends from the barrio taunted her and called her a "Coconut"—someone brown on the outside and white on the inside. It was the Latino equivalent of a black being called an Uncle Tom, although not quite as severe.

Apparently, Cammy's more radical Chicano friends felt that, by becoming a cheerleader, she was succumbing to the conventions of the biased white society that had banished them and their parents to the barrios and treated them so harshly. These taunts led to a bloody fight with a gang of girls in front of her house one day.

What Cammy's friends didn't understand was that her father had filled her with a fierce pride. He made her feel that despite being poor and of Mexican descent, she had no reason to hang her head, ride in the back of the bus, or defer to anyone. He made her believe she could be anything she wanted to be—and that included becoming a cheerleader.

On one occasion, someone firebombed the small Garcia home and nearly killed the entire family. The culprits were never caught. They were rumored to be either local drug dealers her father had tried to chase from the neighborhood or off-duty police officers who hated her father because of his politics.

Cammy also told me that she was a Christian, a religious belief that I knew virtually nothing about. She said that her mother was a believer and that she herself had become a believer when she was in junior high. Since then, she told me, she had relied heavily upon her faith to get her through hard times. Rather than being turned off by all this talk of faith in God, I found myself wanting to hear more, maybe because it was Cammy talking. Or maybe something else was at work inside of me. I wasn't sure.

What I did know was that I was fascinated by Cammy's story, and after learning about who she was and what she had experienced, I liked her even more. Would she be shocked when she found out who and what I was? Of course I had no intention of telling her—at least not just yet.

We left Shooters and hit another place, a glitzy Fort Lauderdale disco called Faces. When Cammy excused herself to go to the ladies' room, a man started hassling her on the way. One of my men, a muscular, two-hundred-seventy-pound brute named William Ferrante, saw what was going on and came over.

"You want me to take care of him, chief?" he asked.

I shook my head no. Cammy had already begun to notice the unusual allegiance I commanded. She had figured it was just because I was the producer of the movie, and I wanted to keep her thinking that way.

The dance music at Faces was so loud that it made conversation impossible. I reacted by merely staring at Cammy, taking in her innocent beauty. This time, she stared back. We looked at each other for what seemed like an eternity. Finally, she took a half-step closer, stood on her tiptoes, and kissed me on the cheek. This sent a charge through my body.

Watch it, Franzese! I thought. *You're not only falling in love, you're falling hard.*

– 87 –

The sun was already breaking in the eastern sky when we got back to the hotel. We walked to Cammy's door, and I gently kissed her.

"Good night," she said.

I didn't move, and she squirmed.

"Good night," she repeated.

I stood firm, but I could sense how uncomfortable this made her. Her father had been right: she wasn't used to this kind of thing. She was so innocent that it strained belief.

I smiled and mussed her hair as if she were a puppy.

"Good night, Camille," I said and walked away.

But Cammy's innocence did not discourage me. To the contrary, we were inseparable after that, having lunch and dinner together every day. I enjoyed taking her to expensive restaurants and showering her with gifts. This was all so new to her that the smallest thing excited her. I had grown accustomed to having so much money that for me it had lost its thrill, but a $100 lunch made Cammy rush to a telephone to call and tell her mother. Through Cammy Garcia, the thrill of having so much money now returned to me.

Our relationship progressed rapidly in every area but the bedroom. I didn't understand this at the time, but it didn't bother me in the least. I sensed that there was already no turning back. I would be with Cammy Garcia forever, and she would change my life. Just how much she would change me, I could not yet imagine.

"I want you to know that you're very special to me," I told her at dinner one evening. "We don't have to rush anything. If it takes a week, a month, a year, it doesn't matter to me. Whenever you're ready, that's fine."

There was another reason I was not rushing things. I felt that before we consummated our relationship, I would have to tell Cammy the truth—at least some of the truth—about my life. I imagined that she might be more concerned about my marital status than about my occupation, so I decided to start there.

The truth was that my marriage to Maria had faded in everything but name. She had told me six months before that it was over, bringing up the subject herself and coming to this conclusion based on my long absences. She had come to realize and accept that we were more like close friends than anything else. We agreed that we would remain friends and do what was right for the children.

But how could I explain all of this to Cammy? And would she believe me?

— 88 —

I chose the perfect backdrop for my heart-to-heart talk, driving Cammy to a beautiful spot overlooking the ocean in Fort Lauderdale. The top was down on the Eldorado, and the sun was just beginning to set. A light summer breeze was blowing in from the sea. It seemed like the perfect moment had arrived.

I took a deep breath and began by telling Cammy that I loved her. It was the kind of opening that screams a stunning "but" will follow, yet she, in her innocence, missed all of the subtle clues about what was to come. By the time I got to the heart of the confession, I had softened the blow the best I knew how, and so I waded right into the matter at hand. I told Cammy that I was married and had three children. I explained to her that the marriage was now in name only and had essentially ended years earlier, mainly because I was hardly ever home anymore. When I was home, I told her, I stayed in my son's room (and that was the truth). I had never had a reason before to legally end the marriage, but now I did, I told her, and I would.

To my surprise, Cammy accepted everything I told her, believing me without question. My revelations didn't seem to dampen her spirits in the least. I later learned that accepting my past life had not been as easy for Cammy as it initially appeared to me. She had strong and long-held views about marriage and had vowed never to date a married man and never to marry someone with children by another marriage.

At the moment of my confession, however, Cammy Garcia had made a determination that would affect us both for the rest of our lives. She believed that God had sent her to me for my salvation, and she was not about to let anything stand in the way of our future. So, from that moment on, my former life, for her, simply would not exist. Everything that came before was of no consequence because everything was new. This was a totally new concept for me, and it certainly proved to be revolutionary.

Although I had no way of understanding at the moment all that Cammy was feeling, I was extremely relieved to see that her feelings for me had not changed. Should I now go further and tell her more? Although my confession to this point had gone far easier than I expected, I decided against proceeding. Cammy would have to know eventually who I was and what I did, but why rush things?

She had hints. For instance, a new movie had just been released that I wanted to see, and I took her. The move was *Once Upon a Time in America*, a mob film starring Robert De Niro. In her room later that evening, her friend Katie asked her how the date had gone. Cammy mentioned that we had seen a movie.

"What film was it?" Katie asked.

"*Once Upon a Time in America*," Cammy answered.

"It figures," Katie had said.

But despite the hint, nothing seemed to register for the innocent Cammy.

Another time, she was talking with *Knights of the City* director Dominic Orlando by the Marina Bay swimming pool. He was telling her about his future projects.

"I'd like to do a Mafia movie," he said. "There's a lot of good material available."

"I like movies like that," she told him. "I find the men so attractive. They're really men. They have this powerful aura about them."

Orlando looked at her, startled for a moment, then laughed a big, hearty laugh and said, "You just might be closer to that than you think!"

Cammy later told me that she thought he had been referring to himself.

At that point, many of the cast and crew knew, or at least had heard rumors, about their producer's sinister background. Cammy was probably the last to hear these rumors. When she did, she simply pushed them out of her mind. After all, the rumors about her sleeping with me had been wrong. She decided that these new rumors were nonsense as well. In her eyes, it was unthinkable that I could be a criminal.

— 89 —

Although Cammy knew next to nothing about me, she was placing a lot of faith in a month-old relationship. A telephone call late one afternoon forced her to examine that relationship and make a major decision.

"Cammy!" an excited voice said to her that day. "You've got a shot at something big here! Can you catch the next flight out?"

She had been taking an afternoon nap when the phone awakened her. She tried to clear her head and sort out what she was hearing. The voice on the other end of the line belonged to Cooly Jackson, a dancer on the syndicated television program *Solid Gold*. He was calling from Los Angeles. Cammy had auditioned for a position with the program's dance troupe a few months before. There had been more than a hundred hopefuls vying for a few open positions, and she'd made it until the final cut. Now, apparently, one of the dancers had been injured or quit or gotten married—or something—and one of the to-kill-for positions was again available.

But what should she do?

"Do I have to come now?" she asked.

"We need someone right away," Cooly explained. "There's a private audition. It's between you and two other dancers. It's now or never, Cammy. This is the chance of a lifetime!"

She begged him for time to decide, but Cooly insisted that she must call him within the hour with her answer.

After hanging up, Cammy paced the hotel room as she agonized over what to do. She carefully weighed her options. *Solid Gold* was indeed the chance of a lifetime. What more could a dancer want? The *Solid Gold* dancers were probably the highest-profile dancers around at the time. The international television exposure involved in such a role would lead to a succession of jobs—a career's worth. The experience would light up her resume like...well, like solid gold.

But what about us? She felt that our embryonic love was too fragile to disturb. If she abruptly left Florida to begin a demanding, time-consuming career, it could kill our rapidly blossoming relationship. She was sure of it.

Then again, the *Solid Gold* audition was a reality while I was definitely a gamble (in more ways than she could ever have imagined). Something compelled me to call her in that moment.

"Hi, Cam," I said. "I just wanted to tell you again how much I enjoyed our date last night. I'll see you at eight for dinner."

She gently put the receiver down, paused for a moment, then quickly lifted it again. Her decision was made. She dialed Cooly Jackson in Los Angeles, thanked him for considering her, and told him that she couldn't make it for the audition.

– 90 –

The filming on the set continued to go well. Aside from Leon Isaac Kennedy, the movie starred Stoney Jackson, *Diamonds* star Nicholas Campbell, soap opera actress and future star of television's *Northern Exposure* Janine Turner, and veteran actor Michael Ansara. I even signed Sammy Davis Jr. and Smokey

Robinson to play cameos, though Davis' part was later edited out of the final version of the film, much to my dismay.

Cammy was penciled in as one of "Jasmine's Bad Girls" and had to prepare for a climactic dance scene near the end of the movie. Jasmine was played by Wendy Barry, and both Cammy and I appeared in the dance-contest segment hosted by Smokey Robinson near the end of the film. I was standing with Robinson when he was introduced, and Cammy was one of Jasmine's backup singers.

Despite the excitement of filming a movie, most of my attention was focused on Cammy. It seemed as though we had burrowed ourselves inside of some novel. Every date was magic, every day a thrill. Cammy was so enthralled that she saved the napkins and matches from every restaurant where we dined and every nightclub where we danced. A thousand little moments were etched into our memories forever, and a thousand hints of a troubled future were banished from our minds during these moments.

"I love you, Michael," she said to me, snuggling close as we drove from Delray Beach one evening.

"I love you, too," I responded. "That sounds really crazy, Camille, because I've only known you a few weeks, but I'm really in love with you."

"Michael, someday you're going to marry me," she said. "Someday soon."

I was sure that she must be right.

For the last few weeks of shooting, I moved the cast and crew to the Konover Hotel, an oceanfront concrete tower on Miami Beach. A Konover showroom had been rented for the talent contest sequence, and it was more economical to move the entire production there. As the move was accomplished, I took the liberty of moving Cammy's growing bounty of personal belongings into my master suite. When she discovered what I had done, she was very angry. Although we had shared many evenings together and had vowed our undying love in an array of tropical settings, we had yet to consummate the relationship.

"I can't move in with you!" she exclaimed.

"You can stay in the other room," I countered, motioning to the second bedroom in the suite.

"What happens if my mother or father call? And the operator says, 'Oh, that must be the young lady staying in Mr. Franzese's suite'? They would kill me!" she protested.

I understood her point. After all, I had promised her father I would look out for her. I had fulfilled that promise, but in ways I was sure Mr. Garcia had never intended. I picked up the phone and reserved another room for Camille. This was getting interesting.

— 91 —

As our relationship began sweeping beyond rumor into reality, Cammy felt the heat of the other dancers' jealousies.

"He's just using you," one sour-faced woman said.

Another added, "He'll dump you when this is all over."

"You're going to get your little heart broken," chided a third.

"This happens on every movie, and it never lasts," jabbed the first dancer again. "What are you going to do—be his mistress? The guy's married."

These taunts stung, and Cammy ran to her room in tears. Joanna Tea, the brown-haired woman Cammy had originally thought was my girlfriend, witnessed what had happened and followed Cammy. They sat together on the bed and talked.

"Don't listen to them, Cammy," Joanna said. "The girls are just jealous because it's very obvious to everyone that he really loves you. Don't worry about what anybody says. Gossip is part of this business, and you're going to have to get used to it. Just be happy and enjoy yourself. If they bother you, just tell them to get lost!"

Intermingled with the continued sniping, Cammy received encouraging reports from some of my associates.

"You know something, I think my friend's in love with you," Frankie Cestaro told her one evening. "I've known Michael a long time, and I've never seen him like this."

"I sat with Michael during your rehearsal today," reported Emily La Rosa, the makeup woman. "All he did was talk about you. He's like a schoolboy in love. 'Look at her hair!' he said. 'Look at her beautiful eyes! Look at the way she moves!' If you handle this right," she assured Cammy, "I think you'll really have a good thing going."

As the weeks progressed, my love for Cammy continued to build. We sat together in Miami's Little Havana and watched Orlando and Kutash direct the big Busby Berkeley-style dance number. When it began to rain, Cammy made a move to leave. I pulled her back.

"You look so beautiful in the rain," I said. "The way your hair is curling, I've never seen you more beautiful."

"Would you please just get in the car? It's pouring!" she laughed.

Despite the gossip on the set, we headed into our second month in love still not having consummated our relationship. To me, Cammy seemed to be moving at a snail's pace in this regard, and I wasn't at all sure why. Fortunately, I was amused by it all, not angered. I adored Cammy, and I was sure she had a reason for moving so slowly. Someday, I would know it.

— 92 —

Eventually, Cammy and I did become physically intimate, and after that night, I loved her with an obsession that was limitless. Nothing could be more important to me than her or than my being with her, and she felt the same about me. Her devotion was soon to be tested.

Michael at age two, on a
pony ride in Brooklyn, N.Y.

Michael at age twelve,
a seventh grader at
St. Ann's Catholic School
in Garden City, N.Y.

An army of heavily armed police officers and detectives nervously shadowed my father's every move during a string of arrests in 1966. He was charged with everything from bank robbery to murder. (*Newsday*)

My father, out of prison for a brief time on parole, attended my arraignment in 1985 with my mother, Tina.

Iorizzo's "daisy chain" gas tax scheme brought us unprecedented riches. A federal aerial surveillance photo shows my former estate in Brookville, Long Island.

I married Cammy and promised that I'd give up my Cosa Nostra empire, accept a prison sentence, and quit the mob. She made me an offer I couldn't refuse. (Lawrence Lesser)

One of the last photos taken of me as a member of the Colombo crime family. I walked to the altar, said "I do," and vowed to do the impossible—quit the mob. I've never had a moment's regret. (Lawrence Lesser)

The last picture taken of Cammy's mother Irma before her death from breast cancer in May of 2001.

Irma shared a special relationship with her daughters, seen here in their last picture taken together in the spring of 2000.

A recent photo of Michael
at home.

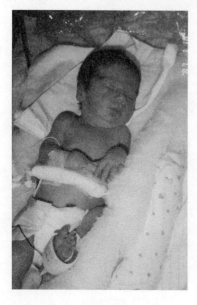

My precious Julia
struggling after her
premature birth in August
1998. I really turned to
God in prayer during her
ordeal, and my prayers
were answered. She is truly
a blessing.

Michael addresses students at Chino High School in California as part of his "Breaking Out" program for at-risk youth.

Irma's prayers for her family were answered in the "Agape House of Prayer." In the midst of Disney's Anaheim, Michael and Cammy are pictured with their family, who built the church under the leadership of Pastor Joaquin Garcia.

Still very much in love after all these years, Michael and
Cammy believe having God at the center of their marriage
has gotten them through all the difficult times.

One day, the movie set started humming with the juiciest gossip yet. Cammy's boyfriend, a painter named Eddie Chacon, had appeared unannounced from California. "And he's got a gun!" everyone was saying. The word quickly spread through the production.

The young man had deduced from the increasingly impersonal tone of Cammy's few letters that something bad was happening in South Florida. Checking with her mother, he had learned why. Crushed, he decided he had to try to win his girlfriend back.

Eddie located Camille on the set by the bandstand, and she nearly fainted when she saw him.

"I missed you, Cammy," he said. "I haven't seen you in so long."

"I've got to rehearse," she said, darting off. "We'll talk later."

My men had also heard the gossip and were taking it very seriously.

"You want us to take care of him?" they asked.

"He's just a kid," I said.

"They say he's got a gun."

"I don't think he has a gun. Leave him alone," I ordered.

Fortunately, I was secure in Cammy's feelings for me. But I was so consumed by my love for her that I don't know what I would have done if I had felt threatened. I might very well have used the life-or-death power I commanded against a perceived rival for Cammy's affections.

It was just such a potent mixture of passion and power that unnerved me. There had to be a balance. Until then, I had successfully juggled the influence of La Cosa Nostra with the unprecedented amount of money I was making. Now, suddenly, my all-encompassing love for a young Mexican-American girl had upset that critical balance. My emotions were on fire, and I knew that I had to be extremely careful.

My men obeyed my hands-off order, but they were on the alert later that afternoon when Eddie came walking toward my car.

"Hi, I'm Eddie, Cammy's friend," he said, extending a hand. I shook it.

"Really nice meeting you, Michael," he said. Then he promptly turned and left.

"See, he's just a kid," I repeated, shrugging.

That evening, Eddie and Cammy met, and as nicely as she could, she explained that their year-long relationship was over.

"I kind of figured that when I didn't hear from you," he said. "You were never in your room when I called, and you never returned my calls."

"I'm sorry," she said, offering a weak smile. "I always wanted to see Miami."

Neither said a word for the longest time.

"Are you sure, Cammy?" he ventured.

She nodded.

"Can we see each other when you come back?" he asked, but she shook her head no.

"I guess I always figured I wasn't enough for you. You're a good girl, Cammy. You deserve the best. Just be careful. If it doesn't work out, come home and call me. I'll be there," he offered.

She fought to hold back her tears, and Eddie just stood there for a while longer. The damp air inside the room was infused with grief. Finally, he turned and left.

Cammy was still weeping softly in her room when the phone rang. It was Eddie calling from the airport.

"Are you sure you want me to go?" he said, making one last-ditch effort at winning back his girlfriend.

"I'm sure, Eddie," she told him.

Cammy was still crying when I picked her up for dinner that evening.

"Don't worry, he'll get over it," I said. "He's young."

The banishment of Eddie Chacon from her life was a cross-road that bonded Cammy and me even tighter, as she had now cut her ties with the past. We were now emotionally intertwined on a fairy tale level and deeply in love, while in reality we knew very little about each other. She certainly didn't know about me, and I was sure I had much more to learn about her.

I quickly learned about the Latin temper.

Michael Markowitz flew in to discuss the joint purchase of a Miami restaurant called Martha's, and we arranged to meet the owners of the bistro after it closed at midnight. We spent three hours with them, eating and then negotiating the purchase. When I returned to the Konover, it was after 4:00 A.M.

Cammy had been waiting for me, growing more furious with each passing minute, imagining that I was out with another woman. By 2:00 A.M., she had made her airline reservations to leave later that morning, and by 3:00 A.M., she was packed and ready to go. When I returned, I found her door bolted tight, and she refused to listen to any explanation.

Later that morning, I tried again, and this time she let me in. She sat upright on her bed, clutching a pillow and pouting like an angry child. I tried to explain that I had been working.

"Working? You don't work at night," she said.

"I don't have normal business hours," I responded in a classic understatement. "I do things at night. Yes, I work at night."

I explained that I had to meet with the owners after the restaurant closed so we wouldn't be interrupted, but she wasn't buying it. We argued for a few moments until she dropped her angry facade a little.

"The only reason I'm still here is that you have all my paychecks in your briefcase," she said. "Otherwise, I'd have been just a memory!"

"No way, Cam," I said, a chilling edge of seriousness cutting through as I kissed her. "I could never let you go."

And I meant it.

— 93 —

I had gone to Florida in part to escape the troubles that were mounting in New York, and Cammy provided that escape in ways I had never imagined. Still, the turbulence in New York refused to give me peace. The joint task force continued to slave away, fueled by Roy Rogers hamburgers, unlimited federal resources, and skilled manpower. But they had become almost too effective. The ambitious scope of their investigation, combined with the vastness of my operations, left them with handfuls of dangling threads to follow.

Prosecutor Ray Jermyn said, "The biggest problem we encountered was that every time we met, there were ten new crimes to report and dozens of new accomplices to add to our lists. Michael had so much going on—car dealerships, bank loans, money laundering, unions, gas taxes, gas terminals, insurance fraud, counterfeit bonds, loan-shark operations, construction businesses, movies, credit card scams, the Russians, you name it. One week, he'd be in California making a movie, the next week he'd be in Florida getting the key to the city, which really blew us away. Here we are hunting this guy who's a Mafia captain involved in dozens of criminal activities, and the mayor of Miami Beach gives him the key to the city and puts his police force at his disposal. Incredible!"

In April of 1984, an unrelated incident worked to renew the task force's vigor and link some of the disconnected fragments of its case. My friend Larry Iorizzo was tried on past charges relating to Vantage Petroleum and was convicted of grand larceny, tax evasion, and mail and wire fraud. His sentencing was set for June.

The conviction of a close criminal partner is always a bad omen, especially when the partner is the less desirable target. I was uneasy when Iorizzo went down, but I trusted him like a brother. In the ensuing months, he repeatedly told me not to worry; he would find a way out of the mess.

As the sentencing hearing approached, however, Iorizzo's attitude changed.

"I don't want to go to jail, Michael," he confided to me. "It doesn't make sense. With all my money, why should I be in jail? We've got solid connections in Panama."

In addition to registering his companies in Panama and hiding his money there, Iorizzo owned a large estate in the Central American country. One of the reasons we had chosen Panama in the first place was because the country did not have an extradition treaty with the United States. We had been paying millions to an acne-scarred Panamanian general named Manuel Noriega in return for banking connections, personal security, and other services.

"I'm not going to stick around for the sentencing," he announced. "I can run the operation from Panama. I've got it all set up."

"That's insane, Larry," I advised. "Once you run, you become a fugitive, and that's a whole new ball game. You should stay and fight for bail. Your lawyer says you have a good shot at beating the charges on appeal. I'd stick around."

But Iorizzo didn't want to listen, and I didn't insist.

"I'm set to leave the night before the hearing," he said.

In June, the day before the hearing, Iorizzo showed up at my home in Delray Beach. Frankie Cestaro, Louie Fenza, and assorted other associates were there, too. Iorizzo had everything worked out. He was taking the Learjet with Wife II. The "girl-friend" wife had apparently been designated as official fugitive wife. The pilot had prepared a phony itinerary that had them hopping around various Caribbean islands, including Port-au-Prince, Haiti, to muddy the trail. Cestaro provided Iorizzo with a phony passport under the name Salvatore Carlino, and Iorizzo gave him $5,000 for his troubles.

That evening, we shared an emotional farewell dinner at Iorizzo's nearby mansion in Boca Raton. I invited Cammy to go along. The multimillion-dollar oceanfront home was the largest she had ever entered. Touring the house, she spotted one of Iorizzo's belts hanging over a chair. She couldn't believe its length. It looked more like a bullwhip than a belt.

At the end of the evening, Iorizzo and I embraced and offered warm good-byes. Not only had we made millions together, but I had also grown to consider him to be one of my closest friends. But when I walked out the door of his home that night, it marked the last time I would see him as a free man—or as a friend.

– 94 –

Iorizzo's plan of running Galion Holdings out of Panama worked for the next two months, but he was not a smart fugitive. He called the United States every day, leaving himself open to phone traces. He flew around the world "as if he had a license to be a fugitive," one associate put it. He began setting up an operation to steal gasoline-tax money in Austria, and he tried to entice me to join him in the foreign operation. "The tax on gas in Europe is $2 a gallon. Can you imagine the money we could make?" he said, giddy with excitement.

"I'm not committing any crimes in Austria," I said. "For all I know, they probably shoot thieves there. If I would get in trouble abroad, do you think Uncle Sam would help me? He'd probably say 'Keep him. Shoot him. We don't want him.'"

Iorizzo's arrogance as a fugitive seemed to be limitless. He scheduled his daughter's wedding in Austria and made arrangements to charter a jetliner to carry three hundred guests there from New York. A flood of wedding invitations announced the gala.

That was the last straw. In October, the feds negotiated an agreement with the double-dealing Noriega to flush out Iorizzo, and a team of Noriega's soldiers swept in and dragged Iorizzo from his fortress. He was tossed into a stone dungeon with no bed, and there he languished for three days—until the FBI "rescued" him.

Iorizzo was flown to Miami and stashed in a wretched prison overflowing with crazed Latin drug dealers and a swarm of additional Cuban and Central and South American psychos and criminals. Within weeks of the arrest, word was out that Iorizzo had cracked and was going to turn.

A relative of Iorizzo personally delivered a disturbing message to me.

"Larry's always considered you his ticket out if he got into trouble," the man explained. "He has a file on you six inches thick. He's kept every clipping that appeared in the newspapers and kept records of every illegal transaction you and he ever made. Watch yourself. This could be big trouble."

I refused to believe these suggestions, because Larry Iorizzo and I had been so close, but as more information filtered back from Miami, the unthinkable began to look more and more thinkable. Prison is a hard place for a four-hundred-fifty-pound man. Iorizzo couldn't sleep on the narrow prison beds, the food was killing him, and his fellow inmates were torturing him. There were reports that the guards had stripped him and forced him to walk down the corridors as the inmates jeered.

I met with Iorizzo's son, Larry Jr., at the Howard Johnson's on the Jericho Turnpike and assured him that I was doing everything in my power to help with his father's case. As I delicately questioned the twenty-year-old, I sensed that the stories about his father's rough prison stay were true.

Shortly before Iorizzo was scheduled to be transported to New York, an associate paid me a visit.

"Larry's been driving me crazy with his calls," he said. "He has a plan, and he begged me to present it to you."

The way he reported it, Iorizzo figured that there would be two U.S. marshals escorting him to the Eastern District courthouse at the corner of Cadman Plaza East and Tillary Street in

Brooklyn. His plan was for me to have a car waiting there when he arrived. I was to dispatch a hit squad to kill the marshals on the steps of the courthouse and free Iorrizo. If I refused to go along with this plan, then it was understood that he had no alternative but to roll over on me.

The consequences of either choice could be severe. Iorizzo's testimony could put me in prison for a long time. But murdering two U.S. marshals was not an acceptable alternative.

"Is he out of his mind?" I said. "The guy must be cracking up."

This scheme was the last contact I had with my former partner and friend. Word was that Iorizzo was singing his lungs out, and I was the lyric.

Cammy knew nothing about any of this, and I didn't want her to. She was my salve, my pressure release. When I was with her, it seemed like New York had never existed, and the stress lifted from my neck and shoulders. Cammy was a portal to another world, and now I just wanted to enter that world and never come back.

— 95 —

Near the end of the filming, I sent Cammy home to Los Angeles for a short visit. Back in her home and back to reality, the glow of Florida began wearing off. Distancing herself from the romance that had intoxicated her, she could see that what had happened in Fort Lauderdale was wrong—morally and religiously—and her mood alternated between elation and remorse.

She wondered about my children. If I was rarely home, as I'd said, they must miss me terribly. And if things between us did work out, she might be taking me from them permanently. They surely would blame her for the loss of their father.

She also hadn't acted like much of a Christian in Florida, and she was now ashamed of herself. She had been swept away by a married man and allowed her religious and moral beliefs to be trampled in the process. She hadn't lost them entirely, but she had suppressed them for the time being so that she could enjoy an affair that flew in the face of everything she believed and stood for.

She had rationalized it all by telling herself that it was a special love and that God not only approved of it, but He had actually sent her to me because He wanted us together. But was this really God's will? Or was it just her way of glossing over the truth?

She fell to her knees by her bed, and tears streamed down her cheeks as she prayed.

"Dear God, what should I do? I love Michael so much, but I don't want to offend You. I believe You brought us together, but I know what I'm doing is wrong. Please, tell me what to do."

Insecurity tormented her as well. I clearly wanted her, but why return to me just to get hurt in the end? The taunts from the other dancers still stung..."not serious," "happens all the time," "love ends when the movie ends," and the worst one of all, the word she hated most, "mistress."

I didn't give her much time to let these dark thoughts fester, calling every few hours we were apart.

"I love you," I said, "and I don't ever want to be without you."

The words sounded wonderful to her, and the attention I was showing her was comforting. Still, she was afraid and unsure. When just fourteen, she had made the vow never to marry a man who had been married before. Of all her father's twenty-two brothers and sisters, only one was divorced. And Cammy Garcia was convinced that this was the way marriage should be.

She had also vowed never to marry a man with children, so I failed on both counts.

"I'm doing exactly what I said I'd never, ever do," she sighed to herself.

She fished around in a small suitcase and removed an envelope. Inside were eight checks for $500 each. In typical poor-girl fashion, she had saved all her paychecks while in Miami, cashing only her per diem checks to get her through the week. Looking at the check on top, she examined the swirled signature of the person who authorized them—Michael Franzese.

Then it wasn't a fantasy. Everything I had ever said to her had come true. Every promise I had made to her had been kept. She felt in that moment that she simply must trust me and keep believing that things would work out.

She cashed her stack of checks and treated her family to dinner. It felt good, and she was able to delight them with stories about Fort Lauderdale and Miami Beach and her new boyfriend. But she couldn't tell them the whole truth—not even as much of it as she now knew. If she did, she was afraid, they would never allow her to return to Florida—and to me.

— 96 —

The *Knights of the City* wrap party was the high point of my professional life. All the forces that had molded my past and those that would direct my future converged during the glittery event staged at a Fort Lauderdale skating rink.

Although the $2 million, independently-produced movie was small by Hollywood standards, the wrap party was first-rate. I was still new to the movie business, but I was a pro at throwing parties. I spent more than $150,000 on food, spotlights, liquor, and decorations. The local media was invited to the all-night event and turned out in force, blinding everyone in the bright lights of the television cameras and flash photography. To add to the festive atmosphere, the big dance numbers from the movie were displayed on giant screens around the room throughout the evening.

Also present were most of my crew, including Michael Markowitz and a contingent of his Eastern European men. The combination Hollywood/Cosa Nostra/Russian affair made for some unusual scenes. Not only was I fawned over by the movie's cast and crew and all the wannabes who conned invitations, but for the first time in Florida, I was openly honored in Cosa Nostra fashion by a squadron of men greeting me with the traditional kiss on the cheek. Any intelligent person observing this should have immediately noticed that something was out of kilter. Few, if any, did. Movie parties have always been strange affairs—even under normal circumstances.

Cammy had returned to Miami earlier that afternoon. I picked her up at the airport, and we drove to my home in Delray Beach. There she changed into one of her favorite dresses, a traditional Mexican style with lots of colorful layers, and she said she felt like Cinderella going to the royal ball.

At the party, Cammy bumped into a large, graceful man who turned and smiled. It was Muhammad Ali. Across the room, she spotted Emmanuel Lewis, the little fellow who starred in TV's *Webster*. She spent half the night talking with her dancer friends and the other half by my side. She was too immersed in her "Cammy in Wonderland" dream to notice anything out of the ordinary.

Several local politicians gave speeches. Archdiocese of Miami Auxiliary Bishop Agustin Roman presented me with a Bible signed by Pope John Paul II, praising me for offering jobs and hope to disadvantaged youth. The bishop had arranged for the signing when he read about the movie in the *Miami Herald*.

The entire night was a great victory celebration, but that victory was about to be spoiled. Early in the morning, about 4:00 A.M., a substitute publicist informed me that a crew from the Miami NBC affiliate, WSVN, had waited all night for a chance to interview me. I had been cautious about doing interviews that evening because my regular publicist, Richard Frisch, was out sick. Frisch was under strict orders to screen all requests, to weed out the knowledgeable New York media, along with any non-entertainment journalists who might be snooping around.

The substitute publicist pleaded the case for the patient WSVN crew, and I relented. I grabbed Zimmerman, and we were both wired for sound and placed under the bright lights. We expected to field some fluff questions pertaining to the movie.

Only this crew was not from the local NBC affiliate. These were top guns from NBC news. Instead of a puff-piece entertainment reporter, the correspondent was Brian Ross, a tough network investigative journalist.

After a few polite questions, Ross zeroed in on his real subject.

"Michael, isn't it true that you are the stepson of Sonny Franzese, an underboss in the Colombo crime family, and that you yourself are the capo in that family?"

"What?" I asked.

"And isn't it true that you are financing this movie with stolen gas tax money?"

I fought to stay cool because I knew my reactions were being taped.

"And Jerry," Ross said, turning to Zimmerman, "isn't it true that you are a convicted felon, convicted of perjury?"

"I'm not taking this," Zimmerman snarled, losing his composure.

The big man stood up, unclipped the microphone from his shirt, and walked away.

Ross turned his attention back to me.

"The FBI says you are a member of the Colombo Mafia family."

"The FBI can allege and say whatever they like," I answered as coolly as I could under the circumstances. "They've been doing this for many, many years."

When Ross tried to continue, I gently cut him off.

"Mr. Ross, it's very late, and it's been a long night. If you would like to continue this interview at another time, I'll be happy to accommodate you."

He ordered the cameras to follow me as I walked away, and in the process, a late-arriving underling greeted me with a kiss. I cursed the bad timing. When the television lights shut off, I located the publicist and chewed him out royally. I then scolded my inner circle for allowing a network bulldog to walk in undetected.

Cammy had observed what had happened from across the room, but she hadn't been close enough to hear Ross' revealing questions. Judging from my reaction, she feared it was something terrible, so she asked to go back to the Konover immediately. I had Louie Fenza drive her.

When I arrived at the room about an hour later, Cammy didn't ask me for details, and I didn't volunteer any. I also didn't warn her of what it all meant. Ross was obviously being fed information by a New York prosecutor, probably Rudolph Giuliani or one of his assistants, and had come to Florida to prepare a report on a pending indictment.

I instructed my attorney to contact NBC and arrange another interview, wanting to have my say, but more importantly, wanting to know what information Brian Ross had. He subsequently interviewed me for an hour at my Houston Holdings office. I denied that I was a mob captain and said that the movie was being legitimately financed. I also denied that my father was in the mob. Ross deleted all my comments when the damning segment aired on NBC news a few weeks later. It was the first of a half-dozen network news reports about me that would be broadcast over the next twelve months. The walls of my underworld existence were starting to crack.

What now?

– 97 –

When the film wrapped, I felt unusually vulnerable and wanted Cammy to remain close. I encouraged her to stay with me in Delray Beach longer than she had planned. When she was around, I was able to forget, at least temporarily, the serious charges I knew were pending.

After a few weeks, Cammy went back to California and I returned to New York. I felt tense and agitated there, however, and I was being followed everywhere I went, so I decided to go to California to see her. California was even farther from New York than Florida, and that was an added advantage. I checked into the Westwood Marquis Hotel in Los Angeles, called Cammy, and asked her to meet me there that evening. In the meantime, I had a meeting with some of my people.

When my meeting ended, I rushed to my room to see Cammy, but she wasn't there.

"In here," a voice echoed from the bathroom.

I laughed when I saw her standing in the dry bathtub, marveling at its huge size. It was the biggest bathtub she'd ever seen. I jumped in and hugged her tightly.

"I missed you so much!" I said, kissing her all over her beautiful face. "What have you done to me? What have you done to my life? I can't think. I can't work. How did this happen?"

I withdrew from the embrace long enough to lead Cammy out of the tub over to the dresser. There I removed a long, black felt box and handed it to her. Inside was a gold necklace with the word "Michael's" spelled out in fat diamonds, including the apostrophe. She nearly fainted.

"For me?" she asked, clearly delighted with the gift.

— 98 —

I had suspected from the start that Cammy didn't live in Beverly Hills, but when I parked my green Jaguar sedan in front of her parents' house in Anaheim, I had to look around a few times before leaving the car. The neighborhoods had steadily declined in quality as she had directed me through Anaheim, where her family had moved from Norwalk. For Cammy, the perspective was entirely different: it could have been a lot worse. She could have been taking me to one of her former homes in the Norwalk barrios.

The Garcia house was small and overflowing with people. There were nine members of the immediate family, plus a swarm of friends and relatives. Cammy's brothers and their friends were break-dancing in the garage. Although it was crowded, it was a lively, happy place that obviously was the center of neighborhood activity.

I took Cammy's parents out to dinner that night to a spruced-up Black Angus in Anaheim, and there I spent a great deal of time talking with her father. He told me that when he had been a teenager, he had lost five teeth and had been shot in the leg when a gang of Mexican-born drug pushers ambushed him and his friend Alex Moreno after a New Year's Eve party in San Diego in 1959. His face had been slashed with a straight razor and his chest gashed with a flattened can opener. His teeth had been dislodged by a gang member wielding a lead horseshoe stake. The drugged sociopath had been about to crush his skull when Moreno whipped out a .22 pistol and shot him in the stomach. Moreno shot a second pusher in the groin before the gang scattered.

A one-hundred-fifty-pound, fifteen-year-old Moreno then lifted Seferino's bleeding, one-hundred-sixty-pound body from the pavement and carried him six blocks through a thick fog to Seferino's sister Eva's house. There the teenager hid his gun in the toilet tank, along with the .38 Seferino had never gotten out of his belt. Although Moreno had saved Seferino's life, the police were not impressed. He was convicted and forced to do eighteen months in a tough youth prison for his heroics.

Seferino told me he'd ducked the police by traveling across the border to Tijuana and giving a horse doctor a few pesos to carve the bullet from his leg. The doctor had done it without anesthesia while Seferino screamed in pain. Seferino told the veterinarian he'd been shot by the border patrol. He returned to San Diego and was brought to Paradise Valley Hospital, where doctors mended his face, mouth, and chest with 160 stitches. He told the American doctors that he'd gotten into a fight while in Mexico.

After he healed, Seferino said, he plotted his revenge. He hunted the remaining gang members down like an urban terrorist. He and a friend cornered one in the lights of his friend's 1955 Chevy, knocked him down, then ran over his legs, crushing them. Tipped that another gang member had been arrested and was going through heroin withdrawal at the San Diego jail, Seferino had himself brought in and jailed on a minor charge. When he had located the sick and emaciated drug addict, he beat him nearly to death.

It was some story, and Cammy's father had the scars on his face and leg to back it up. After hearing all this, I was even more convinced that when the truth came out about who I was, this family would not be dismayed by it, although Cammy did not personally condone the type of activity her father was describing.

After dessert, I floored everyone by making a little speech. "I want to thank you for allowing Cammy to come to Florida. I love your daughter very much, and I intend to marry her."

Cammy nearly dropped her fork. The first chance she got, she confronted me.

"You didn't tell me you were going to say that, Michael!"

"I didn't intend to," I assured her. "It just came out. Now I really have to marry you," I joked.

— 99 —

After visiting the cramped Garcia home, I decided that Cammy needed her own apartment, and we spent the rest of the week looking at condominiums around West Los Angeles. Every one of them looked perfect to Cammy, but I was more exacting. Finally, I chose an expensive unit in Brentwood, an exclusive area on the west side of L.A. near the beach.

With that done, it was time to bring Cammy to New York so she could be with me while I took care of things there. I put her up at a hotel in Garden City, Long Island. The first morning, I left her a note along with an envelope. The note encouraged her to amuse herself shopping while I worked. Inside the envelope were twenty $100 bills.

"Shopping?" she told me later. "I could buy a store with all that! I could *live* on that!"

I next rented a small, one-bedroom unit in the Fairhaven Apartment complex in Woodbury, Long Island, and moved her into it. I explained the coziness by telling her, "When I'm in the living room, I want to be able to see you in every room."

Soon afterward, I came home one day with an American Express card with Cammy's name on it. She had once said that her dream was to have a credit card.

"This is for you," I said. "Buy whatever you want."

Just touching the cool green plastic seemed to send a charge through her body. She couldn't believe that the card had her name on it, but there it was—in raised plastic letters.

I was a little afraid that Cammy would get what I called the financial bends. We were heading into our third month together, and she already had a condo in Brentwood, an apartment on each coast, and a magical American Express card. Or at least it seemed magical to her. No matter what she bought or how much she spent, the bills seemed to vanish into the stratosphere.

But I couldn't help myself. It made me feel very good to buy her things. I wanted to give her everything, to fulfill her every dream. That's how madly in love with her I was.

— 100 —

After spending a few weeks in California, I was at the Los Angeles airport preparing to fly to New York. I phoned my secretary, and she told me that two men I knew, financier Mel Cooper and Dr. Jesse Hyman, had been arrested with half a dozen others for loan-sharking and racketeering. Included among the others was a rabbi, Chaim Gerlitz, fifty-three, a cantor and teacher at Temple Israel in Great Neck, Long Island.

When I arrived at Kennedy International Airport in New York, Frankie Cestaro was there to pick me up. Two men approached us the instant we left the terminal.

"Michael Franzese, you're under arrest," one of them said.

"Who are you?" I asked.

"FBI," was the answer.

Within seconds, a dozen more agents materialized and surrounded me. I emptied my pockets of my wallet, money, and keys and gave them to Frankie.

"Call Cammy," I told him. "Tell her I've been arrested and I'll talk to her later tonight. Tell her not to worry."

A three-car FBI caravan ushered me from the airport. I was surprised to see the cars head toward Manhattan instead of Brooklyn or Long Island, where I would normally have been arrested (and where the joint task force operated).

"What's this all about?" I asked.

"We're arresting you in the Jesse Hyman case," the lead agent said.

"Are you kidding?" I responded. "What have I got to do with that?"

The agent didn't answer.

When I learned the charges against me, I was amazed. I had been hit with seven counts of loan-sharking and racketeering based upon a Lake Success, Long Island operation run by Cooper, Hyman, and the rabbi. It almost made me laugh. I was reportedly stealing $100 million a month in gasoline taxes, and here's Rudy Giuliani and his Southern District forces trying to toss me into somebody else's loan-sharking indictment.

Actually, the indictment proved to be more complicated than I realized. The Southern District was apparently trying to jump the gun on the Michael Franzese Task Force, the investigative army that I still wasn't aware of.

Cammy was at her parents' in Anaheim when Frankie called.

"Cammy, Michael's been arrested. He's in jail."

"Why? What for?"

"He'll explain when he bails out. He's okay. He just doesn't want you to worry."

Cammy initially took the call in stride. After all, her father had been arrested eight times, and some of her uncles had been arrested and jailed. So it wasn't a total shock to get a call saying that her fiancé had been arrested. She viewed this as she had come to view everything having to do with me: I would take care of it, and everything would be perfect again.

I put up my Brookville home, where Maria and our three children were living, to cover the $350,000 bail bond slapped on me, and was released within hours of the arrest. I called Cammy and was surprised at how well she was taking it. It wasn't until later that I realized she had figured my arrest would be like those of her father and uncles. They had gone to jail for a day or so, and that was the end of it. My trial was certain to be long, grueling, and stressful for all of us.

— 101 —

The next day Cammy caught a jet to New York. Once she arrived, I sat her down and tried to explain why I had been arrested. She didn't understand what either racketeering or loan-sharking meant. I explained that racketeering was a pattern of at least two criminal acts committed within a ten-year period. Loan-sharking, I said, was lending out money at unlawfully high rates of interest. I passed these both off as "white collar" charges that businessmen often get slapped with and assured her that they were false charges.

My first move in my defense was to take a shot at trying to talk my way out of the still-pending indictment. I had been arrested on "an information," a legal maneuver that allows police and prosecutors to round up and process suspects prior to the actual indictment. Such a policy gives them the critical element of surprise. The twenty-one-day gap between arrest and indictment offered me room to prepare a defense strategy.

I contacted my attorney, Harold Borg, and had him schedule an appointment with prosecutors Bruce Baird and Aaron Marcu, and FBI agent Stanley Nye. At the meeting, Borg and I spoke for two hours trying to convince our adversaries that I was innocent and should not be indicted. They all listened attentively and took notes.

While awaiting the prosecutors' decision, I received a call from infamous attorney and fixer Roy Cohn. Cohn said that he could help me and invited me to his Manhattan office to talk. With dramatic flourish, Cohn assured me he could get the indictment dropped.

"I'm good friends with Ed Meese," he said, strutting about and dropping the name of the current attorney general. "I have contacts everywhere. It'll be a snap. I'll need $50,000 cash up front and then $200,000 when the indictment is dropped."

"I'll tell you what," I countered. "I'll give you $500,000 if you can get the indictment dropped. But you get nothing up front."

Cohn continued to demand the advance. Suspecting that it was nothing but a cheap hustle, I held firm in my position.

"I'm offering you twice what you wanted," I explained. "All you have to do is wait a few weeks. If you can do what you claim, that should be acceptable."

I never heard from Cohn again.

Neither Cohn's alleged connections nor my arguments before the prosecutors had any effect. I was indicted along with the others.

When I read the indictment, I was surprised to discover that I was again portrayed as Mr. Big—just as I had been in my college days. I was accused of providing most of the money—more than a million dollars—and the muscle for the loan-sharking operation.

The seriousness of the charges was not to be underestimated. Regardless of my innocence, I faced one-hundred-forty years in prison if convicted.

As I studied the names of my codefendants, the confusion started to lift. There appeared to be two separate groups involved in the case. The first was a band of eight men, headed by four Jews. The second group was a disconnected mix of seven Italians. From what I could tell, the Jewish group, including the rabbi, had the greatest exposure. It was their operation. The Italians, which included several made men and associates from four of the five New York Cosa Nostra families, were probably innocent, or at least well-insulated. I guessed that the Italians had been swept in at random for their publicity value. Indict four Jews and the media yawn, but salt the proceedings with seven Italian gangsters and the press goes wild.

Despite the arrest, or maybe because of it, my whirlwind romance continued unabated. I took Cammy to Las Vegas at the end of August to celebrate her twentieth birthday. We stayed at the Sands Hotel, and I told her to pick out anything she wanted at the gift shop, and I'd win the money to buy it. She chose a molded metal sculpture of a circus wagon and various animals pulling it. The price was $1,000. Twenty minutes and a few blackjack hands later, I had the grand and then some, and she had her memento.

Later that evening, as we looked at the stars from my penthouse suite, an unusual series of patterned lights hovered high in the distant sky. It appeared to us to be a UFO, and it also attracted the attention of the local newspaper and everyone who could pull himself away from the gaming tables.

"I had it fly by just for your birthday," I joked to Cammy as we watched the unearthly looking phenomenon.

— 102 —

Back in New York, I worked feverishly on my case, often arriving home late in the evening. Cammy invited her younger sister Sabrina to fly to New York to keep her company. My late evenings and frequently delayed dinners began to grate on the sisters. I promised to make it up to them one night by cooking a special pasta dish. When I arrived home two hours later than promised, however, Cammy coldly told me not to bother.

In that moment, I had a rare loss of cool.

"Don't you realize I'm fighting for my life here?" I told her. "If I don't win this case, I'll be gone for forty years! If I don't win, you and I will never be together!"

These words seemed to knock down some locked doors in Cammy's mind. She had blocked out my problems the way she blocked out so many negative things about our unusual relationship. Now she was unable to sleep, and she lay in bed crying. She cried off and on for the next few days and steeled herself for the worst, promising to wait for me forever. When you're young and in love, you just don't realize what's really happening.

After that, the good times mixed with the bad like an ever-spinning yo-yo. From the Halloween night I was sworn in as a member of La Cosa Nostra, I knew that one day I'd have to do time. I had accepted it as part of the price to be paid for my underworld membership. Everyone had done it. It was not the end of the world, I knew. I had visited my father enough to know that prison could be survived. Because of that, although I never looked forward to it, neither did I fear it.

But that was before I met Cammy. Now, the thought of being locked up and kept from her for any period of time tortured my mind. This was one of the reasons I had never wanted to fall in love. Love always makes a man dread prison.

I decided to channel my frustrations and my nervous energy into fighting the case. The first step would be to hire another

223

lawyer. Howard Borg was good at what he did—making deals, setting meetings, handling appeals, negotiating and pushing for parole; but a federal court trial was something else. I needed a young, aggressive courtroom fighter who had worked as a prosecutor in the same courts where the legal battle would be fought. I wanted someone who knew all the players on a personal level. I also didn't want to use an attorney like Barry Slotnick, who was known for defending mobsters. The attorney I eventually selected was John Jacobs, a former assistant U.S. attorney in the Eastern District of New York. Jacobs fit the criteria.

I also wanted to find a nontraditional private investigator. My experience with private investigators hired to help free my father had soured me on the breed, most of whom I felt were worthless. I opted for hiring a former IRS agent named Don Taylor, then working for a record company in Atlanta. I liked Taylor, and he was a whiz at paperwork.

My team assembled, I began the difficult task of building a defense. And it was difficult. A guilty man knows where he'll be attacked, but an innocent man is in the dark. I didn't have a clue about what evidence the prosecutors had, nor did I know how they intended to link me to the loan-shark operation. I would have to fight this case blind.

— 103 —

In September, I went to my dentist in Long Island one morning to have a filling replaced, but before I could enter the office, I was swarmed by Nassau County detectives.

"Michael Franzese, you're under arrest."

"What's the charge this time?" I asked.

"Aiding and abetting assault."

"What is that?"

The unusual charge stemmed from a four-year-old incident in which the landlord of my Mazda dealership, Thomas Trimboli, was beaten with a ball peen hammer by a tough, whom one of my men, Frank "Frankie Gangster" Castagnaro, had recruited. Castagnaro, a short, rough guy, earned his nickname because he loved being a gangster. Trimboli told prosecutors that the only reason he survived the hammer attack was that his thick gray-and-brown toupee had cushioned the blows to his skull. I knew little about the conflict beyond the fact that Frankie G. heard that I'd had some heated words with Trimboli a few months earlier and enlisted the guy to score points against me. My only involvement had been to post bond for the assailant as a favor to Frankie G.

The hammer man, William Reese, had been convicted and did nearly four years. For some reason, Nassau County had decided to resurrect the stale case and pin it on me. This was nothing more than an opportunity for Nassau County prosecutors to wrestle some headlines from their counterparts in Manhattan.

As I saw it, there was a disturbing wave of prosecutorial competition sweeping New York. Because I operated in such a wide territory, I had become the target of both the Nassau County and Suffolk County prosecutors, along with prosecutors in two of New York's most powerful districts, Giuliani's Southern District (which had declined sending a representative to the Michael Franzese Task Force) and Raymond Dearie's Eastern District. Whenever one made an indictment, it appeared to infuriate the others and prompt an intensification of their own investigations. In this case, the Southern District's indictment lit a fire under Edward McDonald and the joint task force meeting in Uniondale. McDonald's Organized Crime Strike Force assistant, Jerry Bernstein, was so determined to put me behind bars that he delayed his scheduled move into private practice for three years. With Iorizzo in the fold, Bernstein and friends were certain to come up with something stronger than "aiding and abetting assault."

I dealt with the indictment by plunging deeper and deeper into the sheltered world I had created with Cammy. In late

December, a few weeks before the scheduled beginning of the trial, we went together to Peppone, a romantic Italian restaurant in Brentwood. After dinner, I ordered a bottle of Taittinger Rose champagne, clutched her hand, and took a deep breath.

"I love you, Cammy," I began. "You've changed my whole life, and I want us to be married."

I told her to close her eyes. When I told her to open them, she was surprised to see the soft light sparkling off of a three-carat, emerald-cut diamond ring perched in a black felt box.

"Do you like it?" I asked.

Cammy was so awed that she could not answer.

The waiter spotted the jewel and spread the news about the happy occasion, and a parade of diners dropped by our table to scrutinize the ring and wish us their best.

I told Cammy I wanted to get married before the trial. Then I changed it to during the trial. And finally, I took the more sensible approach and decided to wait until the verdict had been delivered.

— 104 —

Hovering like a storm cloud over the pending marriage were the *New York Times* and *Newsday* stories and NBC television reports that portrayed me as a vicious criminal. They were disturbing, but Cammy refused to accept them. She had the same reaction that my mother had decades before: the man in the newspapers and on television was not the man she knew. This had to be a mistake. Cammy was sure of it, too.

I did something without thinking one evening that forced her to reevaluate her view. She was in her Woodbury apartment when I called and said that I would be coming there, but late, because I was having some business problems. I must have sounded jumpy, and the agitation in my voice made her worry.

She went on to bed, but her worry made her toss and turn, and she kept peering at the clock on the nightstand and wondering what had delayed me. It was 1:00 A.M., then 2:00 A.M., then 3:00 A.M., and still I hadn't arrived. By then, she thought I must be dead.

Shortly after 3:30 A.M., Cammy heard the pounding footsteps of someone running up the stairway into the apartment. I burst into the room, threw down my coat, and began frantically tossing things around. I reached under a bed and pulled out a black handgun. I opened up the chamber, checked to see if it was loaded, snapped it back in place, then stuck the gun into my belt.

Cammy couldn't believe what she was witnessing. It must have seemed as if the man she knew was gone and the stranger in the newspapers had suddenly appeared.

"Michael, what is this?" she said in a panic. "What are you doing?"

"Don't worry. Everything's okay," I said.

"Don't go," she said, crying.

"Got to," I said, grabbing my coat.

"Don't leave me," she pleaded.

I flashed her a brief "you must be kidding" look, gave her a quick hug, and kissed her forehead.

"I've got to run, baby. Everything's okay."

"Call me!" she cried as I disappeared out the door.

She dialed my beeper number so many times over the next three hours that I eventually had to shut it off. She paced the room, then sat on her bed and squeezed a large stuffed monkey. She cried and drank NyQuil in a fruitless attempt to put herself to sleep.

A hundred different scenarios passed through her mind, and the peculiarities of our relationship crystallized. There wasn't a single person she could call in that moment to check on me. She couldn't call the police. And she had never even met my parents. If something happened to me, she would have to read about it in the newspapers.

And what about those newspapers? She opened a drawer in her nightstand and pulled out an article she had saved. Staring down at my photograph and the word "mobster" in the headline, she wondered for the first time if what they were writing about me might be true. I had told her that I was charged with white-collar crimes, harmless paper crimes, and she had, until then, refused to believe that I could be involved in violence, gambling, murder, and prostitution—like the stereotypical gangsters in the newspapers and movies. But what she had just witnessed some-how shattered the illusion. I'd had a look in my eyes that she'd never seen before, and I had brushed her aside and rushed out into the night, packing a pistol.

I didn't come back until 6:30 A.M. the next morning. For me, it had been an uneventful night. But not for Cammy. I found her sitting on the floor in the corner, trembling and clutching the monkey. Her eyes were bloodshot from crying, her face swollen.

She was relieved when she saw me, then quickly became furious. She glared at me and refused to talk. When I finally prodded her enough to speak, she exploded.

"You ask what's wrong? You come here at 3:30 A.M. like a maniac, looking like you're about to strangle someone. Then you pull out a gun and count the bullets right in front of me. You don't explain. You just run off. You don't call. You don't answer when I beep you. I don't know if I should wait, pack up and go home, or what! I don't know who to call to ask about you—to ask 'Do you know where Michael is? Do you know if he's killed someone? Do you know if he's still alive?' How could you do this to me?"

"I'm sorry," I offered. "I couldn't get to a phone."

"Where did you go? Why did you need a gun?" she demanded.

"It was just a raccoon wandering around outside," I said, shooting her a grin. "I didn't want it to get into the trash."

I fawned over her the rest of the day, buying her roses and stuffed rabbits and teddy bears. I never explained what had hap-pened that night, and she didn't ask. I took her in my arms and promised that nothing like that would ever happen again, and she believed me. The man she loved had returned, and the memory of the chilling look in my eyes gradually faded away—until it seemed as if it never had happened.

But it had, and I knew there would be more nights like this one. It was part of the life I had chosen. It came with the territory. And now I knew that Cammy would never be able to handle it.

— 105 —

As 1984 ended, the prosecutors scored another major victory. New York indicted Michael Markowitz on fourteen counts of tax evasion. The Rumanian promptly rolled over—although "flopped around" may have been a better description. Double-talking, selling old news, and veiling himself behind a feigned lack of understanding of the English language, Markowitz gave his captors fits. He also played both ends and alerted me to the state and federal prosecutors' moves. How much of a threat the crazy Rumanian posed to me was impossible to determine.

What was not hard to determine was the effect this was having on the gasoline business. There was apprehension on the street about where the operation was going and who would be going down with it. With both Markowitz and Iorizzo rumored to be singing, and my indictment a reality, the cash pipeline began to shrink.

I kept all of this from Cammy, and she continued to be my respite from the growing nightmare. When we were together, nothing else seemed to matter. My only fear was that the looming troubles might cause me to lose her. I was torn over how to handle that reality. If we married before the verdict, it would lessen the odds of losing her if I was convicted. On the other hand, if I was given a long sentence, marriage to me would sentence Cammy to a miserable life.

The loan-sharking trial began January 7, 1985, on a cold and overcast morning, and lasted through the winter and into the spring. For the first seven weeks, I sat like a spectator as the prosecutors built their case against the Jewish defendants and their cohorts. My name was never mentioned. When they did get around to bringing me into the case, the connection was weak. To bolster their case, they brought in their literal and figurative big gun, the massive Lawrence Iorizzo. While I sat stunned, my good friend and business partner gave a rambling testimony that included charges that I had forced him to hide out in Panama and had tried to kill his son Lawrence Jr. The dramatic accusations had nothing to do with the loan-shark indictment, but they did spice up the tedious proceedings.

Iorizzo refused to look at me while he spewed out his lies, but he wasn't shy about scrutinizing the courtroom gallery. When Frankie Gangster walked in during his testimony, the fat man freaked. He no doubt had a flashback of Frankie G. holding the gun to his head and threatening to kill him if he ever hurt me. Iorizzo's reaction was so extreme that the trial was interrupted and Frankie G. was escorted from the courtroom.

From Cammy's perspective, the four-month court trial was a revealing experience. Her father had regarded the police and prosecutors as the enemy for most of his life, and this attitude had been ingrained in her early. As she matured, it had faded, but now, watching me on trial and hearing the foolish charges being used against me, these feelings grudgingly began to return.

She was allowed to attend only a few sessions because Jacobs felt that her presence—and the silver fox coat that I had bought her—might have an unfavorable effect upon the jurors. What she saw in the sessions she did attend was enough to make her believe me when I claimed my innocence. For instance, after testifying about numerous illegal deals, a witness was asked to point me out in the courtroom. Instead, he pointed to the codefendant Mel Cooper, the financier. The prosecutor quickly regrouped and asked the witness to try to identify me again. This time he pointed to a man sitting in the front row of the audience. The prosecutor had to virtually stand behind me and wave his hands before my alleged "business partner" got it right. The same witness later testified that he beat his wife "only when she needed it," a statement that infuriated Cammy and most of the people in the courtroom, including the jurors.

Another government witness, a loan-shark victim, saw mobsters under every rock. He testified that he knew Catholic priests who were part of the mob. When asked how many people he owed money, the witness responded, "Everybody. I must even owe you money."

I loved that kind of testimony because it helped me a lot.

— 106 —

As with most long trials, there were ups and downs in this one. After a bad day in court, I would be in as dark a mood as Cammy had ever seen. After one such day, I said to her, "I'm worried about you, Cammy. I'm afraid for you. I don't know how this is going to come out. And if I'm convicted, what then? Sometimes I think I should let you go. I'll take care of you, and I'll give you a good start on a new life. I just don't want to hurt you."

"Please, don't make me go home," Cammy begged. "I don't care what happens. I'm not going to leave you. I don't care what you say. If you have to go away, we'll survive. Just give me a child. I want to have something of you to remember for the rest of my life, something to keep with me. Just give me a child, and I'll wait for you forever."

I resisted. Why ruin her life? Why drag a beautiful young woman down with me?

She was unbending.

"I want to marry you, but not with this hanging over our heads," I said. "But if you really want a child, we'll try."

I hardly had time to weigh the ramifications of her request before she made the point moot by becoming pregnant. When I saw a pair of baby shoes in a little box on my bed—Cammy's way of announcing the pregnancy—all my doubts vanished. I also wanted something lasting to spring from our love.

I decided to have the official engagement party a few weeks before the verdict. The rationale was that if I was convicted, I'd at least have one last happy memory in my life. The event was scheduled for April 6 at the Hotel Bel Air in Los Angeles.

Complicating matters was Cammy's rough pregnancy. The severe stress of the trial was tearing her up inside and making her hemorrhage. Her doctors feared she'd lose the child.

On the morning of the engagement party, we woke to find the bed covered with blood. She phoned a doctor and made an appointment for 11:00 A.M. Cammy's luck was with her that morning. The doctor said that, despite the hemorrhaging, the baby was unharmed. If she took it easy she'd make it.

That evening, as two hundred people mingled at the Hotel Bel Air and congratulated us, she stayed in her seat. Despite the energetic music and the exhilaration of the event, she fought the urge to dance.

I put up a solid front, never letting on to Cammy how much I was dying inside. I wanted it to be a memorable event for her, especially if it was going to be our last. I knew her emotions rode with mine. If I let my defenses down and displayed my nervousness over the verdict, her shields would dissolve and she might suffer a miscarriage. I had to keep smiling, keep confident. I had to continue to make her believe that I was invincible.

Behind my smiling mask, I was hurting. I had developed two ulcers from the stress of the trial combined with the fear of losing Cammy. As I had feared all along, I had chosen the worst possible time to fall in love, and I was feeling the consequences. The future appeared darker than ever. If I was convicted on any one of the seven counts in the loan-sharking/racketeering case, I would go away for thirty years.

And surely I would not get off scot-free this time. The law had been after me for too long for me to expect a reasonable sentence. Even if I was acquitted, the Eastern District/Michael Franzese Task Force indictment was sure to follow. And there was now no longer any doubt that Iorizzo had turned. Not only was the fat man ratting, he was lying. They had marched him out during the loan-shark trial as a practice run for his future appearances.

I was also deeply worried about my children. I knew what it was like to lose a father to prison, and the last thing I wanted to do was leave my kids without a father. I loved my children dearly and wanted them to know it. No matter what happened in the future, I wanted them to know me and be proud of me.

— 107 —

Something happened before the end of the trial that, for a few harrowing hours, made the pending verdict, Cammy's rocky pregnancy, and every other problem seem insignificant. It caused me, for the first time in my life, to openly challenge my father, and it had a profound effect on our future relationship. It started with a call from Jimmy Angellino.

"The Boss wants you to come in for a meeting at 9:00 P.M."

"What's this about?" I asked, fearing the answer.

"The Boss wants you in," was all he would say.

But his voice was as lifeless as I had ever heard it.

I immediately called my father, who was again out on parole. As I expected, he had just received a similar call, only his sit-down was scheduled for 7:30 P.M.

"We need to talk, Dad," I said. "I'll be right over."

"No, I'll come there," he said.

As I waited for Dad, I thought about what had gone wrong. My operation was generating an immense amount of money, which in turn resulted in a rapid expansion of my crew. That brought unwanted notoriety. Those elements combined to make my mob associates uncomfortable. There was talk—inflamed by the federal government and local television news reports—that I had broken away from the Colombos and had become the head of my own family. At the heart of these rumors was the mistaken belief that I was making more money than I was telling the bosses in Brooklyn and was holding back millions of dollars.

Complicating this were the actions of my parents. Although Dad applauded my success, Mom was unable to accept the changing of the guard. She seemed to resent my lifestyle, and that of my wife, and that we had created our own identities. From her perspective, when my father had been jailed, her status had also fallen. She hounded Dad about this, demanding to know why he wasn't in charge of my operation and why they were not reaping the benefit of the wealth I was now generating. She was relentless and drove him to question my men about the amount of money we were making.

Dad even quizzed Markowitz and the Russians, who were all terrified of him. They reported back to me, and I confronted my father. I told him that he was telegraphing to Brooklyn that there was a rift between us. Plus, if my own father suspected me of hiding money, what were the mob bosses to think?

"Dad, what are you doing?" I demanded. "You're going to get us both killed."

— 108 —

Dad vehemently denied that he had confronted my men, claiming that they had misread his intentions. As much as I wanted to believe him, I knew better.

Angellino's call had now confirmed my worst fears: both my father and I were in serious trouble. We knew about these calls. It was part of the life. You walk into a meeting like that, and they carry you out.

My senses had suddenly become so sharp, so pumped with adrenaline, that the whole world looked different. Colors were

brighter. Sounds and smells were more intense. I could see everything around me in greater detail. My entire body was powering
up for a fight to the death.

And that was my problem. Instead of Dad and me banding
together and going out in a blaze of gunfire, I knew that he would
want us to walk into that room at our scheduled times like lambs
to the slaughter and passively accept whatever fate awaited us.
Of all the aspects of the mob I had grown to despise, the legendary death summons was the worst. I had long ago vowed never to
willfully walk into a room where someone was waiting to take my
life.

This was the conflict I now faced with my father. We would
engage in a verbal life-or-death struggle that pitted the old mob
values of strict adherence to the code against the saner interpre-
tation held by America's second generation of mobsters. I wondered what argument, beyond blind military-like allegiance, Dad
could use to support his position. His way had brought nothing
but decades of grief, hardship, and heartache to himself and his
family.

When he arrived, we talked in the driveway of my home in
Brookville. It was late afternoon, and the air was chilly. As the
sun set, I was reminded of all those hours we had bounced that
rubber ball off of my grandfather's chimney, each of us fiercely
determined to win our makeshift game. We had a different battle
facing us now, and this time, the stakes were much higher—our
very lives.

"I have a bad feeling about this, Dad. I don't like it. 'You in
first and then me.' This isn't right."

"Michael, this is our life. We've been given an order, and we
must obey."

"Dad, do you hear what you're saying? Do you understand?
We have families. We both have wives and children to support.
There are things that are more important than our oath. All of
this is over money.

"You should never have started questioning the Russians about our activities. Now they [the family] believe something's up, that we're making billions. You know the rumor's out there. So now, they're calling us in, and you know what's going to happen."

"I don't think so," he said.

"Neither one of us is sure, though," I said, "so why should we do this? Why risk our lives?"

His answer was, "This is our way. Whatever happens tonight, happens."

This shook me, and I responded, "Are you kidding?"

For a moment, Dad was shocked. I had never taken that tone with him, and the air was suddenly silent.

He just stood there like a rock, saying nothing, feeling nothing, determined to live by the code right to the end. I could see it.

"Okay, Dad. Okay. I know how you are. I know this is our life and we believe in it. I know what the oath says—if they call us, we have to drop everything and go. Okay. But let's go together. Me and you, together. We shouldn't let anyone separate us."

"We can't do that," he said. "That's not how they want it. We can't change it, and we can't show fear."

"Fear? Is that what this is about? Showing fear? You're going to walk in there and let them stick a gun to the back of your head and blow your brains out so you won't be accused by some punk of showing fear? You're going to let them kill me, your son, just because you don't want to show fear?"

"This is the life we chose," he repeated.

"Dad, you know, I always envisioned it would be me and you, side by side, taking on the world. Me and you, back-to-back, going down like warriors. If we're going to die tonight, let's do it that way. Give me that respect. Give yourself that respect. Let's go out together, fighting."

He looked down and stared at the pavement, but I grabbed him by the shoulders and forced him to look at me. I could feel the power in his body, but I could not feel the will. It was gone.

"Dad, let's do it together."

"That's not our way, Michael. We will go separately, the way they asked. And whatever happens, happens."

He walked to his car and opened the door. "It's the right thing, Michael," he said, standing there with the door open. "We live by the oath. The oath and the life are more important than any two individuals. I'm going to go. And you must follow. You must!"

With that, he got into his car and disappeared into the night.

— 109 —

After Dad had pulled away, I paced the driveway then walked around the grounds of my home. My senses were even more intense than before, but now my mind began to rationalize, desperately trying to make sense of the primal signals my body was sending out. Maybe I was overreacting. Maybe my father was so bravely following his beliefs because he knew something I didn't. Or maybe he knew that he wasn't the one on the spot, that he could disavow any detailed knowledge of my operation. That would be easy because I had specifically kept him distanced to protect him from being violated and having to go back to prison. Now he could use that to his advantage. So what should I do?

The time drew near, and I had no clearer answer than before. I was sure that I should not go, but if I failed to show, I could be sentencing my own father to death. That was my answer. I got into my car and drove to Brooklyn.

I parked on the street and walked to the luncheonette where Jimmy Angellino was scheduled to pick me up. This was telling.

Instead of being told where the meeting would take place and being allowed to drive there myself, I was to be driven to an unknown location by another family member.

Jimmy was cold and distant as we drove. We had been made together and had remained close friends. I felt shaky and empty inside but fought the urge to question him.

We drove in silence for about ten minutes. Then Jimmy pulled up to a large, dark house in Brooklyn, a house I had never seen before. It was a perfect place for a hit. I expected the meet would be held downstairs in a soundproof basement.

At that point, I would face two possibilities. If I opened the door and found the room empty, I was dead. I'd be clocked before I could turn my head. If there were people in the room, that might mean that they were giving me the respect of a hearing first. In that situation, I expected acting boss Andrew Russo (Persico was in jail) and the entire family hierarchy to be sitting around a table.

There would also be a young soldier, a man who didn't belong at such a high-level meeting. He would be stationed on my side, but set back so I couldn't see him if he got up. This person would be my assassin.

I walked down a narrow stairway, took a deep breath, and opened the door. There were people in the room. I found everything exactly as I envisioned it in my second scenario. It was as if I had seen that table, those men—and my death—in forgotten dreams buried somewhere in my subconscious.

The assassin was just as I had imagined—a young, hard-looking man sitting alone at the end of the table on my side. I saw a bead of sweat on his temple.

I knew that Russo—my first captain when I had been a recruit—would give the signal, and I knew that whatever it was, no matter how secret or cloaked the acting boss tried to make it, I would recognize it as clear as a flashing billboard. It would be my last thought.

– 110 –

"We want to ask you about your business," Russo opened as I sat down in the chair to his right.

"Go ahead," I said.

For the next two hours, Russo and other members of the family grilled me on my operation. I answered them firmly in a strong, unwavering voice. I had decided that if I couldn't go out shooting, at least I could wage this war with my wits.

"Ask me all your questions," I told them. "I've held nothing back. If you think I'm making more than I've said, show me the facts and figures. Bring in my accusers, and let me confront them. You're attacking me with speculation, rumors, and conjecture. I've given you the exact percentage I promised. I've generated this money myself, and I've generously shared it. You're listening to lies and reading false stories in newspapers.

"And you're taking Larry Iorizzo's wild statements on their face. He's exaggerating the income to build up his importance as a government witness. It's a routine move by someone desperate to stay out of prison."

Russo grilled me hard about Iorizzo. The fat man had rolled, and he was my responsibility. If Larry fingered even a single one of the other made men, it would cost me my life.

"I've sheltered everyone in our family from Iorizzo," I answered. "He's my responsibility, and he won't be able to take down anyone but me. I doubt that he can even do that. I followed the rules, I've kept my oath, and I've protected the family."

"But your father said...," Russo began.

I had been expecting this move, and I understood it. Like a trial attorney or a homicide detective, Russo was trying to trap me with something I had said that didn't match Dad's story. And he and his associates were also going to put words into my father's mouth to see if they could get me to falter or stumble.

"Don't tell me what my father said," I countered. "Don't play that game with me. Don't put me in that position. I'm not going to go for it. You should never have gotten my father involved in this. He doesn't know my operation. I've protected him for his own good. I've kept him clean. I fought all my life to get him out of jail, and I'm fighting now to keep him out of jail. If you wanted to speak to us, you should have brought us in here together. And if he's going to say something, let him say it in front of me. My father and I are together on this. We've always been together. Don't believe anyone who tells you differently. If you have questions, you ask me. You don't ask him."

With that, the tenseness in the room reached a crescendo, and Russo suddenly gave a signal.

It wasn't the signal I'd been expecting. Instead, Russo motioned for someone to serve the wine. My explanation had been accepted—at least for now.

I turned and subtly glanced at the assassin. He looked relieved.

The wine tasted sharp and bitter. My body had been on such a razor's edge that it had altered my internal chemistry. My "brothers" walked around the room and chatted with me and talked among themselves, but I couldn't concentrate on their words. They were trying to act like everything was back to normal, but it wasn't. Just moments before, they had been about to sentence me to death. I would never forget it, even though I would have done the same thing if I had been in their position. It was the way things worked in the life. It would never be the same for me—not with this family or my own.

— 111 —

"Jimmy, if they were going to kill me, would you have told me?" I asked as he drove me back to my car.

"What would you expect?" he countered.

"I'd expect you to tell me!"

As I said it, the truth drained from the words, and Jimmy picked up on it.

"If they were going to kill me, would you tell me, Michael?"

"No," I said. "That's sick, isn't it, Jimmy? What kind of friends are we? What kind of life is this?"

"It's our life, Michael, the life we chose. We knew what we were getting into. You especially. You've lived with it from the day you were born."

That was true. Who better than me to understand the life? My father had acted just as anyone would have predicted—in absolute, blind adherence to the code.

"I tell ya' something, Michael," Angellino said. "You got some courage. If I were in your shoes, I don't know if I could have taken it. You were ice. Man, you were ice. You sat in this car like you were going to dinner."

"Don't think my heart wasn't pounding," I admitted.

Before I got out of the car that day, Jimmy made a rare and unexpected confession. "I wouldn't have told you if you were a dead man tonight, but I can tell you now that you had a serious problem. Both you and your dad. You somehow talked your way out of it. Brilliant performance. But I'll tell you something, and this is between you and me. It goes to the grave with us. Your father...he didn't help you in there tonight."

"I can't believe that," I said.

"Believe it," Angellino insisted.

I knew Jimmy wasn't lying, and I knew what my father had done. He had played dumb. It had been the right move to make in that situation. In fact, I had set it up that way. But still, it hurt to know that he had done it. He could have taken a stronger stand and told them that everything between us was okay, that everything else was lies. But that wasn't Dad's way, because it wasn't the mob's way.

My father probably went to sleep feeling proud that night. He had obeyed his oath under the most trying circumstances. He had faced death without showing fear. He had done his duty. I wished I could have viewed it the same way. Instead, I felt like a sap, like I was the ultimate sucker. I should never have gone to that house. I should never have risked the future of my children and my future life with Cammy by playing this insane, deadly game. I had violated my own vow by willingly marching into a death chamber. And for what? To stay true to the oath? To justify my life to my "brothers"?

In Dad's own way, there was a measure of courage in what he did, but our family, the bond between him and me, should have come first. He should not have asked his son to go into that house unless he knew all along what the outcome would be. Because of that, I felt a great sense of loss. Although we had escaped with our lives, something had died that night. An insecure little boy had lost the blind hero-worship of his father.

The one positive thing I did take from that evening was the knowledge that I could face death without succumbing to fear. I could maintain my composure enough to survive on my intellect. But the next time, if I did confront death again, I would go out fighting.

A sweetly ironic epitaph to this event is that a few years later, the tables would be turned on Andrew Russo, my chief interrogator. Russo's brother-in-law turned undercover informant and rolled on eight of the top Colombo bosses, including Russo, Carmine Persico, Young "Allie Boy" Persico, and Jerry Langella— sending them all to prison. When Russo was released from prison sometime in the mid-1990s, might he expect to be summoned to an empty room? The truth is that he's back in prison on a new charge, and his sentence this time is heavy.

— 112 —

By the time the jury began its deliberations, the snow had melted, and the breezes turned from bitter to warm. On the morning of the verdict, Friday, April 19, I stared at Cammy for hours, wanting to burn her image into my brain so that I would never forget it. I wanted to memorize every fleck of color in her eyes, every crease in her lips, every contour of her smooth skin. I felt that the visual information I stored that morning might have to carry me through the rest of my life—a bleak, depressing life spent locked behind bars.

The jury had been deliberating since the previous Monday, and I had told Cammy that they wouldn't come back with a verdict until the following week. That wasn't true. I expected them to reach their decision on Friday. Jurors don't like to be held over the weekend. I had flown Cammy's mother to New York earlier in the week to be with her—just in case the news was bad.

Driving to the courthouse that morning, I talked with Cammy over the car phone the entire way.

"I love you, Cammy, don't ever forget that."

As I sat in the courtroom, awaiting the verdict, all I could do was think of her. I replayed the still fresh memories of Florida, from the first moment I had seen her at the pool.

At last, the verdicts were read. "Count one, Franzese, not guilty."

All seven counts, not guilty.

I couldn't believe what I was hearing. I had escaped again. I rushed to a telephone and called Cammy.

"Baby, it's over," I said. "Not guilty!"

"What?"

"Not guilty! Not guilty! Can you believe it? All the Italians were found not guilty!"

She screamed for joy and hugged her mother, and they both bounced up and down on the bed.

When the scorecards were tallied, the result was a split decision. All of the Jewish defendants and their associates were convicted, while all of the alleged mob members were found innocent. For once, I felt, the system had worked perfectly. The jury had somehow managed to wade through the government's misrepresentations and separate the guilty from the innocent.

U.S. District Judge Leonard B. Sand handed down stiff sentences. Hyman and Cooper were each given thirty years and fined $160,000. Hyman rolled over and entered the Witness Protection Program. Cooper escaped from prison and spent nearly two years on the lam before he was recaptured in Florida.

There was one notable exception to the tough prison terms. Judge Sand went easy on the rabbi and gave him only five years' probation and two hundred hours of community service. As I drove home that day, the tension that had built up inside me over so many months was released in a burst of laughter. How ironic! It was the rabbi's money that had helped float the entire operation. The singing rabbi had been Mr. Big. *Such is justice*, I thought to myself. Anyway, I was a free man, and I was so very happy about that fact.

– 113 –

In June of 1984, while I had been busy falling in love and filming *Knights of the City*—in that order—Dad completed his two-year parole violation sentence and was released. I interrupted my activities to present him with a new Mercedes to celebrate the occasion.

I had long given up hope that he would return to his 1960s stature, but it didn't matter much anymore. I had enough money to make kings out of ten thousand fathers. I just wanted him to live out his life in comfort and dignity.

Dad wasn't free long before his other family decided to undermine the second part of my master plan. In an extremely rare decree, Carmine "the Snake" Persico demoted Dad from captain to soldier. The Colombo boss said the move was intended to take pressure off of Dad by easing him into retirement and decreasing the chance that his parole would be violated again. Few believed that story. Persico could have allowed Dad to lay low with his title intact, and most saw the demotion as a direct message to me that regardless of how many millions I was making on Long Island and how large my army was growing, Persico was still the boss.

I was furious because I viewed this latest act as a continuation of the insults heaped upon my father by the "brotherhood" he had sacrificed half his life to protect. He could have made a dozen different deals with the feds to finger them and wipe away his own conviction, but he had always followed the oath and maintained silence.

"Let it go, Michael. Let it go," he told me. "What can you do?"

But it was another broken strand in the fraying rope that bound me to New York and to the mob. My life was now Cammy and California, sunny skies, warmth, and the Pacific Ocean. I stored the disrespect shown to my father in the growing file I kept in my mind detailing the mob's hypocrisy.

Free from the burden of the trial, I quickly got back to the business of settling my life. I worked out a divorce settlement with Maria, giving her the million-dollar Brookville home along with a million-dollar interest-bearing account that paid $10,000 a month for the living expenses of her and the children. We were able to settle the matter ourselves without the intervention of attorneys. I didn't, however, tell Maria about Cammy. Nor did I tell my mother, whom I feared would run to Maria and complicate matters.

Shortly afterward, I arrived at Cammy's condo in Brentwood carting a dozen yellow roses and a big smile.

"My divorce is final," I told her. "Now we can get married."

– 114 –

Cammy scouted the best hotels in the Los Angeles area for the wedding celebration and decided on the Beverly Hilton because of the stunning ballroom and the professional manner of Lina Kent, the Hilton's director of party planning. She also consulted with Dr. Myron Taylor at Westwood Hills Christian Church and determined that July 25, 1985, would be the best date for him to conduct the ceremony at the church. We had spotted the lovely church and decided that was where we would like to be married.

During the second week of May, Cammy, her mother, and five-year-old sister, Raquel, traveled to Las Vegas to visit her grandfather. I met them on the third day of their stay and joined them at Caesar's Palace. The following day, we took Raquel to Circus Circus, the giant casino-hotel that features a lively indoor circus and circular carnival arcade. As we walked to the arcade, Cammy's mother spotted the Chapel of the Fountain, the hotel's blue-bathed wedding chapel.

"Why don't you two get married now?" she said.

Cammy and I joked that we were both too chicken, but her mother persisted, no doubt motivated by the advancing state of her daughter's six-week pregnancy and the always volatile status of my professional life.

"You two are in love, so why wait?" she pressed. "You should make it right."

"Okay," I said.

"Okay," Cammy agreed.

We approached the chapel and looked inside. It was tiny but attractive. It looked like a miniature church.

"Wait a second," I said. "Let's go back to the hotel and think this over."

Back at the hotel, we teased and goaded each other some more. Finally, I picked up the phone and made the necessary appointment.

"It's set for tomorrow at 3:30," I told everyone.

As that hour approached, we eased our nervousness by continuing our strange game of marital chicken.

246

"I'm getting ready. Are you ready?" I said, searching the closet for my clothes.

"I'm getting ready. Are you?" Cammy parroted.

We repeated the banter with each item of clothing.

"I'm putting my socks on."

"I'm putting on my stockings."

Once dressed—me in black pants and a black-and-gray plaid shirt, Cammy in a white dress with blue flowers—we gathered up Mrs. Garcia and Raquel and made our way to the chapel. My palms became clammy, and my knees buckled a little the moment I entered. Cammy stayed cool until she started walking down the fifteen-foot aisle.

Much to Mrs. Garcia's delight and Raquel's boredom, we made it to the altar and were married. We celebrated by seeing Bill Cosby and Sammy Davis Jr. perform that evening at Caesar's Palace.

After the show, Cammy called her father to give him the good news, but he wasn't pleased.

"Why didn't you tell me?" he protested. "I could have flown down!"

He was not angry that we had gotten married, but that he had been left out of the happenings.

"Don't worry about him," Mrs. Garcia said. "He'll get over it." I was sure he would, but I understood his anger. What father would not like to be at his daughter's wedding? Well, at least we had the official wedding he could look forward to.

— 115 —

In the days and weeks following the Las Vegas wedding, I had very mixed feelings about what we had done. The $100 ceremony had been so quick and offbeat that it hadn't seemed real. And we had done it more for Cammy's mother than for ourselves. I had been glad to do whatever was necessary to assure her and everyone else involved that my intentions with Cammy were honorable, but now I faced another dilemma.

While the Vegas wedding was legal in the eyes of the law, the July wedding at Westwood Hills Christian Church would be a union in the eyes of God. That thought somehow troubled me. I hadn't given much time to considering God and His place in my life until then. I'd been much too busy for Him.

When I was younger, I had relied upon the Church and the parochial schools I attended to handle that part of my life. But after two decades of Masses, communions, confessions, Lent, ashes on the forehead, priests, nuns, sacraments, dashboard saints, Hail Marys, and rosaries, it seemed that nothing much had taken root in my heart. Then, once my schooling ended and my father stopped driving me to church, religion had faded in importance in my life. There were too many other important things to attend to. Making money and being a good mob soldier had become prime considerations in my daily existence.

Cammy's faith was real, and early in our relationship, she began to water all the dormant spiritual seeds in my soul. Calmly and patiently, she had outlined to me her beliefs and gently pressed me to join her as a believer in Christ. I wasn't so sure I wanted to do that. I listened to her, but mostly out of politeness—nothing more.

After all, I reasoned, I was born a Catholic, and I would die a Catholic. I couldn't have told anyone why I was a Catholic, but I was a Catholic nevertheless, and we just didn't change.

As the wedding approached, it became necessary for the two of us to go and sit down with Dr. Taylor for a counseling session. I was a little reluctant, but it seemed that I had no choice in the matter.

Well, okay, I thought. *Let's get this over with.*

I was surprised to find that I liked Dr. Taylor very much. He was clearly a people person, and he treated us with great respect. I was not offended when he spoke to us of the need for true Christian commitment and abiding faith in Christ, or when he spoke of God's grace being extended to sinners and the need for forgiveness.

In fact, I was so intrigued by what Dr. Taylor was saying that after a while, I found myself wanting to confess to this man everything I had ever done and ask him to help me make things right with God. It was apparent that I was facing a long prison sentence, and that thought had sparked something in my spirit that now surprised me. There was a new tenderness, a spiritual vulnerability that I had never felt before. And I liked it.

I asked Cammy if she would mind leaving the two of us together for a while so that I could speak to the minister alone, and she gladly agreed, going on home. Once Cammy had left, I said to Dr. Taylor, "You talk about forgiveness, but you don't know who I am or what I've done. For God to forgive me would be a real stretch."

Dr. Myron Taylor was not phased at all by this statement.

"Have you heard of the apostle Paul?" he asked.

I indicated that, of course, I had.

"Well," Dr. Taylor said, "he was a murderer. As a devout Pharisee, it fell to him to kill the troublesome Christians. That was his job. Still, God chose to forgive him and save him. God's grace is for everyone."

That was good news indeed, and I was enjoying hearing it so much that Dr. Taylor and I talked for the next several hours.

Eventually, I was convinced that what this man was saying must be true. Cammy had told me before, but it just hadn't sunk in. Now I was beginning to understand. And I was ready to become a real Christian.

— 116 —

"Okay," I said to Dr. Taylor, "I'm convinced. Now what do I have to do?"

"All you have to do is accept Jesus," he answered.

"Okay," I said, "but what do I have to do?"

He assured me again that all I had to do was accept Jesus as my Savior.

"Well, how do I do that?" I insisted.

"It's very simple," he assured me. "Just invite Him to come into your heart."

This is not going to work, I was telling myself. *It's much too easy.*

But I listened.

Dr. Taylor opened his Bible and read to me from John 3:16. I remembered seeing that on banners or posters near the end zones at professional football games. Usually when one team kicked an extra point, there would be someone in the crowd behind the goalposts waving a sheet that said "John 3:16." I had wondered what it meant at the time, but I was never curious enough to track down a Bible and look it up. Now I was hearing it for the first time. It said,

> *For God so loved the world that he gave his one and only Son, that whoever believes in him shall not perish but have eternal life.*

I found this to be a very powerful statement, and it seemed to address me directly.

"Whoever" meant Michael Franzese.

It was immediately clear to me why, of all the verses in the Bible, the football stadium Christians had chosen this one to flash into the nation's consciousness. This was a summation and a confirmation of everything Cammy, and now Dr. Taylor, had been telling me. This was the Christian experience in a few words.

I told Dr. Taylor that I was ready to accept Christ as my Savior and asked him to help me pray. The prayer he led me in that day was very short, but it was also very powerful. It went like this:

Dear God,

I know I'm a sinner and only Jesus can save me. I'm willing to turn away from my sin and submit to Your will. I believe that You sent Your Son, Jesus, to die on the cross and shed His blood to pay the price for my sins and that He arose again. I ask You, dear God, to come into my heart and save me. I ask that Jesus Christ become the Lord of my life.

Amen!

There, I'd done it, and I wasn't sure how to feel about it. Michael Franzese was not one to spend time talking with God, but I had just done it.

"Are you sure that's it?" I said. "That's all I have to do?"

It seemed much too simple.

"That's it," Pastor Taylor assured me.

"Isn't there something else I could do?" I asked.

"Well, yes, there is," he explained. "You and your wife both need to be baptized in water."

Ah, finally, I thought to myself. *Here's something I can understand, a ritual that I can wrap my arms around. That will surely have more of an effect on me than a simple prayer.*

"Yes, let's do that," I said to Dr. Taylor, "at your earliest convenience."

As I drove home that day, I couldn't help comparing what I had just done with the other oath I had taken, with the other time I had been "born again." That oath had been shrouded in ceremony. There had been a half-circle of men, dim lights, blood, and fire. Many wiseguys had waited years for a chance to be inducted into the family, and now my minister was telling me that my name had just been written into the Book of Life and that I would live forever in heaven because of a simple prayer I said in his office. He said that it didn't matter what I had done in the past or how much money I'd stolen.

Wow! This was overwhelming. I was now a real Christian.

Book 2

The New Life in Christ

— 1 —

So I was now a true Christian believer! Or was I?

Although I had really wanted to receive cleansing from my sins the day I spoke with Dr. Taylor in his office, I was still very skeptical of many things he and Cammy had told me. Before I could make a complete commitment to Christ, I would need to see more evidence. I could not blindly accept someone else's word for it. In the meantime, I would study the Bible and pray to God, but just in case this Christian thing wasn't for real, I would hedge my bets and continue life pretty much as before.

God was certainly doing His part to prove Himself. The morning following my prayer of acceptance of Him as Savior, a very strange thing happened. I was lying in bed with blackout shades drawn, when a bright beam of light suddenly flashed before me. I jumped up and searched for its source, but I couldn't locate it or even surmise how it might have been created. I wanted to believe, however conveniently, that it had been a sign from God to Cammy and me of His continuing love and concern for us, that He was telling us that everything would be okay. That experience buoyed our spirits for weeks, and whenever one of us became depressed, the other mentioned the light. To this day, I can't say for sure if God gave me a sign to comfort me or I just imagined it to be one. Whatever the case, He did touch my spirit that morning. He put it in my heart to search for more evidence, to diligently seek the truth about His Son Jesus.

There was nothing depressing about our church wedding. The wedding and gala reception had been planned for Cammy's family and friends. I invited only a few people from New York, including a brother and a sister of mine, but neither of them was able to attend. The reason for the New York blackout was again my mother. I still didn't feel comfortable telling her about Cammy. I also didn't want the matter to be thrown in Maria's face. I did tell Dad what I was doing and why, and he understood. Since I wasn't inviting Mom, I couldn't invite many others from back East, lest she find out. So, like everything else in New York (aside from my children), I just blotted it out of my mind. I was starting a new life in California, in more ways than one. No need to spoil the moment with any reminders of the past or of potential future troubles in New York. If friends and family members later felt insulted or betrayed, I'd deal with it then. This day was for me and for Cammy. This was our moment.

But I had other worries. Although I had already married Cammy once in Vegas, I was somehow extremely nervous about this second ceremony. I wiped the sweat from my brow and paced up and down the church hallways. The fact that I had no relatives and few friends of my own to talk with only added to my anxiety. Unlike Vegas, this was a real church. And this was a real marriage, one that was certain to change my life forever. I wasn't yet sure what this all meant. All I knew was that I wanted this young woman more than I had ever wanted anything else in life, more than I had ever thought I could want anything.

I shouldn't have worried. The ceremony went off without a hitch. The moment the music started, Cammy floated down the aisle in a $5,000 white wedding dress made of lace, satin, and silk, and dotted with pearls. A ten-foot train trailed behind her like a snowstorm. A pearl and sequined headpiece, specially ordered from Italy, was woven into her long, dark hair. A relative of the Garcias sang "Endless Love" while the rest of the overflowing Garcia clan watched. It was magical.

The reception at the Beverly Hilton's grand ballroom featured caviar, escargot, and separate tables of Italian and Mexican food set under each country's flag. The name of every guest was displayed in Swiss chocolate at the tables, while a basket spilling over with an assortment of rich chocolate served as the centerpiece.

The master of ceremonies that day was Leon Isaac Kennedy. Michael Jackson and Prince impersonators performed, as did a full orchestra. Later in the evening, a disc jockey played dance music as Cammy's brothers and friends entertained the crowd by break-dancing. During the dollar dance, a Mexican tradition, guests pinned dollars to Cammy's dress and danced with her. Female guests similarly paid me a dollar for a dance.

The public celebration over, we honeymooned in Hawaii at the Hilton on Maui. The island paradise reminded us of our days in Fort Lauderdale and Miami. We shopped, swam, danced, ate, loved, and watched glorious sunsets. Even losing a race with a wicked tropical thunderstorm in an open jeep failed to dampen our spirits.

Returning home to California, we were greeted by a court summons. It wasn't as bad as it could have been. It was from the seamstress who had made the bridesmaids' dresses for the wedding. She had sued, claiming she hadn't been paid enough for her services. She would win the suit by default, for by the time the case reached court, my presence was required in a higher court on another coast. This time, the stakes were much higher. Little did I realize then how much I needed God in my corner.

— 2 —

During the next three months, I had to split my time between New York and Los Angeles. Despite this hectic schedule, I managed to attend the Thursday night Lamaze natural childbirth classes with Cammy for six straight weeks without missing a session. Sometimes, I'd fly in from New York just for the evening class, then leave that same night on a red-eye flight to get back.

While I was practicing breathing exercises with Cammy, the Michael Franzese Task Force continued its basement meetings in Uniondale, intensifying its efforts to put me away for good. By then, I knew that Ed McDonald of the Eastern District was on my trail, but I still didn't know about the interagency task force muscle he had behind him.

To get closer to its prey, some of the task force meetings were held at the IRS criminal investigation office in Smithtown, Long Island, a few blocks from Peter Raneri's restaurant, where some of my crew, including Iorizzo, Markowitz, and the Russians, frequently ate. Agents mounted video cameras in the trees around the restaurant to monitor the activities.

McDonald's investigation was so intense I could feel the heat all the way to California, and most of my energy was directed at preparing for the next indictment. I began constructing my defense long before the arrest came. Although I was 5-0 in trials, I knew that my luck was bound to run out sometime, and I sensed that the moment was nearing.

To evade the forfeiture provisions of the impending racketeering charges, my lawyer advised me to liquidate all my assets, including my boats, jet, and helicopter, and place double and triple mortgages on my real estate holdings. If the government seized them, they'd have to deal with the banks.

I instructed John Jacobs to assure all the investigating bodies that I would voluntarily surrender when the indictments were announced. This included notifying the prosecutors who were investigating me in Florida. There was no need, I had Jacobs explain, to send a storm of troopers to ambush me. I wanted to spare my wife and our California neighbors from the sudden police invasions that had scarred my life as I was growing up.

During one of my New York trips, Frankie Cestaro met me at the airport and said there was an important meeting we needed to attend at Shelly Levine's office on Long Island. Gathered there were Levine, Joe Galizia, Michael Markowitz (free on bail), David Bogatin, and several others in the gasoline business.

I sensed that something was wrong the moment I entered the building. It felt like I was walking into a trap, which I was. Cestaro was unaware that the Long Island Organized Crime Oil Industry Task Force had wired Levine's office for sound and rigged the building's entrance for video. In a battle of espionage and counterespionage technology, the task force had planted state-of-the-art miniature audio receivers in the office that could not be detected by the weekly electronic bug sweeps performed by a retired police detective Levine had hired. They were also not affected by the white-noise emitters installed in the office to jam listening devices.

Instead of going to Levine's office, I anchored myself at a table in the coffee shop downstairs and ordered Cestaro to tell anyone who wanted to see me to meet me there. I advised my associate to return immediately after delivering the message.

Police detectives and prosecutors, including oil task force spearhead Ray Jermyn, head of the Suffolk County Organized Crime Bureau and a member of the joint task force, listened to the entire meeting. Jermyn dispatched teams of detectives into the building to find out where I was. They spotted me in the coffee shop. Jermyn kept sending in fresh teams to see if I was making any movement toward joining my associates upstairs. The investigators reported back that I was reading the stock market listings in the *Wall Street Journal.*

By the time the meeting ended, everyone in the room upstairs had made damning admissions of criminal activity. Included among the self-incriminated was Frankie Cestaro, who had lingered in Levine's office for more than an hour instead of returning as I had ordered.

As rumors of an indictment swirled, my men began to panic. Two of them came to me one afternoon on Long Island with a request to hit James Feynman, the operator of the Babylon Cove Marina. Feynman had testified against me in the loan-shark case and was expected to give further testimony about a credit card scheme in the pending case.

"We can get to him," they said. "We know where he is. Just give the word, and it'll be one less problem for us."

I was torn. I had an allegiance to my men and to my sworn oath to protect the business of the family. But I thought of the prayer I had said to become a believer, a follower of Christ. Although I still wasn't quite sure about the strength of my convictions, it was an oath I took very seriously, just as I had my previous oath. I knew that God could understand some lapses and failures in the smaller areas as I tried to escape my old life, but how could I order someone's death? I had avoided doing that even before I was a Christian. Feynman certainly might hurt me, but I quickly realized that there was no way I could order the man killed.

"No," I said, shaking my head. "That's never been my way. We can't start killing all the witnesses. It will just create more heat on all of us."

— 3 —

Back in California, my first child with Cammy—Miquelle— was born on November 25, 1985, at Cedars Sinai Hospital in Beverly Hills. It was a difficult birth. Cammy was in labor for twenty-two hours, gritting her teeth and sucking on ice cubes and lemon drops. She taped pictures of our wedding on the wall by her bed to provide inspiration and take her mind off the pain. At one point, the agony was so great she began clawing at her face. I told her to tear at me instead. She accepted, and her nails dug into me.

When the child finally arrived, I was allowed to cut the umbilical cord. That evening, I slept in the hospital in a bed next to my wife. Two days later, on Thanksgiving, I cooked the turkey for my wife and infant child, slaving away in the kitchen with a towel draped around my waist. At one point, I caught a glimpse of myself in the bathroom mirror, holding a large spoon and knife, and wearing a makeshift apron.

"Can you believe this?" I asked Cammy. "I almost don't know myself."

Cammy, who still didn't have the full picture of who I had been, merely laughed. The following day, when Frankie Cestaro called, Cammy explained that I was busy vacuuming.

"Don't tell him that!" I scolded.

"Why? It's the truth," she countered.

The Long Island don had not only become born-again, he had also turned into California's "Mr. Mom." The strange thing was that I was loving every moment of it.

– 4 –

On December 16, 1985, just a few months after my decision to accept Christ, Paul Castellano, boss of the Gambino family, was gunned down in what was believed to be a power play for family leadership, and my flea market rival John Gotti ascended to the Gambino family throne. The New York media ran with the story, soon making it a banner week for mob news. The infamous Gotti would later be convicted of the murder and sentenced to life in prison, where he died tragically of cancer in the summer of 2002.

Three days after Castellano's bloody death, I was awakened at 5:30 A.M. by a call from Frankie Cestaro.

"I have friends at my home," he said.

The "friends" of which he spoke were FBI agents. The joint task force had decided to make their move, and they would be coming for me at any minute. I quickly dressed and left the house. Calling New York from a pay phone, I learned that an army of twenty agents, along with an NBC television crew, had swarmed the Brookville home before dawn looking for me. Maria told them that I no longer lived there, and they accepted her explanation and left.

The feds obviously had ignored my request to come in on my own. They were bent on staging an arrest, preferably in view of network television. I called John Jacobs and told him to inform everyone that I would surrender on January 2, after the holidays. Jacobs argued that the feds weren't about to wait and advised me to come in and post bond. I told him it wasn't going to be that easy this time.

I had gotten wind of investigations concerning old charges, including my alleged death threats against Dad's probation officer. I was certain that the prosecutors were building a case to paint me as "a danger to society" in order to keep me in jail without bond, up to and throughout a trial. They were wary of my past success at ramrodding through my defense, and now they wanted me locked up so I couldn't mount another winning effort. Jacobs disagreed, assuring me that I would be able to make bond.

Cammy met me that afternoon for lunch, and I was cheerful and acted like nothing was wrong. She had an appointment at a local beauty salon to get her hair trimmed, so I offered to drive her there. On the way, the phone beeped in my white Mercedes, and Cammy's heart sank when she heard my end of the conversation.

"Who else was arrested?" I asked without thinking.

When I finished, Cammy forced herself to ask what had happened, hoping that what she suspected was not true.

"The fireworks went off in New York," I said. "Everyone's been arrested. They want me to turn myself in."

"Now?" she asked, incredulous.

"Now," I told her.

"Oh, not again!" she responded, bursting into tears.

The phone rang a second time, and it was Cammy's sister Sabrina. She said that FBI agents had surrounded our Brentwood condo. That scared Cammy even more. Policemen she understood, but FBI agents? That had to mean I had done something really bad.

"Is this the way it's going to be the rest of our lives?" she asked through her tears. "Every six months, FBI agents coming to our home?"

The FBI agents grilled Sabrina, but she clammed up, pretending to be a baby-sitter. I circled the area and explained to Cammy that I had decided to surrender in Florida. I expected that the feds were acting in bad faith, so I would steal their thunder by giving up to the state authorities in Fort Lauderdale instead. I dropped Cammy a block away from our house and told her I was going to the Bel Air Sands Hotel.

"Don't try to come there," I warned. "You'll just lead the FBI to me."

As I had expected, two agents met Cammy at the door when she got home. She told them I had already left for New York. They asked if they could come inside the apartment, and she said sure. The agents questioned her about herself, her marriage, the baby, and anything else they could think of. Cammy played the part of the totally ignorant wife (which wasn't difficult, since I still hadn't told her much about my life). Satisfied, the agents left but continued to stake out the area.

When I learned what Cammy had done, I was angry that she'd let the agents in.

"You never, *ever* let them inside the house," I said. "You meet them at the door and leave them there."

Meanwhile, Sabrina was standing on the balcony of the first floor condominium chatting with a handsome Italian FBI agent. He asked the pretty, tousled-haired teenager if she was an actress or a model and was a few smiles away from asking her for a date when Cammy had to go out and rescue her.

"I'm sorry we have to do this, Mrs. Franzese," the agent said. "We're just doing our job."

"Yeah, great job!" Cammy snapped, pulling Sabrina inside.

"These guys are here to put my husband in jail," she exclaimed, "and now they're making advances at my sister! I can't believe it."

I drove to the Gap clothing store in Westwood and bought a pair of jeans and a striped shirt for the trip to Florida. While I was shopping, Cammy made a test run to Ralph's supermarket on Wilshire Boulevard to see if she would be followed. She was. She noticed that the agents waited outside in the parking lot instead of going into the store, and the wheels began to spin in her mind. She could drive to a mall, go in one end, come out the other, and catch a taxi to get to me. Like me, she had a premonition that this time I wouldn't be coming back.

Returning home, Cammy packed some of my clothes and stuffed them in a garment bag. As the hours wore on, the number of agents surrounding the building dwindled. The Italian outside the balcony had departed. Cammy sent Sabrina out for a walk to survey the situation, and she reported that the remaining agents were staking out the apartment entrance.

Cammy went to the balcony, dropped the garment bag to the grass below, and then climbed down the balcony wall. She braced her feet on a garden hose reel, then jumped the final distance to the grass. She picked up the garment bag, ducked into the parking garage, hopped into the midnight-blue Nissan 300ZX I had bought for her at Thanksgiving and sped out of the building.

— 5 —

Cammy drove around for the next hour, darting in and out of traffic, stopping to get gasoline, and weaving across parking lots to determine if she had a tail. As far as she could tell, there was none. She drove to the Bel Air Sands, slipped into the elevator as unobtrusively as possible, and found my room. She tapped on the door.

The knock nearly sent me through the roof.

"Who is it?" I asked.

"Me," she responded.

"Are you alone?"

"Yes."

"Are you sure?"

"Yes, Michael. Yes. Let me in."

I opened the door and looked sternly at my impetuous wife.

"Why did you take such a chance?"

"I don't care," she said. "I had to see you."

I waved her in, locked the door, and squeezed her tightly. After we had spent some time comforting each other, I said to her, "I couldn't find a flight to Miami. I tried to charter a jet, but none was available."

She grabbed the phone in one hand and the Yellow Pages in the other and began calling every airline. Eventually, she found an Eastern flight that could get me to Fort Lauderdale with two stops. She made the reservation in the name of her younger brother Cuauhtemoc Garcia, a name I couldn't even pronounce. In those days, before the tragedy of 9/11, you could travel under a different name without much difficulty. It's quite different, of course, today.

We ordered room service, shared a solemn dinner, then lay on the bed for two hours hugging each other and crying.

"Who's going to take care of me if you go away?" Cammy whimpered.

I hadn't even left yet, and she already felt terribly lonely and afraid.

I brushed the tears off of her cheek and looked into her huge, frightened eyes. She was just a baby, a scared child.

"We'll get through this," I promised. "Just try to be strong. I'll call you as soon as I can. Have your family stay with you. I don't want you to be alone—not even for one night."

Cammy cried the whole way to the airport, and it tore me up to see her in such anguish. As I drove, tears also ran out from under my glasses and down my cheeks.

"Don't cry," I said, ignoring my own tears. "Everything will be okay."

At the departure ramp, I gathered my things, said good-bye, and walked away. I stopped, turned, and gave Cammy a last wink. I had to be strong. She needed it in that moment.

While I was on my way to Florida, federal agents were wisely searching airline listings to try and intercept me. They stationed men at the airports in Miami and Fort Lauderdale, but those agents were looking for Michael Franzese, not Cuauhtemoc Garcia. Cammy's quick thinking had helped me foil their plans.

During a stopover in Dallas, I passed by a row of newspaper boxes and was struck by a headline in *The New York Times* announcing my indictment. I fished in my pocket for some coins, dropped them into the slot, and removed a paper. As I flew to Fort Lauderdale, I read about the mounting troubles of a young Cosa Nostra capo. The weariness of the all-night flight caused the words of the story to intermingle with scenes from my life. It was such a contrast, and I found it difficult to comprehend that I was the hunted criminal being written about on the front page of one of the world's most prestigious newspapers.

— 6 —

Arriving in Fort Lauderdale, I hid my face as I walked through the terminal. I flagged a cab and directed the driver to a nearby McDonald's. Jacobs had arranged for me to meet a Broward County detective at the fast-food restaurant. The friendly detective led me to his car and drove directly into the garage area of the courthouse to dodge the FBI agents staking out the building. They were intent upon intercepting me on the courthouse steps, pulling rank on the local police, and shanghaiing me to New York. Since the local Florida police didn't like the FBI's Gestapo tactics any more than I did, we were uneasy allies in that moment.

Inside, I was charged with sixty-five counts of Florida's massive one-hundred-seventy-seven-count tax evasion indictment. I posted ten percent of a $124,000 bond and satisfied the state obligation.

"I know," I then told the detectives after being symbolically released. "The feds are waiting downstairs."

A heavily armed band of grim-faced FBI agents took over from there. With me in tow, they set off for the Metropolitan Correction Center in Miami, a civilized federal facility. On the way, however, a message squawked over the car radio: "Divert the prisoner to Dade County." I sunk back into my seat. They were going to take me to the same Miami hellhole that had caused my former associate Larry Iorizzo to crack.

I arrived at the North Dade Detention Center, was assigned a cell, and quickly began to understand why Iorizzo had turned. The place was filthy, the inmates were filthy, the food was terrible, and hardly anyone spoke English. It was like being imprisoned in a third world country.

All weekend long, the television blaring in the county jail broadcast news reports of my arrest, in English and Spanish. My fellow Florida inmates had never seen a real-life mobster before, and loony as they seemingly were, they were impressed. They treated me like a celebrity. Many asked in broken English how they could join "the famous American Mafia."

Upon Jacob's advice, I waived extradition to New York. He wanted to have my federal bond hearing there instead of in Florida. In retrospect, it was a questionable decision. The authorities hardly knew me in Florida, so I would probably have made bail

266

more easily there. In New York, I was a certified, second-generation, blue-blooded gangster, so they would fight very hard to keep
me locked up.

Three long, miserable days after I arrived in South Florida,
two task force members, Suffolk County Police detective Frank
Morro and U.S. Postal Service Agent John LaPerla, flew to Miami.
They had come to escort the "Long Island don," as the United
States Congress had dubbed me, back to New York. Morro and
LaPerla were decent and didn't bother to handcuff me until we
arrived at Islip Airport in Long Island. Even then, the handcuffs
were a show for the crowd of reporters waiting to record my arrival.
The reporters aimed their cameras and shouted questions at me
as I was taken to a waiting car. I was then driven to the federal
courthouse in Uniondale, Long Island, and taken to a courtroom
a few floors above the same basement conference room where the
Michael Franzese Task Force had worked to seal my fate.

— 7 —

By what seemed like some stroke of very bad luck or some
devious coincidence, the judge assigned to my case was Jacob
Mishler—the same Jacob Mishler who had presided over my
father's cases and sentenced him to fifty years in prison nearly
two decades before, the same Judge Mishler who had overruled
our appeals attempting to prove that my father had been framed,
the same Judge Mishler whose daughter I was said to have
planned to kidnap, and the same Judge Jacob Mishler whom
Mom had once sarcastically applauded in open court, screamed
insults at, and openly accused of being part of a vicious scheme to
frame her husband.

Great! I thought. With Mishler on the bench, the odds of my
getting a fair trial were about a hundred to one.

John Jacobs immediately filed to have Judge Mishler removed
from the case, citing his long, stormy history with the Franzese

family. Despite the logic behind this motion, I wasn't in complete agreement with it. There was no question that Mishler would be tough during the trial and devastating during sentencing, and under him I'd be lucky to get a "mere" fifty years like my father. On the other hand, Judge Mishler had always been lenient in awarding bail. He had allowed my father to remain free on appeal for three years following his bank robbery conviction. More than anything else, I wanted to make bail, and the way I saw it, we could motion to have Mishler bounced *after* the bond hearing.

Jacobs remained adamant that Mishler had to go without delay and continued to push hard to have him ousted. Mishler countered that he hardly remembered my father's case or the threat against his daughter and that he could be fair with me. Jacobs continued to protest and demanded a speedy trial, a calculated move based upon the fact that Judge Mishler was scheduled to sit on the bench in South Florida as part of his rotating federal jurist duties. Mishler finally relented and gave up the case. It was reassigned to Judge Eugene Nickerson.

Judge Mishler's courtroom had been in the wide-open spaces of Uniondale, Long Island, but Nickerson's courtroom was in Brooklyn. Despite my attempts to escape to the sun of Florida and California, I had come full circle. I was back in mob territory.

In Brooklyn, I was finally able to read the twenty-eight count racketeering indictment produced by the fourteen-agency joint task force headed by the Eastern District of New York. Indicted with me were most of my top associates: Louis Fenza, Frank "Frankie Gangster" Castagnaro, Frank Cestaro, Harold Sussman (my accountant), financier Gerard Nocera, Allied International Union boss Anthony Tomasso, union attorney Mitchell Goldblatt, and Walter Doner. Doner, my Rumplik Chevrolet partner, was a Catholic deacon and Little League baseball coach and was totally innocent. He just had the misfortune of being caught in the drift net with the rest of us.

Once again, I was astounded by the charges lodged against me. I was accused of conspiracy, mail fraud, obstruction of justice, extortion, uttering a counterfeit security, violating federal anti-kickback laws, embezzlement, and wire fraud. The companies I was said to have defrauded of $5 million included such blue-chip corporations as Mobil Oil, Citicorp, General Motors, Mazda Motors of America, Merrill Lynch, Chemical Bank, Beneficial Commercial Corporation, and Allied International Union.

The bulk of the charges involved wild accusations of fraud and extortion in my auto dealerships and in my association with the security guards' union. There was even a charge for credit card fraud based on a $500 rubber raft someone had given me as a gift. There was just a single count pertaining to the gasoline business and only $3 million allegedly stolen. Part of that was based upon Iorizzo inflating the figures on a financial statement filed for a fuel-tax bond.

I was charged with knowing the statement was false—which I hadn't. I rarely saw that kind of paperwork. Similarly, I had no idea that the $100,000 treasury note that was put up as collateral for the $500,000 Rumplik floor plan loan was counterfeit. I thought it was stolen.

The last count of the indictment was a "Kline conspiracy," a blanket accusation that every business I was ever involved with was created for the sole purpose of stealing taxes. The indictment indicated that I owned twenty-one separate or related businesses spanning the construction, auto, and motion picture industries, and traced the spending of millions of dollars.

The one-hundred-seventy-seven-count Florida indictment listed twenty-six codefendants—including Austrian Duke Henri Alba-Teran d'Antin—and dealt solely with the gasoline business. I didn't know a dozen or more of the codefendants, including the duke, and had no idea why they were included. Others I knew well. They included Frankie Cestaro, Vincent Aspromonte, William Ferrante, Sebastian "Buddy" Lombardo, Peter Raneri, Jerry

Zimmerman, Michael Markowitz, David Bogatin, and Leo Pers-its.

My first thought upon reading the indictments was that I could beat these charges. The union embezzlement charges were imprecise, and I was insulated from them. The rest of the charges were a mishmash of truth, fiction, other defendants' crimes, and routine business practices. The accusations could easily be attacked. Despite the millions I had been stealing in gasoline taxes, it appeared that the government was still unable to build a solid case against me.

− 8 −

I was among friends at the Metropolitan Correctional Center (MCC) in New York. Included among my fellow inmates on the ninth floor were family boss Carmine "the Snake" Persico Jr., Colombo underboss Jerry Langella, and Genovese family boss Anthony "Fat Tony" Salerno. It was said that there were more of us in MCC than there were on the street at the time.

We were all there because Rudolph Giuliani, then U.S. Attorney in Manhattan and later mayor of New York City, had indicted the bosses of all five families for racketeering in what came to be called the "Mob Commission Case." Under his tenure, there was intense and unprecedented scrutiny of the mob as he was determined to bring it down.

Also in MCC at the time was a band of Sicilian mobsters awaiting trial in the "Pizza Connection" drug case. My cellmate was a terrorist who had been involved in a number of bombings in Chicago and New York. Although he explained his organization, motive, and cause at length, it meant little to me. These men did not make for pleasant company.

Cammy and I argued about whether or not she should fly to New York. I didn't want her to suffer through my ordeal, but she wanted to be there with me, and in the end, she prevailed.

Cammy, Sabrina, and the baby flew to Kennedy Airport the next day. John Jacobs booked her into the Lombardy Hotel, an old stodgy structure that was nevertheless quite expensive. Cammy found it so gloomy that she called around the next day for a brighter hotel and found three she liked. I vetoed them, saying that they were too close to wretched Forty-Second Street, a thoroughfare infested with pimps, prostitutes, muggers, street crazies, and aggressive panhandlers and winos. We finally agreed that she would stay at the Parker Meridien Hotel off Central Park.

The first time she visited me at MCC, Cammy was roughly searched, had a handheld metal detector run up and down her body, and was ordered to check her fur into a locker. She filled out some forms, squeezed herself into a packed elevator, got off at the ninth floor—the mob floor—and was directed to a cramped visiting room overflowing with people. When I appeared, she rushed to me. I gave her a restrained hug and explained that emotional displays were frowned upon at MCC. She asked if I was okay, and I said I was.

Cammy remained in New York for the rest of December and all of January, as my bond hearing kept getting postponed and extended to accommodate Judge Nickerson's vacation and to enable the prosecutors time to build a stronger case. She was allowed to visit me only for an hour every Tuesday and Thursday, and during that time, her mood alternated between enthusiastic optimism and complete despair. Most of the time, however, her mood reflected mine. When I was up, she was up, and when I was down, it plunged her into despair.

The various members of the Garcia family took turns staying with her. When Sabrina had to leave, her mother, father, or brothers flew in to take her place.

MCC was a real drag. We were locked down all day with no exercise, activities, or even a breath of fresh air. One afternoon, I watched as a pair of Chinese Dragon gang members, in prison on murder charges, beat a bulky weight lifter bloody with a pair of broomsticks. The bodybuilder was a bully who threw his weight around, especially in the telephone area, and the Chinese guys had finally had enough. They were as quick and deadly as mongooses and ended up breaking the bigger man's arm.

What was more disturbing to me, however, was the fate of my fellow mobsters. They kept going to trial, losing, and getting hammered with harsh sentences. Every other day, it seemed someone was coming back with a thirty-, forty-, fifty-, seventy-, or even one hundred-year sentence. The city seemed to be engulfed in a wave of mob hysteria, and the prosecutors were on a roll. This didn't bode well for me, especially considering that it was the ringleaders who were being hit the hardest. And I was the youngest of the clan.

During my bond hearing, the prosecutors dredged up every damning indictment from my past, including the alleged death threat on my father's probation officer. Iorizzo was hauled out to repeat his lies that I had tried to kill his son and had ordered him to hide in Panama. This time, he added that I had also threatened to kill him. (On an interesting side note, this same Lawrence Iorizzo was convicted of gasoline-tax fraud some ten years later, in 1996. His son Larry Jr. testified against him at trial. He was sentenced to serve one hundred eighty-eight months in federal prison, where he resides today.)

Taped conversations from various points of my life materialized as if by magic. I learned for the first time that Luigi Vizzini, one of the men who had tried to entice me into offering a bribe to national parole board director Benjamin Malcolm, had been an informant and had taped our conversations. Vizzini had later been murdered, and the prosecutors implied with their questions that I had found out about the setup and had killed Vizzini. It made for a nice story, but it wasn't true. I hadn't known until that court proceeding that I had been set up. I hadn't even been aware of the fact that Vizzini was dead.

The prosecutors trotted out everything they could to try to convince the judge that the "Yuppie Don" was actually an old-fashioned, blood-and-guts mob killer who was a menace to society and unworthy of any bail, and by calling witnesses who twisted the facts, they were doing a pretty good job of it. When the hearing ended, Judge Nickerson reserved his decision until an unspecified date.

It didn't surprise me when he ruled, a week or so later, that I was to be held without bond. By comparison, John Gotti and a gang of his associates were, at the same time, awaiting trial in Nickerson's court for charges ranging from murder to drugs, and none of them had been remanded. How ironic! Except for a few poorly supported extortion counts, I had been charged with white-collar crimes. My continued detention was difficult to accept. Quite honestly, it wasn't God I turned to. I knew that I had some serious work cut out for me if I wanted to hit the streets and be with Cammy again.

– 9 –

Cammy took the judge's decision even harder than I did, and her ordeal made my predicament seem even harder. It was exactly what I had not wanted, exactly the kind of situation I had always avoided getting myself into. I had wanted to do my inevitable jail time clean, without destroying anyone else's life. I had witnessed firsthand how my father's imprisonment had devastated my mother and ruined the lives of my younger brothers and sisters. And here I was, doing the same thing to my families. I was confident that Maria would be strong and would be able to take care of our children. She was mature, steady, resourceful, and in control of her emotions. Cammy, on the other hand, was a totally different creature. Although she was street-tough and a fierce fighter, she was extremely emotional and empathetic. She would be dying each day I spent in prison.

I had to get out of jail, at least for the stressful time prior to and during the trial. There had to be a way, so I again reviewed all the angles.

Another inmate told me about a new law that allowed prisoners with complicated cases to be released for part of the day to work on their defense. Since my Florida indictment included twenty-seven coconspirators on top of my twenty-eight count federal indictment, I figured I was a natural to test the law. Jacobs, my attorney, discouraged me, calling it an extreme long shot and a "frivolous motion." I wrote most of the briefs myself and ordered Jacobs to present the request to the judge.

We were all surprised when the judge granted my request and even granted me more free time than I had sought. I had asked for six hours a day, five days a week, but the judge awarded me ten hours a day, six days a week. I would be transported from MCC to Jacob's office at 10:00 A.M. on each of the six days, watched over by U.S. marshals, and then returned to the jail around 8:00 P.M. that night. I was only the second inmate to have such a motion granted. Of course, Jacobs claimed the credit, after the fact, for filing the motion. As for me, I began to wonder if God had His hand in all of this.

John Jacobs's office was a prison of another kind, but it beat the total lockdown of MCC's ninth floor. I could eat better food, see my wife and child, and fight my case. It could have been a whole lot worse.

Studying all the charges against me and considering what was happening with other mob defendants, for the first time I began considering the possibility of working out a plea bargain. One of my codefendants, union boss Anthony Tomasso, had already rolled over. That was significant, because the union activities were an area where I was at risk. And even if I had been able to mount an effective defense against Tomasso and Iorizzo, the current indictment was merely another in what appeared to be an endless string the task force was prepared to bring against me. Brooklyn's organized strike force chief, a sharp prosecutor named Laura Brevetti, was even then busy working on a gasoline-tax indictment. She was thus closing in on my most vulnerable area—the money we had made stealing taxes. That was the one indictment I truly feared.

At this point, Cammy was beginning, on her own, to understand more about the nature of my business. And as her understanding grew, it struck me that I had made the same mistake I accused my father of making when I was a child. It upset me that when he was going through his legal problems, he had never sat the family down and explained the newspaper stories, never explained to us what was happening. I felt he should have told us what to expect and who and what he was. But when it came my turn, I, too, never sat my families down to explain. Instead, I took the same silent route as Dad had taken. Even as close as I was to Cammy, I never admitted to her who I was or gave her a history of La Cosa Nostra.

What bothered her most now was what she perceived as the savage cannibalism of the crime families themselves. From her perspective, she had more to fear from my friends than from the prosecutors, and she had a point. Vincent Rotondo, a DeCavalcante capo she'd met when he was a codefendant with me in the Hyman/Cooper loan-shark trial, was blown away in front of his Brooklyn house while his wife and children huddled inside. Rotondo's body was covered with the fish he had purchased for dinner from a nearby deli. It was widely believed that he was killed because Jesse Hyman was his associate, and he had introduced Hyman to other made men. When Hyman became a government witness, Rotondo was finished.

Veteran mobster Johnny Irish Matera, a close friend of my father's, arrived at Kennedy Airport one afternoon from North Miami and drove to a meeting in Brooklyn headed by Persico. He failed to notice that he had an FBI tail. Because of this, Persico's parole was revoked for associating with felons, and Johnny Irish paid for the mistake with his life.

My initiation ceremony cohort, Jimmy Angellino, would later incur the mob wrath by trying to muscle in on the Gambino family's interests in New York's billion-dollar garment industry, which surrounds the Empire State Building. He was taken for a ride by his Colombo family brothers and was never seen again.

Rotondo's death and the murder of Gambino boss Paul Castellano hit Cammy especially hard. She envisioned me going out the same way, in a puddle of blood in front of our home or on a dirty New York sidewalk outside an Italian restaurant. She decided that she'd rather have me in prison in California than free in New York.

That feeling, and her acceptance of my being in prison, made agreeing to a plea bargain a great deal easier. I was concerned about her increasing fears and had decided that I never again wanted to come home and find my emotional wife on the bedroom floor, trembling, crying, and clutching a stuffed monkey. All else considered, I would have fought the indictments in court, where I had always won. But even if I had been able to dodge yet another bullet, I would merely have doomed Cammy to a life of tormenting anxiety. And I'd be putting my children through the same hell my father's lifestyle had put me through.

For Cammy, I was ready to give up my criminal empire and go to jail, and even to attempt the impossible—sever my ties to La Cosa Nostra. With those private goals in mind, I concluded that my best position would be to offer an all-encompassing plea that settled everything, past and future. Over the next six weeks, I hammered away at the prosecutors until they agreed to a deal we could all live with.

— 10 —

As part of the plea bargain, I agreed to plead guilty to two of the twenty-eight counts filed against me—federal racketeering and tax conspiracy. I was given a ten-year prison sentence, was forced to forfeit nearly $5 million in assets, and agreed to be fined an additional $10 million in restitution.

I also agreed to plead guilty to the sixty-five counts charged against me in Florida, which included racketeering, grand theft, conspiracy, theft of state funds, and failure to account for taxes collected. The nine-year Florida sentence would run concurrent with the ten-year federal sentence. A $3 million Florida restitution fee would come from the $15 million federal agreement.

In addition to the pleas, I privately promised to quit the mob.

Publicly, I sang a different tune, one in keeping with my oath.

"I am absolutely one hundred percent not a member of organized crime," I told The Associated Press. "It's because of that label that I've had all these problems. I'm willing to give the government a pound of flesh if this will be the end of it."

In return for my "pound of flesh," the slate would be wiped clean. The sentence would cover past crimes and future indictments, and clear me of everything I had ever done—except in the case that I was found guilty of murder or perjury.

The feeling among the multitude of prosecutors and law enforcement officers who had hunted me varied widely on the plea. Those who supported it felt it was a major victory over a criminal who had proven difficult to convict. I would go to jail, my billion-dollar operation would be shut down, and I would have to pay what they saw as an enormous restitution fee. Plus, when I finally let it be known that I was turning my back on the family a short time later, they viewed my vow to quit the Mafia as the clincher. That, they believed, was an automatic death sentence.

"He's agreeing that he'll forever owe the federal government $14.7 million," Brooklyn strike force and joint task force prosecutor Jerry Bernstein told reporters. "That's very meaningful."

"I'm very pleased with the disposition," added strike force and task force Chief Ed McDonald. "We've convicted a major organized crime figure and forced him to make a significant restitution."

The United States Department of Justice was also pleased. It awarded each member of the Michael Franzese Task Force a plaque commemorating each one's accomplishment.

In Florida, the official response was similar.

"We were lucky. We caught our problem early. In New York, they're saying $500 million may be missing," said Robert Dempsey, commissioner of the Florida Department of Law Enforcement (FDLE).

"That is a tremendous departure point," agreed Rolando Bolanos, FDLE chief. "Normally, when the head of the organization falls, the backbone will follow."

Those who fought the plea bargain believed that I got off much too easy. The detractors pointed to the deal made by junk bond king Michael Milken in April 1990 as a comparison. Milken agreed to pay a staggering $600 million in restitution, then later received his own ten-year prison sentence. "And Milken stole less money than Franzese," noted one bitter prosecutor.

"He got the deal of the century," said Suffolk County district attorney and organized crime specialist Ray Jermyn, a key joint task force member. "The government was suckered, just like he's suckered everybody else. The guy's amazing. Everybody loves him. He smiles, steals them blind, and they still love him."

In public, I strongly disagreed with this assessment, reminding everyone that not only had the government fined me $15 million, but it was also taking four to ten years of my life—depending on my conduct in prison.

"In simple terms," I stated for public consumption, "I lost and the government won. The score might have been closer than some wanted, but I lost nevertheless. The task force achieved its stated goal of destroying my organization and putting me behind bars. And never, even in my most private moments, did I feel that I suckered anybody. I came to realize that the life I was living was wrong, and I was glad to be paying my debt to society and starting a new life."

In reality, although I felt that the disposition was fair in many ways, I was sure that I had dodged a major bullet that could have landed me in prison for life. My plan was working perfectly.

− 11 −

After the plea agreement had been signed, I was allowed to fly back to Los Angeles with Cammy and our baby. The only difficulty we encountered was getting her baggage home. She had come to New York in the dead of winter with little more than a sweater and parka to fight the cold. Her sister, mother, and brothers, all lifetime Californians, had also lacked winter clothing. Because of this, Cammy had purchased so many bulky coats and sweaters during her sojourn that she now had to hire two taxis just to get her bags to the airport. She ended up having to ship most of her belongings as unaccompanied baggage on a cargo plane.

During the flight home, my U.S. marshal escorts let me sit with my wife and child. I hugged Cammy and played with Miquelle as we made the five-hour trip. Then, when we arrived in Los Angeles, I was allowed to spend the weekend at home before reporting to the U.S. marshal's office for phase one of my punishment.

Among numerous riders I had been able to negotiate into my plea agreement was one that enabled me to spend the three months prior to my sentencing in a Los Angeles halfway house. Halfway houses are set up, in part, to prepare long-term inmates nearing the end of their prison stay to reenter society. I took the position that I needed to prepare to *leave* society, and I was thus assigned to the Suicide Prevention Center/Community Treatment Center on Menlo Avenue. I arranged it so that I could be out

Michael Franzese

from 6:00 A.M. to 11:00 P.M. each day. Basically, all I did was sleep at the place.

I wasn't totally free during the day, for U.S. marshals did monitor my every move. Because of the imprecise language in the plea papers, however, I was able to dictate the terms of my watch. The agreement stated that I was to pay the salaries of the officers on the twenty-four-hour detail, a sum that amounted to $4,000 a week. This apparently led the U.S. marshal's office to view it as a sort of "rent-a-cop" situation. They asked me how it was supposed to work, and I quickly laid out the least intrusive scenario. The marshals were to follow me in a separate vehicle on my daily rounds. They would park outside the buildings where I stopped but would not follow me inside.

In New York, the prosecutors were under the impression that the order meant I was to be bodily surrounded by marshals at all times, and I was aware of this perception. So, whenever any of the New York prosecutors came to California, I had the marshals stick closer to my side. Then, when the prosecutors left, the marshals were sent back to the trail car.

This unusual arrangement with the U.S. marshal's office allowed me to become almost a friend of those who shadowed me. They were decent men who worked hard, and I liked them, so I did my best to make their job easy and let them know that I wasn't going to get out of line. I even alerted them in advance of my schedule so that they could be properly attired.

"I'm going to the beach tomorrow, so bring your shorts," I advised them one afternoon. The marshals appeared the following morning dressed in swimsuits and carrying picnic gear.

"We're going to see the Dodgers tonight," I announced a week later. "I've got box seats for everyone."

On one occasion, the officers became disoriented by the plethora of white Mercedes in Los Angeles and followed the wrong car. I had to double back and hunt them down. Cammy and I chased them up Wilshire Boulevard.

"Hey, where are you guys going?" I shouted at a stoplight. "I turned on Beverly Glen!"

They followed us sheepishly and thankfully.

When Miquelle was christened at Westwood Hills Christian Church, we invited the marshals and their wives to the event and to the party afterward.

– 12 –

Cammy was happy about the halfway house arrangement. The only negative aspect was the knowledge that the clock was ticking with each day. We used even this knowledge to our advantage, making good use of our time together.

Being unable to spend the night with her was unpleasant, but we adjusted. I'd arrive around 6:30 A.M. and slip into bed beside her so we could wake up together. It was during this time that Cammy became pregnant again. This time, the news depressed her. She wanted only one baby at a time, and I was on my way to prison for up to ten years.

I didn't share Cammy's dismay over her pregnancy. As the home pregnancy kit registered dark blue, a big grin formed on my face.

"That's the bluest blue I've ever seen," I quipped. "I don't think there's any doubt."

We celebrated by moving from the condo in Brentwood to a luxury apartment in the exclusive Mirabella building on Wilshire Boulevard in Westwood. I wanted a complex with security guards, and the Mirabella, with its elaborate closed-circuit television security system, seemed perfect.

One evening, as we huddled in our new bedroom, watching television, I flipped through the channels and caught the beginning of the classic movie *Spartacus*. I remembered having enjoyed it years before and wanted Cammy to watch it with me. For the next four hours, we sat mesmerized as Kirk Douglas and Jean

Simmons played out the tragic love story of the former Thracian slave who led an uprising against the Roman Empire in 73 B.C.

I was especially moved by a scene near the end where, prior to going to battle, the powerful gladiator/warrior Spartacus tells Varinia (Simmons) that his love for her has weakened him and made him feel fear for the first time in his life. Varinia responds that he is so strong he could be weak with her. Those lines really hit home. I had avoided falling in love all my life because I equated love with weakness—specifically, the loss of control and the fear of doing jail time. I was now in the grip of a still new love and weeks away from prison. Yet somehow, I felt I would be all right. When the burdens facing me became too heavy to bear alone, I could let my guard down and tap into Cammy's strength. That didn't make me weak, and it didn't make me any less a man. Jean Simmons had assured me of that. Like Spartacus, I was strong enough to be weak with Cammy.

As I watched the tortured Spartacus dying on a cross and Varinia standing below him, crying, clutching his feet, and lifting their baby son so the gladiator could see the child before he died, my mood shifted between the sorrow of the movie, the uncertainty of my own life, and the comfort that I didn't have to face the future alone.

"With you, Cammy, I can be a man and be weak," I told her, echoing Spartacus. "I can be strong, and I can cry. I never thought I could be that way with anybody."

— 13 —

The halfway house segment of my sentence was to last three months, but my intention was to extend it for as long as possible. In fact, my ultimate goal was to spend my entire sentence that way. I argued that I couldn't earn the government its $10 million if I was in jail. Better I be given the freedom to make movies and build profitable new businesses, I reasoned.

Whether the feds intended to accept this or not, my limited freedom ended abruptly when Brian Ross and his NBC news crew flew to Los Angeles to update their viewers on "The Franzese Story." Ross and company spotted me cruising down Wilshire Boulevard in a white Eldorado convertible, all but singing Frank Sinatra's "Summer Wind." They videotaped me from a van, then later shot my marshal friends abandoning their post in front of my condominium to go on an extended coffee break. (I had told them I wasn't leaving the house anymore that day.) Ross and his producer, Ira Silverman, intercut my seemingly carefree L.A. lifestyle with scenes of shackled inmates in grimy federal prisons. When the segment aired, Ross pointed out the contrast between how most federal prisoners do time and how I was doing time.

The moment I saw the broadcast, I knew my freedom had ended. Sure enough, the following day I received a call to report to the U.S. marshal's office in Los Angeles. I told Cammy that I just might have to return to New York. I tried to hide my great disappointment at this turn of events and my concern over what it meant, but she could tell that I was very troubled.

As I was leaving, I walked the long hallway of our condominium like I was going to the gallows. Cammy stood and watched me from the door. Just before entering the elevator, I turned and flashed her a weak smile.

"I'll be back."

I would keep that promise—but only after forty-five months.

At the marshal's office, I was cuffed, driven to the airport, and put on an American Airlines flight to New York.

"Relax, pal," I told a nervous American Airlines clerk at the gate. "I'm in for tax fraud. I'm not a murderer or anything."

The passengers similarly gawked at my handcuffs as the marshals paraded me through the cabin to my seat in the back.

In New York, I was brought before the miffed Judge Nickerson, who had no doubt seen the NBC news report. Not surprisingly, the judge ended the halfway house arrangement and ordered me back to prison. I was bused to the Otisville federal corrections facility near Middletown, New York. My freedom had ended so fast that I had been unable to schedule the water baptism I so desired.

— 14 —

Otisville wasn't bad. It had a large exercise yard and reminded me somewhat of Hofstra University. Half the prisoners were Italian, and a good percentage were mob guys or mob associates. One of my crew members, Frankie Gangster, was there. The Italians and the Chinese controlled the kitchen and took turns making lunch and dinner. The food was excellent.

The plea agreement had stated that I would be allowed to serve my sentence in California, but the final decision lay with the Federal Bureau of Prisons. The prison authorities were not held to plea bargain deals. Once they had me, they owned me.

"I've got good news and bad news," I told Cammy over the phone. "The good news is that I'll be coming home. The bad news is that I don't know when. It looks like it's going to take a while to get back to California."

"Then I'm coming there," she said.

"No, don't come," I pleaded.

"I want to see you," she insisted. "I'm coming."

Cammy, Irma, and the baby flew to New York, then took a limousine to the upstate prison. She stayed a week at the Holiday Inn, eating her meals at Swensen's and Denny's.

The only negative point at Otisville came near the end of my two-week stay there. One day, just before I entered the visitors' area to see Cammy, a guard came over.

"What are you doing with that ring?" he asked, pointing at my diamond wedding ring. "That's not on your personal belongings list."

"They must have overlooked it," I said. "I'm only going to be here a few more days."

"You'll have to give it to me," he said.

"No way," I argued. "I'll give it to my wife in the visiting room."

"I've got to take it," he said. "You don't know what can happen. An expensive ring like that—Another prisoner might cut off your finger while you're sleeping and take it."

"Give me a break!" I said. "I'll take my chances. Nobody's going to take my ring."

"Turn it over," he insisted.

We argued for a few minutes, but he refused to allow me to give the ring to Cammy. That really made me angry. Finally, I relented because Cammy was waiting and I thought the guard might cancel the visit if I didn't hand over the ring. That was the last I ever saw of the $2,000 ring.

After Cammy returned to California, I was transferred to a federal prison in Lewisburg, Pennsylvania, and was assigned to K-Dorm, a basement dungeon out of some Stephen King novel. The bottom floor at Lewisburg had previously been condemned, but had been reopened after a riot at a nearby Washington, D.C., prison ended with the prisoners burning the place down. They shipped two hundred fifty of the one-thousand-plus D.C. prisoners to Lewisburg and dumped them into the basement, which was nothing more than a large army-style barracks with exposed pipes and rows and rows of filthy bunks. There were no bars or individual cells. Everyone just wandered around, made noise, argued, picked fights, and got on each other's nerves.

The food was so bad at Lewisburg that I ate only one meal a day. In fact, it was such a hellhole that I insisted that Cammy not visit me there.

I did have some friends on the more civilized floors above us. Among them were Tony West and James "Jimmy the Gent"

Burke. West owned a bar and restaurant next to my brother-in-law's Italian restaurant, Trattoria Siciliana, on Second Avenue and Twenty-Ninth Street in Manhattan. Burke was the Lucchese family associate Robert De Niro played in the movie *GoodFellas*. I wasn't sure why West was in, but Burke had been convicted of murdering Richie Eaton, one of his partners in the infamous $6 million Lufthansa Airlines theft at Kennedy Airport in 1978. Eaton had been found frozen solid in a refrigeration truck. Burke would place cigarettes, candy bars, books, or postage stamps in a small bag, tie a long string to it, drop it out an upstairs window, and lower it to me through a window in the shower room. I didn't smoke, but cigarettes and candy were like money in prison. I was able to trade them to other prisoners in exchange for their phone time.

K-Dorm was a holding area for prisoners being sent somewhere else. The flights out were every Tuesday and Thursday, and the list of those scheduled to leave was posted after midnight the same morning. Everyone wanted to get out of there so badly that we all awoke after midnight on those mornings and trudged to the board to see if we might be on the list. Finally, after three weeks, my name was posted. I took a two-hour bus ride to an airport somewhere, then turned around and took a two-hour ride right back to the prison. Apparently the plane had broken down. I could not get out until the following day.

I was being sent to El Reno, Oklahoma, another paradise. There I was placed in the hole (in isolation) for an entire week. I passed the time reading my Bible. I was certainly interested in learning more about God at that point, but my Bible reading had not yet reached the level of impact or intensity that it would later.

Cammy surprised me by flying in from Los Angeles. When I was told that I had a visitor, I thought it must be a mistake. When I eventually realized that it was no mistake, I asked permission to shower before seeing her because I was so grubby from my incarceration. Even then, I must have presented a horrid sight. My hair was long and unruly, and my beard was dark and stubbled. I was wearing baggy pants with huge cuffs, black shoes with rubber soles, and a khaki shirt, and I had lost fifteen pounds.

"You look like a homeboy," Cammy joked.

"You should have seen me before I took a shower," I said. "I couldn't come out that way."

— 15 —

Meanwhile, back East, things were looking grim. Undercover agents spotted my father having dinner at Laina's Restaurant in Jericho, Long Island, with a convicted gambler and loan shark named Joseph Caridi. According to Nassau County Assistant Director Attorney Elaine Jackson Stack, Caridi interrupted his meal to collect a usurious loan payment from one of the agents. My father's parole was subsequently revoked for the second time, once again for associating with known felons. He was shipped to a federal penitentiary in Petersburg, Virginia, for eight more years, beginning in April 1986.

Mom was beyond grief. For the first time, both her husband and her son were in prison. And corrections officials made sure that Dad and I were never at the same prison. I felt helpless. Locked away myself, there was nothing I could do for him. That hurt as much as anything else.

After my week in the hole at El Reno, I was transferred to a new prison facility, this one in Phoenix, Arizona. That was as close to California as I was to get for the next four months. Because of its newness, the Federal Correctional Institution in north Phoenix was sparkling clean.

"My mother could do time here," I joked to Cammy, trying to ease her mind.

The farther I got from New York, the more my mob background seemed to affect people. The day I arrived, the prison's chief lieutenant summoned me to his office.

"This is mah prison," the beefy Texan drawled. "You ain't gonna come here and take ovah."

"Hey, I don't recall sending you a resume for a job," I countered. "I'm just a prisoner. I'm not taking over anything. In fact, you can keep me in lockdown twenty-four hours a day if you want. Just slip my food in the door and let me out for visits. I just want to do my time and get out of here."

After that, the guards and I got along fine.

Cammy flew in every weekend on America West Airlines and stayed at the Westcourt Hotel. Her visits were made doubly pleasant by the prison's outdoor patio area. As the two of us enjoyed the sun and the beautiful Arizona winter, we amused ourselves by observing the domestic situation of one of my fellow inmates. The American Indian was married to twin sisters and had a girlfriend on the side. The three women visited him every weekend, sharing their time and presenting him with an assortment of children.

At Phoenix, I met and befriended Jeffrey MacDonald, the former Green Beret captain and military doctor convicted in 1979 of killing his twenty-four-year-old wife and two daughters, ages two and five, at their Fort Bragg, North Carolina, home in 1970. I found the doctor to be a pleasant man who frequently worked out in the prison's exercise yard and staunchly maintained his innocence despite a best-selling book, *Fatal Vision*, and television movie that claimed otherwise. Since Dr. MacDonald was more intelligent and educated than the average prisoner, we were able to converse on a wide range of topics. For the most part, I believed MacDonald's claim of innocence. But every once in a while, when the setting sun hit the doctor's eyes, I detected a strange glint, an odd spark that made me wonder.

"Cammy, that man two tables over, to your right—that's Jeffrey MacDonald," I said during one of her visits.

Cammy, who had read *Fatal Vision*, shuddered as if a breath of frigid air had blown over her.

"He gives me the chills," she said, oblivious to the irony that Dr. MacDonald could point me out to *his* visitors, and they would probably get worse chills.

Despite the pleasant visiting circumstance and the almost college campus atmosphere of Phoenix, the distance from Los Angeles made the trips tiring for Cammy, and when she was eight months pregnant, her doctor ordered her to stay put. I told my attorneys to push harder to get me to Los Angeles. Finally, the order came through, and I was sent to Terminal Island, a federal facility near San Pedro that was a forty-five-minute drive from the Mirabella.

"Baby, I'm home," I told Cammy over the phone after I arrived.

"Home" was better than most of the other prisons I'd been in and was certainly survivable.

My new home, however, turned out to be anything but a pleasant experience for Cammy. The facility was grossly over-crowded, and she would often have to wait in a line of unruly visitors for up to two hours every time she wanted to see me (three times a week). By the second week, she realized that it had taken less time and stress for her to fly to Phoenix and take a cab to the prison there than it did to see me at Terminal Island. But after fighting so hard to get close to Los Angeles, it was too late for me to ask for a transfer. I wouldn't have anyway. Knowing Cammy was nearby compensated for the poor conditions.

— 16 —

I requested and almost was granted permission to attend the birth of our second child, but two days before Cammy went into labor, the New York prosecutors overruled that decision, deeming me to be such a high-level organized crime figure that I should not be afforded any privileges whatsoever. Fortunately, this time Cammy didn't need her human scratching pole. She was in labor only four hours, and this birth was a breeze compared to the first. We had a second Cammy-look-alike daughter, Amanda, born January 22, 1987.

"I hope you're not upset that it's not a boy," Cammy said when I called.

"No, baby, I'm not upset at all," I assured her.

Since Terminal Island was my long-term facility, I was given a job there. After some basic training, I was designated a "psychiatric aide" and was assigned to B-Dorm, the prison's psychiatric ward. It was just like *One Flew Over the Cuckoo's Nest*, only worse. Every day, I'd have to ride herd over the crazies. I'd assist the doctors, prevent the patients from attacking the nurses or each other, and do my best to keep things at a tolerably insane level. None of that was easy.

The characters in B-Dorm were unbelievable. One guy had taken female hormones in preparation for a sex-change operation, then he changed his mind at the last minute and took male hormones to reverse the effect. The male hormones made him grow hair all over his body, and he looked like a monkey. This seesaw act with his gender must have cooked his brain, because he was a mess. One minute, he would be a woman, giggling and flirting with some of the men, and the next moment, he'd be a macho man. He was in prison because he had written a threatening letter to President Ronald Reagan. He hadn't signed the letter, but his boyfriend turned him in after they had an argument.

Another man thought he *was* President Reagan, and he played the part pretty well. He was a mad professor type with disheveled hair and clothes, but he talked intelligently about government and world affairs. It sounded like he'd once been a real politician. His main problem was that he had a thing about stuffing trash into mailboxes, and that's why he was in prison. He was caught dumping garbage into a blue postal box. In prison, he'd sound good one minute, espousing his presidential decrees, then the next minute, he'd try to sneak off and dump junk down the prison's mail slot.

"Hey, Prez," I'd say. "What are you doing?"

He'd get this weird grin on his face and try to hide the garbage behind his back.

"I'm carrying out my presidential duties," he'd say.

"No, you're not," I countered. "You're stuffing trash in the mail slot again. Cut it out now. That's how you got in trouble in the first place. What's with you and this garbage thing?"

He never offered an explanation.

For a while, the constant tension and anxiety of never knowing what some B-Dorm lunatic was going to do next made the time pass and helped get me through the long days. After about eight months of that, though, it had become so mentally and physically taxing that I requested a transfer out of there before I began stuffing trash down mail slots along with the Prez.

I was able to form a long-lasting friendship with Kelly Hamilton, another psychiatric aide. Hamilton was better known in the Northwest as "the I-5 Bandit." The way he told it, he was watching the Steve McQueen and Ali MacGraw movie *The Getaway* one afternoon and decided to spice up his life by becoming a bank robber like McQueen. A bright guy, Hamilton successfully robbed a string of banks along Interstate 5 before getting caught. He never used a weapon. He just handed the teller a note demanding cash, smiled, and made off with the money, usually just a few thousand dollars—enough to get him to the next town. He was tried, convicted, and sentenced to twenty years. Character-wise, the I-5 Bandit was the most stand-up guy I met in prison, and our daily battles with the denizens of the psychiatric ward helped solidify our friendship. Hamilton was released from prison in the mid-1990s, after serving some fourteen years. To this day, I consider him to be a very decent human being and a most trusted friend.

There were other prisoners at Terminal Island who I wanted nothing to do with. One afternoon in the prison yard, I ran into someone who looked familiar. When he saw me, he nearly freaked out. It wasn't until later that I realized it was Henry Hill, the lowlife Lucchese family associate from the book *Wiseguy* and the movie *Goodfellas.* I barely recognized Hill because he now looked so old, broken, and haggard. He was no Ray Liotta, the actor who played him in the movie. Hill had wandered in and out of the Witness Protection Program after ratting on everybody he knew, including my friends Paulie Vario and Jimmy Burke, and he was now in jail for crimes he'd committed while back on the street.

Soon, the prison's chief lieutenant, Henry Navarra, called me into his office. "Michael, Henry Hill spotted you in the yard and came in here as white as a ghost."

"I thought I recognized him," I said.

"He demanded to be put into solitary," Navarra told me. "He says you'll kill him."

"I'm not gonna touch that guy," I said. "He's got nothing on me. He's not worth killing."

But Hill remained so terrified that they shipped him out within the week to another prison facility.

— 17 —

The officers at Terminal Island treated me well—sometimes too well. Some of them offered to take me out for a night on the town. They were actually going to sneak me in and out of the prison. I told them they had to be crazy. I always tried to treat them with respect. In return, they would afford me some perks that were small by social standards, but huge within the confines of prison society: extra visits, more access to the telephone, better food, a color television in my cell. One time, a rather grumpy unit manager confiscated my television. While she was giving me a verbal discipline session in her office, another television was being delivered to my cell.

Another time, after being transferred from Terminal Island to the Boron federal prison in Victorville, California, I was allowed to leave on an eight-hour pass. There was a mistake in the paperwork that said I was to return the following day instead of that same evening. When I returned eight hours later, I knew I was going to have trouble. Prison guards don't like to do paperwork unless they have to.

"Franzese, get out of here," the guard at the gate said. "You're not due back until tomorrow. Nobody comes back early. You must be nuts."

"The return date is a mistake," I argued.

"If it says tomorrow, that's when you return. Go home," the guard ordered.

I thought of spending the night with Cammy at a hotel in nearby Silverlake, then thought better of it. Someone could have caught the mistake during the night, and they would have had a fugitive warrant out for me by dawn. They could have arrested me as an escaped felon and ruined my chances for parole. I had to get back inside that prison.

I argued with the guard some more, but he wouldn't let me in. It seemed that the only way I could get back into that jail was to break in. What a twist that would have been! Eventually, I convinced the guard to fetch the lieutenant.

The lieutenant read my orders and told me to come back the next day.

"Look, you can put me in the hole," I offered. "You don't have to do the paperwork until tomorrow. Just let me back in."

Finally, he relented—reluctantly—and I avoided the potential catastrophe.

My fellow prisoners, almost to the man, wanted to join my gang. I never had any problems with anyone in any of the prisons. Made men are considered kings among criminals, and the strict underworld social structure holds true in prison much the same as it does on the outside.

I could have taken advantage of the standard business opportunities in prison, from bringing in illegal contraband to directing criminal activities on the outside, but I declined. All I wanted was extra visits and phone privileges, my television, and sometimes a better meal. Other than that, I played it straight. I wanted to rack up all the gain time I could get. Each day I was a good prisoner, I would get two days knocked off of my sentence. If I stayed out of trouble, I could be free in three and a half years. And that thought consumed me and guided my every move. I had too much to live for now to spend more time needlessly behind bars.

— 18 —

Shortly before Thanksgiving, 1987, I was roused out of my bunk at Terminal Island early one morning by an unfamiliar guard.

"Wake up," the corrections officer demanded. "Pack your things. You're leaving."

I instinctively glanced at my watch. It was just before 3:00 A.M. This was not a good sign.

"Why?" I asked.

"You're on the list, Franzese," the man said, showing me a sheet of official-looking paperwork.

I knew that statement was probably the full extent of the guard's knowledge. Everyone had his job in the rigidly organized prison. The answers that morning would have to emerge in bits and pieces as I was processed through the system.

It took a surprisingly long time to pack, and I marveled at how much I had accumulated in my one-room home. The guard kept rushing me, but I gathered my possessions at my own pace. A shaving kit. Soap. Notebooks. Legal paperwork. Photographs.

Letters and cards from Cammy. A few items of clothing. And my books—*Fatal Vision, Iacocca, Born Again* (by President Nixon's former special counsel Chuck Colson, who served time on a Watergate-related charge), and some escapist novels by Sidney Sheldon and Jackie Collins.

I was escorted through the dark prison and taken to the receiving and discharging room.

"What's going on?" I asked the officer there.

"You're being transferred," he said.

"Where?"

The man looked at me, paused, and flashed a sympathetic expression.

"Marion, Illinois."

I recoiled. Marion means nothing to most people, and few could even find it on a map, but every two-bit burglar knows the significance of the place. Marion was, at the time, the location of the only Level Six federal prison in the United States: maximum security and beyond, absolute lockdown twenty-four hours a day, home for 350 of those whom the federal prison system viewed as their most dangerous inmates.

Marion, Illinois, is also the last whip the federal corrections system uses against recalcitrant prisoners. Even Death Row inmates and lifers have to fear something in order to be controlled, and Marion is the sword of punishment that hangs over the heads of every federal prisoner. This was terrible news indeed.

"What for?" I asked.

The guard shrugged. He didn't know. I was just on the list.

My thoughts spun, and the first of them was of Cammy. She was scheduled to visit me later that same day. If she arrived and found me gone, she'd panic. And then, when she learned where I was being sent, she'd *really* panic. It didn't occur to me that a young Christian girl like Cammy wouldn't know Marion, Illinois, from Omaha, Nebraska. Normally, she wouldn't have, but my wife was no longer the innocent person she'd been when we met. Two years of standing in jailhouse visitors' lines, chatting with wives, lovers, parents, and children of other inmates, had educated her on the prison system. I was sure she must now know what the levels meant and what the differences were between Level One and Level Five.

There was no doubt in my mind that Cammy had heard of Level Six, one level above hell. The guards at Marion were rumored to be as twisted and sadistic as the prisoners. They sometimes wore full riot gear, complete with flak jackets, helmets, Darth Vader face masks, gloves, and heavy boots. They often carried pistols, rifles, and shotguns, along with three-foot-long clubs with ends weighted by steel beads.

I had to call Cammy. I had to ease her fears, even if my own were running wild at the moment. I would ask her to contact my attorney so that he could find out what was happening and then take measures to stop it. This task would not only take her mind off of the perceived horrors of Marion; it would make her feel, rightly or wrongly, that the process could be thwarted. As soon as I could get to a phone, I would call.

As I waited, I tried to guess what had sparked this latest development. An obvious answer came quickly to mind. An edition of *Life* magazine with a lengthy article about me had hit the stands three days before. I had consented to a rare interview, and the story was given big play. *Life* proclaimed me "the mob's young genius" and once again hinted at special treatment.

The *Life* article detailed my wheeling and dealing with the government and my unusual plea agreement. It also claimed that Cammy had given me an ultimatum to quit the mob and had threatened to leave me if I refused. That part of the story infuriated me, because Cammy had made no such demand.

I steered my thinking back on course. Prison officials must have read the article, thought my life was in danger because of its "Quitting the Mob" headline, and decided to ship me off to Marion for my own protection and to avoid liability.

"What can I do?" the receiving and discharging clerk said. "It came over the teletype. It's a writ."

A supervisor appeared, and I confronted him. "How can you writ me to Marion?"

The supervisor seemed surprised. "Marion? Who said anything about Marion? You're going to Chicago."

It had probably been an honest mistake. Chicago, Illinois—Marion, Illinois. The other guy had just assumed that I was being sent to the worst prison in America. Chicago was still too close to Marion for comfort, but the supervisor insisted there was no connection. I was then able to breathe a sigh of relief.

Chicago, welcome as that news was, created a whole new set of confusing scenarios.

"Why Chicago?" I asked.

"I don't know," the supervisor said. "You have to appear before a grand jury on Tuesday, so we have to get you there. That's all I know."

It must be a mistake, I thought.

I had made no agreement to testify in Chicago. I *couldn't* testify. With La Cosa Nostra, to testify was to die, or worse, to be imprisoned in the Witness Protection Program the rest of life.

"I've never been to Chicago," I said.

The supervisor knew what I meant. Chicago had its own mob hierarchy dating back to the days of Al Capone. That was the turf of Anthony "Joe Batters" Accardo and the late Sam Giancana and their crime families. I had nothing to do with them.

It was mid-morning before the prison bus arrived at the small San Pedro airport. I still hadn't been given any answers, nor was I allowed to get anywhere near a telephone. I asked another prisoner to call Cammy and have her phone my attorney. I was confident that by the time I got to a phone, my lawyer would already be on the job.

Handcuffed and manacled, I was herded onto a beat-up 707 sitting on the San Pedro runway. The marshals' jets were generally broken-down machines inherited from some other department or confiscated from drug dealers. The insides had been altered just enough to shift from carrying illegal freight to transporting human cargo. The jet was slowly filling with criminals of one sort or another being transferred around the federal prison system for whatever reason.

By takeoff time, the lumbering jet was packed with nearly a hundred convicts. Most of them quietly accepted their fate. A few, however—those who didn't quite know their fate, those who knew their fate and didn't like it, or those who were afraid of flying—had to be dragged onto the aircraft, screaming in anger or terror.

As the battered 707 lifted off, the anguished wails of those prisoners acted to drown out the disquieting creaks of the old jet's fuselage and engines. In a strange way, that eased the minds of the other prisoners. Screaming was somehow better than rattling motors.

— 19 —

Lunch was served shortly after the jet leveled off. I struggled to maneuver my handcuffs enough to be able to eat the baloney sandwich, apple, and cookie I'd been given. Some of the food ended up on my shirt or bouncing down my chest to the seat or floor. Most of my fellow prisoners seemed to be more skilled at eating with cuffs, and they fared far better.

Shuffling slavelike off to the restroom, I took in a full panorama of society's underbelly. Instead of picture-perfect families, foreign tourists, college students, and the suited businessmen who populate most commercial flights, each seat on "Convict Airlines" was occupied by some craven-faced criminal with hard eyes. Most were forgotten men who'd started life with nothing and had sunk even lower since. I saw the same pathos in every face, and it made me wonder if I, too, now looked that way. I decided the first thing I would do in the tiny restroom would be to get as close as possible to the mirror and search for any sign that prison life was eroding my features.

As it turned out, there was no mirror. A mirror could be broken and turned into a weapon. No one on the plane needed to see himself anyway. After relieving myself, I leaned over to flush the stainless steel toilet. Instead of swirling down the dark hole, the foul water shot back up and splashed across my face, hair, and shirt. I shuddered in revulsion and quickly washed off as much of the fluid as I could. But no matter what I did, I couldn't kill the creepy feeling, or the smell.

"The mob's young genius," I thought as I returned to my seat. The billionaire Cosa Nostra prince, ushering in a new age of smooth, white-collar crime. People were reading those sentiments in *Life* magazine at that very moment. And there I was, getting splashed with rancid sewage on a "Convict Airlines" flight to nowhere.

A couple of hours after takeoff, the jet's whining engines changed their pitch. I could feel the plane descending—apparently by design. It was too early to be arriving in Chicago, but that hadn't been a consideration. Most prison flights landed in El Reno, which acts as a way station for convicts in transit.

I was bused to the El Reno holding pen. No one there had any answers for me either. No one there ever did. El Reno was just a post office for the human equivalent of junk mail.

I was finally allowed to get in line for a telephone at 11:45 P.M. It was Friday night, so the authorities knew a prisoner's chances of reaching a troublesome attorney had diminished. With me, they hedged their bets even further. Phone privileges at El Reno shut down at midnight. Although there were a dozen or so phones up against the far wall, the last-minute crunch had resulted in lines of six or more agitated convicts snaking out from each phone.

For a prisoner, every call is an emergency, and one con's predicament is no more urgent than another's. Pleading for a chance to cut to the front of the line is usually fruitless and can sometimes be hazardous. Still, made men have an advantage, even in unfamiliar prisons. I pulled rank, promptly made it to the front of the line and called Cammy.

She tried to sound calm, but the quaver in her voice betrayed her emotions. Her day had been as emotionally charged as mine. The Terminal Island inmate had come through and called her, and she had immediately contacted my attorney, Bruce Kelton. As I predicted, she had focused her thoughts on coming to my aid, and Kelton had assured her that he would take control.

Cammy was concerned with having to uproot the family and move to Illinois to be near my new prison. Although she was ready to do this without hesitation, she wasn't happy about the prospect. I told her I didn't think a move was going to be necessary. I couldn't elaborate, and she didn't force me to. The conversation lasted only a few minutes. I wanted to save my remaining time for Kelton.

Bruce Kelton was formerly the assistant chief of the Los Angeles Organized Crime Strike Force (OCSF). In the world of attorneys, experience in a specialized government field gives prosecutors valuable training that enables them to do an about-face in the private sector. State prosecutors, skilled at convicting thieves, rapists, and murderers, become defense attorneys and work to free wealthy thieves, rapists, and murderers. Federal prosecutors learn how to free federal criminals. Drug task force prosecutors learn how to best defend drug kingpins. IRS attorneys learn how to defend against IRS investigations.

In the old days, this legal seesaw didn't impress the mob. The first-generation mobsters were too full of rage, revenge, and paranoia to trust a former government attorney. They preferred to rely on traditional mob lawyers or family members with law degrees. That changed as the second-generation mobsters became educated and sophisticated, and as the overcrowded court system became even more of a legal casino. Instead of public trials, prosecutors and defense attorneys increasingly faced off in cubicles and plea-bargained. In such an atmosphere, those in need of a good defense attorney learned that connections were more important than sharp legal minds or courtroom skills.

Bruce Kelton had given notice of his pending career change in March of 1986. He was well-liked by his bosses and well-respected by law enforcement agencies, and his credibility and ethics were unquestioned. I had been alerted to his professional movements by New York OCSF man Jerry Bernstein, the same Jerry Bernstein who had hunted me so feverishly. Bernstein recommended Kelton. Kelton retired from the Los Angeles OCSF on May 1, 1987, and I contacted him on May 2 and hired him a short time later.

I reached Kelton now just before midnight at his Los Angeles home. Cammy had called him late Friday afternoon. With the week quickly winding down, he had been unable to learn more than the Terminal Island supervisor. There was a writ and some hoped-for grand jury testimony, but the subject remained a mystery. He told me to hang tight and he'd stay on the case.

The corrections officer began barking orders to end all the telephone conversations, and the prisoners in line grumbled. I ignored the guards, talked for another thirty seconds, and then hung up. The worst was yet to come.

— 20 —

At the federal detention center in Oakdale, Louisiana, known as "La Isla Bonita" for its unusually colorful décor, and at the notorious Atlanta federal penitentiary, the fallout from the ill-fated 1980 Freedom Flotilla between Mariel, Cuba, and Miami, Florida, was about to explode.

On the Friday I was flown to El Reno, the United States and Cuba reached a tentative agreement for the deportation of some three thousand Cuban prisoners, whom Fidel Castro had shipped to America among the hundred thousand refugees who arrived during the flotilla. In a reverse of John Milton's statement about preferring to rule in hell rather than serve in heaven, the Cubans preferred to be incarcerated in an American prison rather than roam free in Castro's Cuba. With baffling speed, these prisoners took control of both prisons, taking 122 hostages and torching sections of the historical Atlanta facility, the jail that had once housed Al Capone.

The rioting Marielitos had a ripple effect across the entire federal prison system, and everything was frozen while officials dealt with the Cuban crisis. For me, being in transit during a prison riot, even a distant riot, was like being in an elevator in a tall building when the electricity goes off. I was suddenly locked in place in the massive receiving and discharging corral at El Reno. Cots were brought in so the masses of stalled prisoners could sleep. It was a mess—even for a prison.

On Monday, Kelton was able to trace the writ to Howard Pearl, a federal prosecutor in Chicago. Kelton knew Pearl from his strike-force days and called him. Pearl, knowing he was speaking with a former strike-force prosecutor, didn't bother with coyness. He told Kelton they wanted me to testify in the Norby Walters case.

Pearl didn't have to explain what this case was about. Norby Walters was a onetime bar owner, entertainment manager, and booking agent. By then, he had become a successful sports agent. He was a longtime friend and music business partner of Dad's, and he partied with other top mobsters at his various bars and nightclubs. Walters was flamboyant, gregarious, and quick to entertain friends and strangers with an endless supply of war stories culled from a lifetime of colorful activities. One of his favorite stories was how he got his name.

Born Norby Meyer, Norby and his brother Walter opened a jazz club in Brooklyn in 1953 called Norby & Walter's Bel-Air.

The ampersand on the club's neon sign burned out, and the brothers didn't bother to replace it, so everyone began referring to the club as "Norby Walter's." Quick to jump on a good thing, Norby changed his name to Norby Walters, and his brother likewise changed his name to Walter Walters.

Norby Walters' biggest claim to fame was managing or booking superstar black recording acts through his successful agency, Norby Walters Associates. His main associate was his silent partner, my father. They set up the agency in 1968 and were fifty-fifty partners. Norby acquired a notable list of clients, including Janet Jackson, Rick James, Dionne Warwick, Lionel Richie, the Commodores, the Spinners, the Four Tops, Cameo, Miles Davis, Luther Vandross, Patti LaBelle, Kool and the Gang, the New Edition, and Ben Vereen. Although he was a Jew, Walters had a special talent for communicating with blacks. He could slap hands, talk and walk jive, and blend in with his clients. He was quick to provide his stars with seed money to help launch their careers, and this endeared him to them.

Walters' latest venture had been to buy his way into the sports agency business. It was a perfect target—lucrative and totally unpoliced. Anyone with a smooth tongue or some ready cash could convince a disadvantaged athlete to let him be his agent. Once the talent was signed, the agent could cut himself in for a five percent share of a professional sports contract that might total as much as $20 million. Better yet, there was little skill or knowledge needed for this work beyond recruiting the athletes. The top players' agents set the market each year, depending on how high a player was drafted by the professional teams. All that the other agents had to do was wait until the veteran agents set the year's price range, then sit back and catch the rain of dollars that resulted.

Walters teamed with Lloyd Bloom, a crusty young man with a thick New York accent and a smattering of sports connections. Bloom had been a bouncer at New York's Studio 54 nightclub, once a hot celebrity party favorite. Even though the pair had personalities that clashed like snake oil and ammonia, Walters and Bloom threw in together and formed World Sports and Entertainment, Inc. In 1985, they set out to become big-time sports agents.

Not long after the company's creation, I became a partner in the operation. Aware of the huge contracts being awarded to professional athletes, I felt that it was a solid investment. And what better way would there be to feed the family's gambling and booking operations than to be in direct control of the careers of college and professional athletes? Cammy's brother Dino acted as the bag man for the delivery of my initial investment and took a grocery sack stuffed with cash to Walters' office in the Brill Building on Broadway in Manhattan—the former office of music biz powerbroker Morris Levy, the mob associate my father had chased away from Buddah Records two decades earlier.

For a time, it was money well spent. Business boomed, and within three years, Walters and Bloom had signed forty-three top athletes. Among their catches were such big-name professional football players as Rod Woodson of the Pittsburgh Steelers, Tim McGee of the Cincinnati Bengals, Reggie Rogers of the Detroit Lions, Brent Fullwood of the Green Bay Packers, Tony Woods of the Seattle Seahawks, Terrence Flagler of the San Francisco 49ers, Ronnie Harmon of the Buffalo Bills, and Paul Palmer of the Dallas Cowboys.

During the recruiting process, Walters talked such fluent jive that many of the black athletes who spoke with him over the phone thought the New York Jew was black. And that was no small feat. One athlete told *Sports Illustrated* that Walters affected a walk complete with a juke in his step, like a hip black man.

It wasn't all walk and talk. Walters bragged about introducing the athletes to all the famous music superstars he knew. He sent several of them on trips to New York and Los Angeles, where they mingled, wide-eyed, with the stars. He even took Palmer, a Heisman Trophy candidate, to the Grammy Award ceremonies.

The trouble was, according to prosecutors, the National Collegiate Athletic Association, *Sports Illustrated*, and the targeted athletes, Walters and Bloom went after sports stars the same way Walters had gone after entertainers. They showered the prospects with cash—a total of $800,000 worth, according to Bloom—to get their attention. After that, it was easy to get their signatures on the dotted lines of postdated contracts. This last measure was taken to skirt the law and preserve the athletes' amateur status until they completed their college eligibility. Bankrolling a prospect was perfectly legal when dealing with a hot new singer down at the local club, but it was illegal when dealing with college athletes.

— 21 —

To complicate matters, whenever Walters and Bloom would hit a snag, they invariably brought in some muscle. In the early music days, my father had provided this muscle. His appearance at a meeting was usually all it took for Walters to iron out contractual difficulties, keep an unhappy act from jumping ship, or keep the entertainers' noses out of the books. After my father was imprisoned and I was made, I replaced my father as Walters' muscle.

When Dionne Warwick wanted to cut her ties to Walters in 1982, he called me. I hopped on a jet to Los Angeles, met him, and the two of us went directly to the Sunset Boulevard office of Joe Grant, Warwick's manager. After a few minutes of listening to Walters talk his jive and of Grant explaining that Warwick sought a more "prestigious" agency, I took over. I asked Walters to leave so that Joe and I could chat alone.

"I don't like what I'm hearing." I explained. "I want you to do me a favor. Stay with Norby another six months. Then, if you still have complaints, we'll talk about it again."

Warwick stayed with Walters.

A similar visit between myself and the Jacksons manager, Ron Weisner, nearly resulted in Walters bagging the group's 1981 tour, headed by the skyrocketing Michael Jackson. An unrelated snag killed that deal, allowing another booking firm to take over. I was also called in to lay down the law to the manager of the New Edition when that super group wanted to dump Walters.

Since such activities are commonplace in the mob-saturated entertainment industry, our activities drew little attention. The same couldn't be said for the undeniably corrupt, but less visibly so, world of big-time college sports. The feds got wind of Walters' new sports agency venture, tapped Bloom's telephone, and turned up a bonanza. They taped Bloom threatening to have his mob pals—presumably me—break the valuable arms and legs of a few college football stars who figured they could take the money and then pull a double cross on Walters by signing with another agent. Other athletes told the National Football League Players Association they had received similar threats from Walters. The Packers' Fullwood took it one step further. He testified before a Chicago grand jury that Bloom had threatened to kill his agent, George Kickliter.

In the midst of all these threats, which Walters and Bloom steadfastly denied, Kathe Clements, an associate of Chicago sports agent Steve Zucker, was roughed up in her Chicago office by two hoods wearing ski masks and gloves. Clements, wife of former Notre Dame quarterback Tom Clements, had squabbled with Bloom over Zucker taking three of World Sports and Entertainment's clients. The feds suspected that Walters, Bloom, and their muscleman—me again—were responsible for Clements' beating and intensified their investigation.

Then an incredible thing happened. In March of 1987, Walters had the gall to file suit against some of his former clients for breach of contract—contracts that were illegally postdated and gained through illegal cash payments (which he now wanted repaid). Then he followed this strange action by telling the *Atlanta Constitution* that the players had wronged him by taking his money. This bizarre act was similar to someone calling the police to report that an acquaintance has robbed him of his cocaine stash.

When the authorities came down on Walters and Bloom, a nasty scandal erupted that quickly became national news. Sports reporters dubbed it "Jockgate" and covered every angle of it. Walters and Bloom were made to symbolize everything corrupt and evil in big-time college and professional athletics.

The more press it received, the bigger the case became for the hotly pursuing prosecutors. When the lawmen connected Walters to me and my father, they could hardly conceal their elation. The high-octane element of organized crime invading college athletics fanned the media fires even brighter, and the press, fed by the FBI and Chicago prosecutors, had a field day. The hallowed halls of academia, places like Notre Dame, Miami, Nebraska, Pitt, and Oklahoma, were supposedly being invaded by bent-nosed mobsters.

The last thing I needed was a messy national scandal, especially one that starred me as the chief leg-breaker. Walters and Bloom were already becoming household names. If I was suddenly pegged as the pin-striped mastermind behind their operation, it would open me up to an onslaught of media attention that would all but paint yet another giant bull's-eye on my back. Ambitious prosecutors from New York to Los Angeles would come gunning for me again, and any convict looking to make a deal would be quick to sell me out. This was not part of my plan.

What I failed to realize, viewing the matter from my own perspective, was that the Walters and Bloom case had grown bigger than me. They were getting all the press. The case was in Chicago, not New York, where I had become a household name and favorite target of federal and local law enforcement agencies. Therefore, in the Chicago prosecutors' minds, Walters and Bloom were now the big targets. For the first time in my life, I would be on the other end of things. Instead of being the prized red bowling pin everyone wanted to topple, I was now one of the white pins needed to knock over the red one.

— 22 —

Once I understood what was happening, my next move was to get a better grip on the expected grand jury testimony. The problems that such an appearance presented were enormous. Testifying anywhere about anything is against La Cosa Nostra rules. But that giant dilemma could wait. There was a more immediate problem to deal with. The Jockgate trial wasn't scheduled to take place for two years. That meant that in the meantime the prosecutors might try to stash me in some dreary, overcrowded, inner-city, metro correctional center in Chicago with no exercise field and what amounted to twenty-four-hour lockdown. I wanted no part of that, and it certainly hadn't been part of my plea agreement.

"No way," Bruce Kelton told prosecutor Howard Pearl. He went on to explain that I was already steaming about getting stuck in El Reno during the Cuban riots. I would simply play my ace and take the Fifth. Pearl hinted that such a posture could lead to my indictment in the case and could also result in a contempt-of-court charge. If cited for contempt, I would be held in a Chicago prison for up to three years with no credit toward finishing my federal term.

Kelton explained that we were not shutting the door. We just wanted to establish ground rules before we officially opened communications with him. I wanted to go back to Terminal Island. That was nonnegotiable. Pearl would then be invited to pay me a visit and explain exactly what he wanted. We would discuss it and take it from there. Pearl agreed.

Everything had been worked out in Chicago and Los Angeles. In Atlanta, however, things were still festering. The Cubans were hanging tough, refusing, as the weeks passed, to relinquish control of the eighty-six-year-old facility. When they finally caved in, it took another week for the federal corrections system to clean up the mess and get back to its normal pace. Meanwhile, I sat fuming in El Reno for three more weeks before I was sent "home" to Terminal Island.

The worst part of the ordeal was spending a miserable Thanksgiving Day in El Reno. A slab of some kind of compressed turkey was all I received. At Terminal Island the previous year, at least we'd had a complete dinner with fresh turkey, stuffing, and cranberry sauce.

Pearl and FBI agent George Randolph flew to California during the normally slack workweek between Christmas and New Year's. That action spoke volumes about the importance of the Norby Walters case. The prosecutor and the agent laid out their evidence. They even read to me the transcript of a tape on which Bloom had threatened to break a Texas wide receiver's hands if the athlete signed with another agent. Randolph, an honest straight-shooter who didn't play games, knew the extent of my involvement, how much I had invested with Walters, how Cammy's brother had delivered the cash, and the precise details of the Dionne Warwick, Michael Jackson, and New Edition shakedowns. It didn't take me long to realize that the prosecutors had Walters and Bloom nailed.

Although he wasn't saying it, Pearl also knew that I had little to do with the sports agency or the threats against the athletes. In addition, Pearl had nothing to connect me—or Walters and Bloom, for that matter—to the brutal beating of Kathe Clements. There was little doubt, however, that Walters had been readily dropping my name to push his way around the sports world. And even though I was in prison, I remained Walters' prime muscle. That was enough, the prosecutor explained, to indict me and toss me into the sensational case.

And not only me, but my father as well. At the very least, they wanted Dad to testify about his longtime dealings with Walters. That threat got my attention. My first reaction was to protect Dad.

"My dad's been in jail seventeen years," I protested. "He's sixty-eight years old. Leave him out of this."

Pearl made no promises. It all depended upon how cooperative I was, he said. "We don't want your father. Just between us, we don't even want you. I don't know if we can make a case against you, or if it would stick. But we do have enough to get an indictment."

I briefly tried my "I'm out of it, let me do my time in peace" routine, but I could see that wasn't going to get me anywhere. The Norby Walters case was too big. The Chicago prosecutors, Howard Pearl and Anton Valukas, were in a national goldfish bowl on this one.

I also knew what the game was. It didn't matter what I could testify about. My story made no difference at all. My presence was what mattered. All the prosecutors had to do was connect Walters and Bloom with the mob, and the jury would raise their eyebrows, shudder, and convict the pair of anything the government wanted. I merely had to appear, give my name and mob rank, and admit to being a partner in World Sports and Entertainment, Inc. To help the jury members with their imaginations, and to juice the national headlines, the prosecutors would get me to chat about visiting Weisner and Dionne Warwick's guy Joe Grant on Walters' behalf.

That was it. I wouldn't have to admit to any criminal activity. I wouldn't have to say anything to directly implicate Walters or Bloom. I didn't have to finger them in any criminal act whatsoever. I could testify and still stay semi-clean. The prosecutors would take the ball from there. They would be able to take my testimony, stand before the jury, hum *The Godfather* theme, and paint a portrait of Walters' operation that would make Mario Puzo and Francis Ford Coppola proud.

There was only one problem with this: to testify was to die when it came to the family.

— 23 —

Having gathered their evidence, Pearl and Randolph headed back to Chicago, and then I did some investigating of my own. Despite being in prison, my lines of communication were still operational, and what I learned was distressing. Word on the street was that Bloom was dealing and that he was going to roll on Walters. (This information was good. A year later, *Sports Illustrated* reported that Bloom had made a deal with state prosecutors in Tuscaloosa, Alabama, to testify against Walters in a separate but related case involving a University of Alabama basketball player. If Walters was convicted, Bloom would receive some light sentence, like washing police cars for a week.)

That was the final straw for me. It was apparent that the Chicago prosecutors had Walters and Bloom where they wanted them. Everything they had told me was true. They had the documents, the wiretaps, and the dirty athletes to prove their case, and it was getting too much media attention for them to allow Walters and Bloom to slip away. If the case continued to its logical end, it would not only grow but would also start sucking others down into the muck. I knew what I had to do. A one-line order, complete with the official Colombo stamp, was promptly dispatched to Walters: "Take a plea. End it for all of us."

At the time, Walters could have walked away with eighteen months, Bloom less, and he wouldn't have had to turn. Both could have been paroled in three to six months. But Walters refused.

"Tell Michael they got nothin'—nothin'!" he responded. "I ain't takin' no plea. Tell Michael not to worry. I can beat it. Just tell him not to testify."

Then a second, more urgent, message was sent to Walters through the mob courier system—"Michael strongly suggests that you take a plea. End this!"

Walters refused again.

I was infuriated. Walters had benefited from his mob associations his entire life. He used the mob when it helped him and denied it when it hurt. Now he was disobeying a direct order and putting family members at risk.

The Norby Walters mess was hurting my own future. I was determined to do the minimum, forty months, and get out of prison. Now Walters was putting me into the position of possibly having to do the whole ten years. And that was just my current sentence. If I was dropped into the fetid Jockgate stew, I could have another decade or so tacked on—all to save Norby Walters from doing six months soft time in a case he was going to be convicted in anyway.

"I'm not doing one extra day for Norby Walters," I vowed.

But that vow meant doing the inconceivable—testifying.

The trouble was that the inconceivable clashed with the unthinkable—being locked in a prison cell away from Cammy for up to seventeen more years.

"I'll answer truthfully. No lies," I told Kelton. "Just the honest truth. Norby is an associate of the family. I am his partner. I don't know what Norby did. I never met a single athlete. I met Lloyd Bloom one time. I never heard of Kathe Clements. I was in jail when all this happened. End of story."

There! I had started the ball rolling toward the inconceivable! Now what would happen?

– 24 –

I had more than a year to sit in my cell and contemplate my pending testimony. Messages filtered in from other mob associates about my decision. I was reminded about my oath never to reveal or acknowledge La Cosa Nostra. Yet, at the famous Cosa

Nostra commission trials in New York, the heads of the five families had acknowledged its existence. So that section of the oath appeared to no longer apply.

I briefly considered seeking advice from my father, but I abandoned the idea when I realized how tough the communication would be between two prisoners three thousand miles apart. Short messages could be delivered, but the process didn't allow for give-and-take. I felt that he needed a face-to-face, two-way communication to understand my decision.

Being unable to arrange such a meeting wasn't critical. I knew my father well enough to know exactly what he would say. He would listen, nod his head, and agree to all my arguments. He would agree that the price was too severe to protect Norby Walters. He would agree that Norby wasn't worth making any sacrifice for—much less one so grave. But then, after I had presented my overwhelming case, Dad would furrow his considerable brow and advise me not to testify.

In Dad's thinking, testifying just wasn't right. It wouldn't look good. It would embarrass the family. And most of all, it went against the all-powerful oath. Even though my father himself sometimes questioned allegiance to the oath, he always remained loyal to it.

I knew my father so well that I could almost hear him rendering his judgment.

"We took this oath, Michael, and we're just going to have to live by it," he would say, ignoring the dire consequences. "We made our bed, and now we've got to sleep in it."

This is all so crazy, I thought. *How could my father still feel that way after all he has suffered, after a life squandered in prison, after putting his family through twenty years of pain and financial hardship, and after being forgotten, betrayed, and demoted by his own organization?*

I thought about the oath, the blood oath I had sealed twelve years before. It seemed exciting back then—a secret brotherhood based upon honor and integrity. I had repeated the ominous words and become a made man like my father. As I lay on my prison bed now, Thomas DiBella's words echoed through my mind in disjointed segments: *"If your mother is dying and you are at her bedside, and the boss calls, you leave your mother....If you are ordered to kill—even your best friend—even your father—you do it. No questions. If you fail, you will be killed...."* They were harsh words, but such power was supposed to be tempered with a strong sense of evenhandedness and uncompromising honor.

"Those who obey will be protected; those who disobey will be killed." But it hadn't worked like that. Those who obeyed were sometimes killed, and those who disobeyed often escaped unharmed. Politics, money, and power weighed heavily on serious family matters that should have been determined by the "honorable" code hidden in the oath we all swore to. I hadn't failed the oath, I reasoned, however conveniently; the oath had failed me! It had destroyed my father and mother and brothers and sisters, and now it was trying to destroy me and my family.

And even if someone obeyed, if someone followed the oath without yielding, what good was it? My father had blindly followed. He had never bent. He was the ultimate mob soldier. And what good had it done him? He had been framed for a crime he knew nothing about, for twenty years he had rotted in jail, and he still faced thirty more where those came from.

Some had said that the mob set my father up in the first place. Maybe the enemy wasn't the prosecutors and the FBI but the mob itself.

And still, he kept quiet, for ten then twenty years in prison. He was the iron man, a man of rare honor and integrity. Everybody deserted him, but still he didn't testify. He accepted no plea bargains, no deals—no nothing. He had also not received any lasting parole, just fifty years in prison.

And who cared? Who cared about Sonny Franzese rotting in some Virginia prison? And now *I* was supposed to follow in my father's footsteps?

Even my mother waffled on her stance. She had initially supported my decision, expressing a disdain for Walters and inciting me with tales of how Walters had been disrespectful to her and my father. She repeated how Dad's long imprisonment had torn at her and her family. But Mom could shift directions in the blink of an eye. She confided to others that she was repulsed at the thought of her son testifying. She even went so far as to put me in the same class of men who falsely testified against my father. She proclaimed Norby Walters to be a dear family friend and decreed that I should stay quiet and be a good soldier like my father.

Mom's declarations didn't just sting, they hurt me deeply. I loved her very much. We had been through a lot together, and although we had often clashed, sometimes fiercely, it hadn't changed the way I felt about her.

No matter what Mom or Dad would say, I now saw no honor in remaining silent. Norby wasn't a "brother," just a fringe player who boasted about his organized crime clout whenever it benefited him.

And Norby had disobeyed. Norby broke the code by refusing a direct order to take a plea. Norby wasn't thinking of the good of the family. Norby didn't care if someone had to do an extra seven—or seventy—years. He was trying to save himself from a six-month sentence.

And besides, as much as I loved her, my mother's opinions didn't carry much weight with me anymore. They had been supplanted by my feelings for another Franzese woman—Cammy Franzese. And Cammy needed me out of prison.

— 25 —

In March of 1989, two marshals came to Terminal Island, handcuffed me, and clamped leg irons on me. Then they chauffeured me to Los Angeles International Airport for the trip to Chicago. Stopping at the terminal, they ordered me out of the car.

"I'm not going out like this," I protested, nodding toward the leg irons. "You must be out of your mind!"

"We can't do that," the lead marshal said.

"I'm not shuffling two miles through a crowded airport chained like a slave," I protested. "You can turn around and take me right back to Terminal Island."

The marshals huddled for a few minutes. "Okay, we'll take them off, but if you try to make a run for it, remember, we've got guns."

"Give me a break," I said, not happy with the humiliation. "Just get these stupid things off of me."

The trial of Norby Walters and Lloyd Bloom was a star-studded affair played out before a courtroom mobbed with reporters. The media conglomeration at the U.S. District Court in Chicago was a strange mix. The hard-news reporters were there, covering it as a news story. The sports press was there, covering it as a major sports scandal and reveling in the parade of big-time sports stars who took the stand and testified about wads of dirty money and threats of broken legs, arms, and hands. The longhaired rock press also fought for seats, dispatching reports to *Rolling Stone*, *Billboard*, *Variety*, *Cash Box*, and other music magazines about the music biz angle. They perked up when the Jacksons and Dionne Warwick's people, Weisner and Grant, testified about my visits.

In the midst of all this sensational testimony, I took the stand and hushed the courtroom audience with my mere introduction: "Michael Franzese, capo in the Colombo crime family."

Few of the spectators, even among the hard-bitten journalists, had ever seen a real live Cosa Nostra captain up close, and I could feel the jury hanging on every word as I went through my lines. I talked for ninety minutes on direct, and another sixty on cross-examination, about my partnership with World Sports and Entertainment, my father's involvement with Walters, and my visits with Grant and Weisner. I was the connection that would juice the headlines in the newspapers and magazines. I was the link from the mob to both sports and rock and roll.

As the prosecutors predicted, what I said didn't matter, not even with the media. They were able to fill in the blanks.

The show closed after five weeks, the jury huddled and then threw the book at Walters and Bloom. They were convicted of conspiracy, racketeering conspiracy, conspiracy to commit mail fraud, mail fraud, wire fraud, and extortion. The judge sentenced Walters to five years and Bloom to three. (As it turned out, Walters never served one day in prison. His sentence was later reduced to probation. Bloom was murdered gangland style at his home in Malibu, California, before ever serving a day in prison. His murder was believed to be the result of a drug deal gone bad.)

After the whole affair was over, I returned to Terminal Island, and a few weeks later, I was released. I was sure it was all over and that I could now look forward to the future.

At last, I was a free man, and I could get on with my new life.

– 26 –

One of the most important things I wanted to do after my release was be baptized in water. The ceremony was arranged for Sunday, October 15, 1989, and the scene that day has been vividly described as follows by Dary Matera, co-author of my book, *Quitting the Mob*:

> They were standing high above the congregation, waist-deep in the warm blue water. Bronze organ pipes lined the walls on both sides, occasionally crying out

piercing notes. Above them, the ornate Gothic ceiling was too high to make out the carved rafter patterns and checkerboard bursts of color. Down below, in the water, the two men wore white robes tinged pale crimson by the light bouncing off the blood-red carpet that bathed the entire building.

All eyes riveted on the chiseled features of the younger man, the slight, dark-haired parishioner to the right of Pastor Myron Taylor in the small, watery chamber. Many in the congregation knew who he was and what he was. Openly, they had accepted him into their flock. It was the Christian way. There was even historical precedent that demanded their acceptance: Jesus himself had reached out to the man who had hung beside him on the cross. They all knew the story. It was one of the Bible's most memorable tales, symbolizing forever how easily one can slip into heaven, right up to the last breath of life, simply by believing. One can lead a lifetime of greed, evil, lust, and murder and still escape the postdeath sentence of spending an eternity in a fiery lake merely by whispering a deathbed request to be forgiven.

The example was unmistakably clear. They could argue among themselves about other passages, other verses, and other parables, but not about this one. There was no gray area regarding the thief on the cross. They were thus charged with accepting the stranger into their flock, welcoming him with joyful hearts, smiling when they shook his hand, trying not to let their tension reveal itself through muscles jerked tight down the sides of the neck and around the edges of the mouth.

It was God's way.

But, privately, they doubted.

Privately, many were afraid.

The good people of Westwood Hills Christian Church in the trendy Westwood section of Los Angeles weren't used to a young man like this one among the congregation of their stately, nondenominational church. The old-fashioned cathedral, which sits precariously between the glitz of the Westwood Marquis Hotel and the youthful glamour of the UCLA campus, was modeled after ones constructed in Scotland centuries before. Stone arches, varnished pews, and silk-screened shields fill the interior. A large steeple topped by a cluster of sharp-pointed spires dominates the exterior. The church survived as the neighborhood around it grew wild....

Only now, this morning, something dark and frightening, something far worse than the congregation ever imagined, had ventured inside.

It wasn't so much that this man was in a church that was so disturbing. The congregation had seen the movies. They knew such men weren't strangers to churches. On the contrary, many had been portrayed as devout. But it was the Roman Catholic Church that had to deal with them, accept their tainted money, hear their bloody confessions, and minister to their meek, prayerful wives and well-behaved children.

They were the Catholic Church's problem.

No longer. Now, one had come their way. A powerful one. A famous one. One who had been in all the newspapers, made all the network news shows. A thirty-eight-year-old Long Island native who had been part of one of the most infamous Mafia families and had sprung directly from one of the most feared crime bosses: an enforcer so cold-blooded and deadly that he had evoked as much fear among his minions as the devil did among his.

That man's son was now standing before them, participating in their most sacred ceremony. And no matter what they thought, how much they feared, Jesus had ordered them to accept. Not to judge, not to cast stones, not even to question the man's sincerity. They were to accept.

It was supposed to be a quietly joyful moment, a humble rebirth for the man who brought himself into the water. The rite is performed many different ways by many different denominations, but this congregation's method, shared with the Southern Baptists and other Protestant sects, was the most dramatic....Their way was total immersion. In the case of the gangster in the baptistery, the water would surely bubble and turn black as the night.

They also knew about the woman, the one who usually sat among them and was now in the chamber alongside the two men. The story was titillating and romantic. She had brought him here. She had succeeded where all the prosecutors and government task forces and police detectives had failed—she sent him to prison. He went, the story was, out of his all-consuming passion for her. He gave up the money, the power, the family tradition and spent three years locked up because of his love for her.

He put his very life at risk, in the past, in the future, and at that very moment. All for her.

The women in the congregation, those who pondered such things, were skeptical. They couldn't see it. What was so special about this woman? She was pretty, they admitted, maybe even beautiful if one is partial to the dark and exotic. She seemed nice enough and appeared to be a good mother and a faithful wife. She was even a true believer. But to abdicate from an empire, even a criminal empire, for her? To go to jail? To give up millions? For this Mexican woman who sat among them each Sunday with her two little girls and baby son?

The men, those who pondered such things, were less skeptical. In fact, it was the woman who heralded the first ring of truth to the whole bizarre story. She was more than just pretty. They could sense it, almost feel it. Something about her made the heart pound and the knees weak. Maybe she truly had gotten inside him, first making him crazy with lust, then insane with love. The combination could have consumed his every thought and led him down whatever path she desired, including the renouncement of his secret life.

Love can do that. Lust certainly can do that. Combined, they can be an addiction more consuming than money, power, or the strongest drug. Fused together, they can be more enticing than crime practiced at the highest, most profitable levels.

Fanciful thinking. A good story, certainly—the kind of which movies are made. And not surprisingly, Hollywood had called. A television miniseries was in the works. It would be America's version of Samson and Delilah, played out, fittingly, by a mobster and a Latin dancer.

The cynical among the congregation scoffed. Nice story; heck of a movie...now wake up. Lovesickness overtaking a man who reigned over a violent world where the slightest show of weakness could be fatal? Giving up everything and going to jail when he could have kept it all, stayed free, and probably gotten the girl anyway?

Sure.

But the woman had made him weak. Even the cynics could see that. And she made him strong.

Every now and then, the free-floating speculation was interrupted by a scent of death hovering in the distance. Sometimes it floated closer, so close you could feel it pressing against the skin. Would the young man rise out of the water? Would he walk out of the church and make it safely to his car? The underground buzzed with news about the contract. You can't walk away, they say. He had. He had created an unprecedented situation that needed to be corrected. He had violated the Mafia's most sacred oath, the one he had sworn to on Halloween night fourteen years before.

The whispers claimed that his public repudiation had caused such fury that his own father had ordered his death.

Wash away his sins, blow away his life, all in one mad fusion of water and blood and exploding gunpowder mixed with pipe organ music. Keep an eye on the door. Get ready to duck. The assassins feared the other church, the one with the statue of the Virgin. But did that fear hold true for this one? Or would they just come slithering in and take him out right there where he stood, so vulnerable in Pastor Taylor's arms, waist-deep in a pool of warm water in a blood-red Protestant church?

"Michael Franzese, will you repeat after me: 'I believe that Jesus is the Christ, the Son of the living God. Jesus is Lord.'"

The voice that followed was deep and resonant, exactly the voice the congregation expected to hear—a voice more suited to ordering death than to praising a resurrected Savior.

"I believe that Jesus is the Christ, the Son of the living God. Jesus is Lord."

"Michael Franzese, upon the profession of your faith in Jesus Christ, you are baptized in the name of the Father, and of the Son, and of the Holy Spirit. Amen."

Pastor Taylor put a handkerchief over the young man's mouth, braced his right hand against his back, and leaned him backward into the water. Michael Franzese arose a few seconds later, dripping wet, his thick black hair pushed back as if it were heavily gelled for a night on the town. He looked down at the congregation, then over to his wife. She had been immersed moments before....Their eyes locked. She looked more beautiful at that moment than he'd ever seen her before.

The mobster Christian. The born-again don. The yuppie capo, now going onward as a Christian soldier. The senses spin. The brain rejects it. The billion-dollar Mafia swindler. The brilliant schemer who took the blood, guts, and hot lead out of the mob and streamlined it into a smooth, white-collar operation that made money faster than any old labor union, bank, or financial institution, then took down the oilmen. He wrapped himself in crisp button-down shirts, Italian silk ties, and Pierre Cardin suits, smiled, winked, and played a blinding billion-dollar shell game on Uncle Sam.

The son proved to be as lethal in the skyscrapers of the business world as the father had been on the streets.

And even after he turned himself in, after he unbuckled his six-guns, raised his hands in surrender, and looked longingly at the Mexican cantina girl, little changed. He merely put on his open-collar shirts, his California-casual Gucci loafers, his Giorgio Armani suits, smiled, winked, and brought the feds back to the table. Follow the pea. Watch closely. Which shell is it under this time? Switch, shift, roll. The hand is quicker than the eye. I'll cop a plea in return for three years in prison, some of it to be served in a halfway house with weekends off. Switch, shift, roll. I'll pay back whatever I owe. Fifteen, twenty million? Okay. I don't have the money now, of course. The billions? The newspapermen exaggerate. It's all gone! Expenses. The family. Those wild and crazy Russians. Everyone taking their cut. Hardly any left for me. But no sweat. Switch, shift, roll. Just let me out so I can work my magic and turn the money faucets back on. And don't worry. I'll do it clean this time! In Tinseltown! The land of stars and dreams and overnight fortunes! We'll be partners: Michael Franzese and Uncle Sam. Got a nice ring to it. And I'll do all the work. What a deal!

What a deal indeed. Uncle Sam squinted down through his bifocals, turned over the shell, and, for once, thought he'd found the pea.

There remain cynics. Not only among the Westwood Hills Christian Church flock but among the FBI, the Organized Crime Strike Force, and the state attorneys in California, Illinois, Florida, and New York. And especially among the Mafia itself. Could this guy possibly be for real? And what's this born-again thing? Is it another great con? Part of the big picture, the Franzese all-the-world's-a-sucker megascam?

If so, what's the angle? He's out of prison. The extraordinary deal he wrangled out of the feds had been cut. He hadn't used his born-again conversion to impress the parole board. And he was baptized after he was out, his time served, with seemingly no one left to scam or impress.

There was no accompanying media extravaganza like at boxer Mike Tyson's baptism. No CNN cameras to record the moment. Just a private ceremony in a mid-sized Los Angeles church. A public proclamation of faith before a congregation of strangers. A dunking that most people, particularly a man of his stature, would find a bit embarrassing. An event that had indeed made the iron-willed Mafia prince so nervous that he found it difficult to stand.

Where did this religious transformation fit into the master plan? What was the master plan?

Was he doing it for himself? Or was he truly paralyzed by his love for the dark-eyed Latin woman in the wet, clinging white robe? Was this, again, her doing?

Maybe.

Maybe not.

I'm sure the writer was correct in reporting the many opinions others held about my intentions that day. Only I knew the truth. Although I was happy to be publicly declaring my new faith, I was a long way from being a strong Christian. But I was on my way.

— 27 —

Notwithstanding this public declaration of my faith, the months following my release from prison were extremely difficult for both Cammy and me. I had testified in a high-profile case and, in doing so, had openly admitted to my membership in the mob. This placed me under a serious cloud. I was freed and allowed to go to Los Angeles to live, but I would have to live under the threat of death. Cammy lived in constant fear that the next time I went out the door I wouldn't be coming back. I told her not to worry and that I would be fine, but she couldn't be sure. After all, I had been wrong before. And we were often warned by the FBI that my life was in danger.

Because of my parole agreement, I would not be able to make any contact with my former associates, and so, during the coming months, I would remain unemployed (and unemployable). Most of the money I had managed to save in previous years had been spent to support my family while I was in prison, and now I had to find a way to continue to support them and myself. For the first time in my life, I didn't know how I was going to earn a living.

Another complication was the high cost of living in California. Before, I hadn't even noticed it (with all the money I was hauling in), but now it ate at me relentlessly. Because of all of this, things were tense at home.

About a year after my release, I was contacted by two Hollywood film producers who were interested in turning the story of my life into a feature film. Moshe Diamant and Mark Damon had been the successful producing team behind many of kickboxer Jean Claude Van Damme's hit films. Moshe was a straight-talking Israeli whom I was immediately drawn to. He was forever asking me questions about the mob life. My answers would inevitably lead to his telling me what a bad guy I had been when I was a "Mafia don." I found him to be very amusing and actually enjoyed his well-intended criticism.

Through all of this, Moshe and I became good friends. He and his wife Ilana were immediately drawn to Cammy, and our friendship grew. Little did I realize just how important a friendship it would turn out to be for me and my family.

While working together on my film project, Mark Damon approached me about forming a company in partnership with him and Moshe to produce moderately budgeted feature films. I was more than happy to oblige, and the partnership was formed. Unfortunately, my life on parole was much too complicated to allow me to devote the amount of time the project needed. As it turned out, however, my friendship with Moshe and Mark could be considered nothing less than a blessing. Both of them supported me and my family at a time when I desperately needed their help. And they didn't wait for me to ask. Neither of these men are believers, but God used them both to help me get through a crisis, and I am forever grateful to them both.

Along with Moshe and Mark, my ever faithful and loyal friend Robert Schultz was another man who God sent to help me get through what seemed to be my never-ending travails. He worked with me during those dog days of parole and did everything he could to help me get the production company going. I realize now that the company was just not part of the plan God had for my life. But at that moment, a battle was raging in my life, and Bob was yet another ally that God blessed me with to get me through that most difficult period, a period that had only just begun.

— 28 —

Although I was baptized within months of my release and fully intended to try to live the Christian life, I found that I simply was not able to do it. The idea of having God in control of my life—of me not being in control—was so foreign to my thinking that I couldn't receive it. I was so used to doing everything for myself that I now thought I had to somehow get through my probation period by using my own wits. I would have to earn a living (while starting from scratch), appease the government, and dodge any bullets that came from my former associates. I had always been able to accomplish almost anything I set my mind to, and I figured that this would be no different.

Oh, I knew that God would be there if I needed Him (and I loved Him in my own way), but I couldn't imagine that I would actually require His help. I needed to help myself. That's what I needed.

In short, my intentions were good, but I was far from ready for real life. My faith had not yet matured, and I needed the failure that was to come. And it came—big-time.

The truth was that I simply couldn't cut it. The adjustment from mob guy to good guy was just too difficult for me under those conditions. In Los Angeles, I was like a fish out of water, away from the life that had been so much a part of me. As the saying goes, you can take the boy out of Brooklyn, but you can't take Brooklyn out of the boy. I desperately needed God's help, but I was too self-absorbed to ever turn my situation over to His control.

Because of this, everything I did to pull myself out of the hole only seemed to make matters worse. Mob life was still too much a part of me. It had taught me to make my own way in life, not relying on anyone but myself to survive the brutality and treachery around me.

I remembered the joke Little Jo Jo Vitacco had made the night I was inducted into the family: "Hey boss, should we give them their bag of money now?" It was a joke, but it had sent a deadly serious message. The mob wouldn't be doing anything for me. I had to provide for myself and my family—and for *the* family. If I got into trouble with the law, I would have to fend for myself. I would have to get myself a lawyer, fight my case, kill some witnesses, or whatever else it took. It was all up to me. It was the same for all family members. It was the mob way.

Oh, I would get help if I needed it, but I must be the architect, the catalyst, the doer. I could not sit around and wait for a wish to be fulfilled. In the mob, my desire was not some prayer that the family was to answer. I had to make my own way in life.

I had thrived and prospered under this policy, earning my own money (and plenty of it) and vigorously defending myself when I was caught up in any legal troubles. I had gone even further than most made men when it came to directing my lawyers. I never sat around and waited for them to act, like Dad had done.

No, I had fought hard and worked hard to make my way up the ranks. Then, through my own wits, I had engineered a deal with the government to get me only ten years in prison instead of life. I had done it so that I could build a new life with Cammy. I had been proactive, and I had accomplished all that I set out to do.

So how could I now turn everything over to God? I simply couldn't do it.

I would continue to work things out myself. Only this time was different. This time, I failed. Maybe this was my first failure ever, but it was a masterful one. I not only failed, I failed miserably. And it landed me right back in prison, where God went to work on me again.

But this time, I would get it right.

— 29 —

It was the morning of November 13, 1991, and that day would prove to be the most painful of my life. Early that morning, I had spoken with my probation officer from home. He asked me where I would be for the next few hours because, he said, he would need to call me back later in the day to discuss certain matters. I told him I would be going to the bank for about half an hour, then I would return home and wait for his call. He gave me no clue what I could expect to happen next.

I went to the bank at 9:00 A.M. as planned, but as I was leaving the bank, I was surrounded by some fifteen or more state and federal officials and arrested for violations of the terms of my probation. I was handcuffed, placed in a paddy wagon, and taken to Metropolitan Detention Center (MDC) Los Angeles, the federal jail.

I handed the keys to my car to an IRS agent and asked him to drive it to my house and inform Cammy about what was happening. He did. Cammy took the news very hard. She was alone again, this time with three small children. (In 1989, she had presented me with a son, Michael Jr. He was born July 15, two months after I was released from prison the first time. Cammy had become pregnant while I was out on an eight-hour pass.)

At MDC, I was booked and placed in administrative detention—the hole. I still find it very difficult to adequately describe what I was feeling in those moments when I was left alone with my thoughts. What I can say is that I was hurting as I had never hurt before.

Part of what I was feeling, of course, was the dread of spending more years behind bars and of leaving Cammy and our children. But it was much more than that. I felt like I had let everyone down. Many people had placed their trust in me, and I had failed them all.

I had failed Cammy, and I had failed my children, and that hurt. I can't begin to describe the pain this realization caused me. I hated myself for messing up.

But most of all, I had failed God. A soon-to-be-published book about my life was supposed to have been a wonderful way of showing the world what God had done in my life. It portrayed a man who had been about as lost as any one man could be, but who had been changed by accepting Jesus Christ as his Lord and Savior. Now, that testimony was spoiled. I was an embarrassment to myself, to my family and friends, to my associates, and, worst of all, to my God.

As I lay on the cot in that cell, my insides seemed to be bursting. On top of my worry about how Cammy would be handling my latest incarceration and my hatred of myself for failing everyone around me, I was also feeling very sorry for myself. This was something unusual for me, and I struggled with it.

I knew that I needed help, so I asked a guard if he could bring me a Bible. He did.

I started to open the Bible, but just then a wave of anger washed over me. I was not only angry at the system that had put me back in jail, I was angry with God for allowing it to happen. I had a beautiful wife and three small children, and now the arresting officers were telling me that I faced twenty-five more years in prison. I wasn't sure how that was possible, but they assured me that it was.

All my hurt suddenly turned to self-pity, and I grasped the Bible firmly and hurled it against the wall of my cell

"Why, God? Why?" I sobbed in my anguish.

— 30 —

Within minutes, I realized how foolish it was to be angry with God. It was not His fault that I was back in jail. I had no one to blame but myself. Regardless of whether or not the violation had been warranted, I had put myself in a position to be violated. I should have been smarter, more alert, and much more careful.

And besides, I desperately needed God's help now. I had hit bottom in life, and who could pick me up but Him? And if I didn't turn to Him, who could I turn to?

I suddenly remembered the words of my Uncle Joe, who had died nearly twenty years before, and whom I had loved. A hard-drinking forty-year veteran of the merchant marines, Uncle Joe had often told me, "Never feel sorry for yourself. Sympathy is a word you find in the dictionary. Look for it there one time, and don't ever look for it again. Feeling sorry for yourself makes you weak."

I had known instinctively that Uncle Joe was right, and until this point in my life, I had never been guilty of feeling sorry for myself. Now, I vowed that I would never feel sorry for myself again.

Once again composed, I picked up the Bible where it had bounced off of the wall and landed on the floor and began to read it desperately and to pray to God as never before. And as I did, strength began to return to my spirit.

I read the Bible and prayed all night, and, by morning, I was ready to deal with whatever lay ahead. Throughout the night, the Lord had guided me to every possible verse in the Bible that would give me strength. Through His promises, He assured me that He was with me in whatever I faced and that He would never abandon me. I asked Him to forgive me for having blamed Him, however briefly, for what had happened, and I knew that I had been forgiven.

I realized now that I could never have embarrassed God. Never! Overlooking sin was what His grace was all about. Those who made a habit of knocking Christianity because of the behavior of some believers were missing the point. God knew that His children would fail. He knows better than anyone that we are all sinners. Some fall harder than others, but we all fall. Some fall publicly while others fall in private, but we all fall.

What the Bible was showing me was that when we receive Jesus into our hearts, God forgives us for all of our sins—past, present, and future. That's the unique message of the Christian Gospel, and nonbelievers cannot be expected to understand it. This being the case, why should we condemn a perfect Savior because of the actions of His imperfect children?

It was clear to me that God had announced time and time again in His Word that we were all sinners and needed His grace for our salvation. Grace, then, was not meant to make us perfect and without sin, and God never said it would. He, through grace, forgives sin. During that long night in MDC Los Angeles, I began to understand this essential element of the Gospel for the very first time.

It was a very long night, and I'm not sure that I appreciated the great good it was doing me as I was experiencing it. In retrospect, I can say that it was a night crucial to the maturing of my faith. I came to realize that God, who holds all things in His hands, had allowed me to return to jail for a reason, and I sensed that in time I would understand the reason—or reasons.

The reasons were primarily spiritual, of course, but, in time, I realized that my return to prison was probably one of the most important reasons that I was still alive. Judge Nickerson, in sentencing me to four more years in prison (out of a possible five allowed by law), had probably saved my life. My former mob associates had come to fear me because I was publicly renouncing the former life, and they were sure that I would testify against them at some point. Once they (my own father included) realized that I would not be testifying against my former associates, the heat would be off. But it took the thirty-five months I served in prison this second time, most of it in twenty-four-hour lockdown, to cool things off. Whatever the case, I believe it was the Lord's doing.

— 31 —

That first night was just the beginning of my intensive reading of the Bible over the coming months. I had read it before, but now I read it and reread it and read it some more. And what I read began to make a lot of sense to me.

This was remarkable because I was a very exacting critic. Because of my experience with the mob, I had become skeptical of everyone and everything and had developed what I came to call my "proof" test. If someone or something didn't meet my "proof" test, forget it. I wasn't falling for it. For me, there was no such thing as blind faith. I needed proof based on hard evidence before I would put my faith in anyone or anything.

When I use the word "proof" in this context, I am speaking in a legal sense. The terms "evidence" and "standard of proof" had become all too familiar to me over the years. A lifetime of involvement with organized crime had kept me in and out of courthouses, attorney's offices, and prisons for what seemed like an eternity. Being a constant target of law enforcement compelled me to deal with evidence and the legal standards of "proof beyond a reasonable doubt" and the "preponderance of evidence" in criminal trials and legal proceedings for more than thirty years.

I was a criminal defendant in two federal racketeering indictments, five separate state indictments, five criminal trials, numerous subpoenas and grand jury appearances, bail hearings, parole hearings, and appellate court writs. And the outcome of each proceeding was dependent upon the evidence presented to meet the required standard of proof. During my seven-year stretch in prison, I spent countless hours in the law library preparing legal arguments for other inmates attempting to overturn their convictions based on some aspect of the evidence presented during their trials.

In the process, I experienced evidence of every kind: direct, circumstantial, and corroborating, as well as evidence from eyewitnesses, informants, experts, wiretaps, bugging devices, documents, DNA, ballistics, and videotapes. Many times in the past, my freedom depended on my ability to identify such evidence and, along with my legal team, attempt to either destroy its credibility or prove its reliability to a jury in a criminal trial.

One might consider that a lifetime of experience has qualified me to competently evaluate information offered as evidence and determine whether or not such evidence will stand up under the required legal burden of proof. Evaluating evidence is really all about a search for the truth. Is it reliable? Does it support your particular position or conclusion? Can it be believed? Now, based on these legal concepts, I began to put the Bible to the test, and I was amazed to find the evidence to be overwhelming that it truly was the Word of God. It was important to know that the Bible was the Word of God because it declared that Jesus is the Savior and the only way to God. Suddenly, I knew the truth of who He was and what He could do.

I found the stories about Jesus' life recorded in the Bible to be powerful and convincing. I had learned through experience that the most effective type of evidence a prosecutor could produce was eyewitness testimony. That was the reason that police officers worked so hard to develop informants. Although many new types of electronic surveillance, DNA evidence, and other break-throughs in forensic science had changed the face of investigation and trial proceedings, still nothing could prove a crime better than a real person who had witnessed it.

What we had in the Bible were the apostles acting as eyewitnesses, some of them reporting directly what they saw and heard. This, I realized again, was the very best type of evidence available. These men were there. They walked and talked with Jesus. And their testimony was given within a few years of the actual events, while their memories were still fresh. Their testimony was then placed into written form so that it could be preserved as legal testimony for all generations. I later learned, through extensive study and research, that the writings of the disciples were often further authenticated through credible archaeological evidence and that parts of their text were corroborated by the writings of other men who were not even followers of Christ.

I noticed that four strong witnesses had written the life story of Jesus, four men as varied in their temperaments as they had been in their names: Matthew, Mark, Luke, and John. Still, these four men had been able to corroborate each other's testimony in case after case after case. That was powerful and credible evidence that could have stood up in any court of law. Some two thousand years had now gone by, and no one had been able to refute the teachings of the Bible.

I had heard it said that we should render "blind faith" in the belief that Jesus is the Redeemer of all mankind. Now, I discovered that nothing could have been further from the truth. The apostle Paul had specifically told Christians to *"Test everything. Hold on to the good"* (1 Thessalonians 5:21). Apparently, Luke agreed, as he said, *"I myself have carefully investigated everything from the beginning...so that you may know with certainty of the things you have been taught"* (Luke 1:3–4). Jesus Himself had rebuked His opponents for not using the same methods to test His claims as they were accustomed to using to predict the weather (see Matthew 16:1–4 and Luke 12:54–56).

The more I searched for the truth, the more God's truth was being revealed to me.

<h2 style="text-align:center">– 32 –</h2>

Another thing that convinced me beyond any reasonable doubt that Jesus Christ is the Son of God was the willingness of the original disciples to die for their faith. As a mobster, I found this to be overwhelming evidence.

I had often been asked why the new breed of mobsters were not "stand-up" guys like the old-timers before them. The people who asked this question were just not aware of the history of law enforcement and the mob in this country. Certainly, the perception of a new, frailer mobster was out there, but the truth had less to do with the character of the present-day mob guys than it did with the increased arsenal of weapons that law enforcement had at its disposal to combat organized crime.

For example, Al Capone was the most notorious mob figure of the twentieth century. Murder, extortion, and bootlegging were just the more visible of his pursuits, and yet the government never was able to indict him on any of that. Although he ruled the Chicago Mafia and made headlines almost every day, having a much higher profile than John Gotti of more recent times, Capone was convicted of nothing more than income tax evasion. He was sentenced to fifteen years in prison on that charge, and he only did half of that.

For a mobster, that was nothing. A mobster could do seven, ten, or even fifteen years and count it as nothing. Then he got out, and mob business went on as usual.

But if Capone had been around today, I knew, he would be indicted for racketeering, a charge that could include counts for murder, extortion, bootlegging, tax evasion, and all the rest. Capone would be arrested, and, under the provisions of the Bail Reform Act of 1984, he would be held without bail as a "danger to the community." He would thus be forced to fight from the confines of a federal prison against a mountain of charges facing him. And that was much more difficult. Virtually all of the bosses of New York's five families had suffered similar fates in the Mafia commission case of 1985 and in countless other mob cases that occurred in the 1980s and '90s. I knew firsthand, because I had been indicted twice on federal racketeering charges myself.

Once arrested (and the arrest would come), the indictments would not stop until there was a conviction. Instead of fifteen years, Al Capone would have received something more like fifteen hundred years or life in prison. At the very least, he would have received fifty, a hundred, or even three hundred years, like mobsters were getting every day. And, under the new Sentencing Reform Act, he would do eighty-five percent of his time with no parole, no extra time off for good behavior, and no probation.

At that point, Capone would have been finished. If my dad had gotten hit with fifty years in 1967 (long before Rudolph Giuliani declared an all-out war on the mob in New York, a war that eventually caught fire in mob strongholds around the country), what could Capone have expected?

Still, with all the weapons the government had in its arsenal—the racket-busting laws, sophisticated surveillance technology, and lengthy prison sentences—the truth was that none of these weapons would have been nearly as effective if they had not served to develop the single most powerful weapon that was used to cripple the mob—informants.

Giuliani and the feds finally figured out that the mob had to be brought down from within. The new weapons exposed the one weakness the mob really had—a weakness in individual mobsters that caused countless mob defections. And if the same weapons had existed in the days of Al Capone, the results back then would have been the same.

It didn't matter how old a mobster was or what kind of character he displayed, when he was arrested, denied bail, and suddenly faced a lifetime in prison, his mob boss had better pray. Was he loved, admired, respected, and believed in enough that his soldier was ready to give his life for him? Had he been a leader who inspired his followers enough to command complete loyalty under the most severe conditions? Could he hope that his soldier believed in the honesty, integrity, and loyalty La Cosa Nostra purported to represent, now that he was about to be asked to surrender his life for that belief? This was what we were commanded to do when we took the oath, and I had taken it, knowing full well the consequences.

The mob possessed another weapon to inspire loyalty in its soldiers. It was called fear. Fear was a powerful emotion that, in the old days, kept guys quiet. But the feds had learned to use this tool to their own ends. Now, the question was, who should a man fear most: the mob or the feds? All too often a mobster's fear of the family was replaced by a greater fear of the law. The feds, oddly enough, became more feared by mobsters than their own bosses. This resulted in a veritable flood of defections, and since the early 1980s, the number of made men who have betrayed the oath they took when they were inducted into La Cosa Nostra is staggering.

These defections were not limited to soldiers. Captains and bosses from all the families around the country had also traded their loyalty to the mob and to each other for the freedom and protection the government could offer in return for their cooperation in prosecuting their fellow mobsters. We have all heard the names paraded across the evening newscasts. Even John Gotti, the most revered mobster since Al Capone, wasn't able to inspire loyalty in his most trusted ally and soldier, Sammy "The Bull" Gravano, who rolled over on him.

This did not surprise me, and it only served to demonstrate that the very fabric of the mob, the principle upon which it was founded, was weak. It had always been so. That fact just hadn't been exposed until recent times.

The mob asked men to surrender their lives to the family, but it offered no legitimate reason for doing so. So it was no wonder that when push came to shove, when their backs were really up against the wall, individual mobsters were unable to find a compelling reason to remain loyal to the oath.

The oath they took offered them the opportunity to acquire money, power, and an inflated ego, but how quickly that all became meaningless when their lives were suddenly on the line! And once the weapon of fear had been dealt with, there was nothing left to hold a man to his oath. I speak from experience, for I am among the ranks of those who betrayed the oath.

And the mob was not the only organization that had experienced near-wholesale betrayal among its ranks. When President Nixon was experiencing his Watergate travails, it took only twenty-nine days for all of his top lieutenants to forsake their loyalty to the president and begin testifying against him. Imagine, twenty-nine days for some of the most powerful men in the world to run to the law to save themselves. Led by Nixon's most trusted confidant, John Dean, all of his men except for one (ex-FBI tough guy G. Gordon Liddy) opted to save themselves from the threat of some negligible prison time. As a consequence, the most powerful man in the world could not maintain loyalty from his most trusted allies.

— 33 —

Suddenly, as I thought about all this in my cell, I realized that my life in the mob had provided me with very powerful and convincing evidence that proved, beyond any doubt, that Jesus Christ was the Son of God, that He was Lord and Savior of the world. I found this evidence in the lives of the men who followed Him.

These were ordinary people from all walks of life. Many of them had been fishermen, but one was a doctor, and another was a tax collector. Still, all of them had accepted the call of the young carpenter to follow Him.

But what had been their motivation in doing so? Jesus had no other followers, no organization, and no reputation to entice these men to follow Him. And He promised them nothing.

They were not asked to take an oath that day, to shed their blood, or to swear allegiance under penalty of death—as I had been required to do. They were not faced with the fear of retribution from Jesus or His family if they did not obey.

In fact, with the disciples of Jesus, it was the exact opposite. They were threatened with retribution by those who condemned them for following the young teacher. They would be harmed if they *did* join His family. And yet they not only chose to follow Him, they chose to follow Him to their deaths.

Most of the early disciples of Jesus suffered violent deaths according to church tradition. Philip, for instance, was stoned to death. Barnabas was burned to death. Peter was crucified upside down. Paul was beheaded, as was Matthew. Andrew was also crucified. Luke was hanged. Thomas was speared to death. Mark was dragged to his death. James was clubbed to death. And John was abandoned and left to die on the Isle of Patmos.

And why had they suffered so? They had not been criminals and were not bound to a criminal organization. They had done no wrong against the state. They were not violent men, and they posed no material threat to society. Jesus had taught them to obey the laws of the land and to *"render unto Caesar the things that belong to Caesar"* (Matthew 22:21).

No, these had not been evil men, and yet they had all met violent deaths. Why? Each of them had been put to death simply because he believed in something with all of his heart, mind, and soul. That common belief was that Jesus Christ was the Son of God.

All that these men would have had to do to escape the horrible fate that awaited them was to renounce their belief in Jesus— just as I renounced my belief in La Cosa Nostra. There was no indictment hanging over their heads. They faced no jail time. They were not being asked to cooperate with law enforcement officials and give testimony concerning the crimes of their fellow apostles. There were no crimes. So all they had to do was renounce Jesus, and they could walk away with their lives. I was convinced that there wasn't a mob guy around who would not have taken that deal. Still, to a man, the early disciples of Jesus had adamantly and boldly refused to deny Him. In the face of certain death, not one of them had broken rank and agreed to renounce his membership in the army of Christ.

What was even more incredible to me was that Jesus was no longer with them in the flesh. He was gone. No one could ever hurt Him now, and they knew this. So why would they have taken the position they did? What could have made these men react in a way that flew in the face of any logical or reasonable course of action they could have been expected to take? The answer is clear: they were convinced, beyond any reasonable doubt, that Jesus Christ was truly the Son of God.

And if that is true, what convinced them? It had to be the evidence placed in front of them. They were convinced by what they saw with their own eyes, by what they heard with their own ears, and by what their fellow disciples experienced as well. In 2 Peter 1:16, the apostle tells us, *"We did not follow cleverly invented stories when we told you about the power and coming of our Lord Jesus Christ, but we were eyewitnesses of His majesty."* The apostle John clearly corroborates this testimony in 1 John 1:1–5, when he speaks of seeing, hearing, and touching the "life" that came down from the Father in Heaven. None of the disciples were following Jesus by blind faith, but because of hard, cold factual evidence.

Many of these men had seen Jesus crucified on the cross. They saw Him die, and some of them had fled in fear. Then, three days later, they had seen Him again, and He was alive, risen from the dead—just as He told them He would be. If that was not true, how else could I explain their dramatic about-face? Only a few days before, some of them had denied that they even knew Him. This, to me, was strong irrefutable evidence.

All the enemies of Jesus would have had to do at the time was produce His dead body and drag Him through the streets. If they could have displayed Him in the village square for all to see, that would have been the end of His following.

Jesus had plenty of powerful enemies who were determined to stamp out His name for all time. "Kill the myth" was their cry, for they believed Him to be an imposter. He was as dangerous and infamous a figure to His enemies in that day as Osama Bin Laden would later become for the United States. I was sure that a manhunt must have been conducted for the body of Jesus that would rival the hunt for Bin Laden.

We all know that if Bin Laden had been killed in the attacks on Afghanistan and his body would have been found, his corpse would have been displayed on the front page of every newspaper in the world. Then, the enemies of the crazed madman would have proclaimed victory, and history would have recorded it so that all future generations would know the truth. In that case, Bin Laden's most loyal followers would be singing a different tune.

Finding the body of Jesus would have exposed Him as a bold-faced liar and a madman, and it would have made informants of His followers. But there was no body, only a risen Savior, so the would-be informants remained loyal to their "boss" until their deaths.

That day in my jail cell, as I read the story of Jesus as recorded in the Bible, there was no way I could dismiss it as a fairy tale. No credible source had ever been able to refute it, and, in fact, some independent sources corroborated the stories. As I thought about it logically and applied my sense of reasoning, I knew that Jesus was alive or His followers would never have risked their lives to proclaim Him the Son of the almighty God.

If Jesus had not risen from the dead, then the early Christian disciples would have become bigger informants and turncoats than Joseph Valachi, Jimmy "The Weasel" Fratianni, and Sammy "the Bull" combined. And the story of Jesus would have been more infamous than that of Al Capone, John Gotti, or even Adolph Hitler. The fact that the apostles remained loyal to Jesus until their deaths is irrefutable evidence, beyond any reasonable doubt, that Jesus Christ is truly the Son of God.

Case closed!

— 34 —

The more I learned about Jesus, the more I was drawn to His amazing leadership style. One of the most impressive qualities He had as a leader was His absolute and genuine humility, an ability to control His power. I knew that it was what a man held under control that revealed his true leadership, not his ability to dominate and control others. Who was more powerful than the Son of God? No one. Yet He was in complete control of Himself.

When it came to being a leader, I realized that Jesus was the antithesis of the men who ran the mob. We wanted to flex our muscles, show our strength, and be respected by all, while Jesus wanted only to be loved. We wanted to be served, while Jesus made it clear that He came to serve and not to be served (Matthew 20:28). Through His Son, God had shown the world the qualities of a true leader, and as I saw them for the first time, I was genuinely moved.

And what about Jesus' message? All of His teachings seemed to boil down to one crystal clear message, a clear directive as to how we should live our lives here on earth. He taught us to love God first and to love our neighbor as we would love ourselves. If we would apply our sense of reasoning to the everyday experiences of life, I realized, we could quickly see that there should be no other way to live. I tried to imagine what a wonderful place this earth would be if every human being followed those two commands: love God and love one another.

Having been totally convinced of the deity of Jesus Christ based upon this revelation of His style of leadership and His message, added to the evidence I had previously uncovered, I now began to study the Bible with much more zeal.

I became fascinated with the book of Proverbs, the book of wisdom. This was interesting because I had been around many people in my lifetime who I considered to be wise and intelligent.

Living and surviving in the mob doesn't make one ignorant of the ways of life. To the contrary, survival has a way of sharpening the intellect. Some of my former associates were so intelligent that I am sure many of them could have made significant contributions to society in all walks of life had they not chosen a life of crime. Despite that fact, I now realized that I had to honestly admit that I had not found anyone on the face of this earth with the absolute wisdom that was presented in the book of Proverbs. There was no question in my mind that the teachings of that book were not of human origin, but rather from God Himself.

A diligent study of the book of Proverbs will provide a clear and sensible answer to almost any moral, social, or spiritual issue one might encounter in life. You might have heard that mob guys were into Machiavelli, a great Italian philosopher. His book is almost required reading for mob guys in prison. Mobsters believed the Machiavellian way of thinking would help them outsmart the next guy at a "sit-down." Even my dad was into him. If only they would have discovered Proverbs. Who knows what might have been?

Another element that provided concrete evidence of the Bible's divine origin was the fulfillment of its many prophecies, in many cases right down to the smallest detail. I was totally amazed by this factual evidence that provided further proof beyond a reasonable doubt that the Bible was inspired by God. No other religion contained this element of proven prophecy. Entire books had been written on the subject, and the evidence was irrefutable. I was so thankful to God that my prison experience was providing me with this period of enlightenment.

As I expanded my search for the truth, the evidence just kept piling up. Comparing the evidence in support of the Bible to that which was offered to substantiate the validity of other faiths, my research left me with only one conclusion. From the history of creation as told in Genesis to the mystery of eternity revealed in Revelation, the evidence proved beyond any and all doubt that the Bible was truly the Word of God. I was thankful that I had opened my heart to receive that truth, and that the truth was setting me free.

— 35 —

One of the very important elements of my spiritual maturing was the fellowship I enjoyed with other inmates who were believers. There is an expression that is frequently used to describe inmates who become Christians while in prison: "Born-again until they're out again." The "knock" is that inmates look to Jesus to gain favor from the system while in prison. It is imagined that this helps them to receive a favorable nod from the parole board, a better prison job, or some favorable treatment from guards. But, as the theory goes, it's all a con, and once they get out, they'll go right back to their criminal ways. As a person who served time in prison, I consider this concept to be without merit. I cannot judge what's in a man's heart, but my experience has been that most inmates do not seek Christ for these reasons.

Anyone with any knowledge of the prison system would realize that parole boards couldn't care less about whether or not a prisoner is born-again, and neither does the prison administration. A prisoner's religious experience means nothing to them and is never a basis for favorable consideration. Since inmates know this better than anyone, why would they attempt to carry out such a charade?

Why is it so difficult for people to believe that inmates could find strength and comfort in Christ while enduring the trials of incarceration? Prisons are fertile ground for ministry because the men there are broken and humbled, and many of them are searching for some real meaning in their lives.

Many prisoners are ready to mend their ways, ready to repent of their sins, and isn't this the principal message of the Bible— that God awaits such sinners with open arms? I've personally witnessed many genuine conversions in prison and have known many sincere inmates. Christ can claim many successes among His convicted converts, men and women whose hearts have been changed and who now have the strength of character and conviction to stay straight and refrain from criminal activity.

One such success story is that of my dearest friend of some fifteen years now, Barry Minkow. Barry and I met in Terminal Island prison way back in 1987. He was in his early twenties when he came into the system convicted of fraud charges that landed him a twenty-five-year sentence. He was a young Christian back then, but, boy, did his faith grow and blossom during his period of incarceration. Not only did he "earn" an early parole due to his exemplary behavior and achievements after serving the minimum seven years, but he also received a degree from seminary along the way. Today, some seven years after his release, Barry is the pastor of Community Bible Church in San Diego, California. God has blessed his ministry, and he has seen the congregation grow steadily every year since he arrived. Our friendship also continues to grow in Christ. Barry is just one example of the fact that God can live in the heart of an ex-con.

This doesn't mean that their faith has made them perfect. Like all Christians, they will probably sin again. Hopefully, their sins will no longer include criminal behavior. However, we should not be surprised if believers who are ex-cons get into trouble again once released from prison. If they do, one should not automatically assume that their faith in Christ is not genuine. The best of us are not invulnerable to sin, and there is no guarantee that any Christian will never sin again—whether he has a criminal record or not.

While a man is in prison, he is obviously limited in his ability to engage in criminal activity. Once he gets out and the temptation is there, he may give in to it again and commit some crime. But it's no different for the free believer who continues to sin because he or she gives in to temptation.

For instance, some believers struggle with an addiction to pornography. That may not be criminal, but it's surely sinful. Does it mean that they are only born-again until they sin again? Of course not. The presence of sin does not automatically label a Christian a "phony." It only proves that God was right when He called us all "sinners" and extended to us His great love. Believers do sin, and believing prisoners may commit further crimes, but that doesn't change God or His love for us.

Oh, the wonder of His grace!

— 36 —

During this final incarceration, I did time in FCI (Federal Correctional Institution) Englewood, Colorado; FCI Sheridan, Oregon; FCI Lompoc, California; and the L.A. County Jail. While I was in L.A. County, I was housed in a maximum-security area along with the Menendez brothers, who were convicted of killing their parents. It was the same cellblock in which O.J. Simpson was later housed. I was able to witness to the Menendez brothers, since my own faith had grown enough that I could now share it with others.

Even though the opportunity for me to witness to these men was a welcome diversion from the dreary jail routine, the time seemed to pass intolerably slow. Every second seemed like hours and every day like weeks. Cammy and I both struggled with the separation.

In the months prior to my release, I was particularly on edge, anxious for the big day and hoping against hope that nothing would be allowed to spoil it. I had been returned to FCI Lompoc in December of 1993, after having spent eleven months in the L.A. County jail, and I was scheduled for release in November of 1994.

"Please, Lord, let it be," I prayed.

During this tense period, I was contacted by a newspaper reporter in Arizona saying that a former mob underling of mine,

Tony "Tony Limo" Sarivola, had told law enforcement officials that I had paid a bribe of $250,000 to President George Bush Sr. in a New York hotel just prior to his election. The reporter wanted me to comment on the story.

Tony Limo was testifying for the prosecution in Phoenix in a murder trial in a matter unrelated to me. He was a star witness who claimed that a fellow inmate had confessed a murder to him. When news of his prior statements was released to the defense, they wanted to subpoena me to testify against him and say that his testimony regarding the Bush incident was not true. If I testified that Tony's statement was untrue, however, I was sure that the prosecutors would not be happy about it. And yet, I was obligated to tell the truth if I were called to the stand to testify. This was a dilemma I didn't need. When a person was as active and high profile as I was in the life of the mob, it never goes away. Something is always hanging out there, and ten, twenty, or even thirty years later, I could be faced with things from my past. I found it all to be gut-wrenching.

When this situation reared its ugly head, I spent a lot of time in prayer and Bible study, and I was somewhat encouraged.

Dary Matera, the co-author of my first book, also contacted me on behalf of the reporter, and Dary was upset that I hadn't told him this story while we were writing the book back in 1990. It would have added something significant, he felt. I told Dary the last thing I needed while on parole was to create controversy for a sitting president. I was dealing with enough problems at the time. Therefore, I was not willing to either confirm or deny the story.

My position on the matter had not changed when I was contacted by the reporter. I saw no purpose in commenting on the story in the media. If I were called as a witness in the case, I would deal with the matter in the proper forum—the courtroom. I didn't want a newspaper story to somehow get in the way of my release.

The story was eventually written and published, but it quickly blew over and nothing came of it. For me, it was just one more thing to deal with, something to keep me on edge. My former life continued to haunt me. Would it never go away?

Shortly after that incident blew over, I was contacted by a *New York Daily News* reporter who told me that a former Colombo associate had turned informant and was implicating many Colombo mob guys in various racketeering crimes that had occurred in the 1970s. That thought did nothing to make me more comfortable. I was only five months away from release, and now I had something new to worry about. On the day of my release, would FBI agents be waiting at the gate to arrest me for yet another mob-related crime? Was some other indictment brewing in New York? Had the *Daily News* reporter contacted me because he knew more than he was letting on? Was I already being implicated in some other case? For the next four months, I didn't get a single good night's sleep because of worrying about these and other possibilities that might derail my impending freedom.

Although I was so on edge, I refused to let on to Cammy that anything was wrong. I didn't want to worry her. Could she handle yet another crisis that would keep me behind bars even longer? I wasn't sure. The only thing I knew to do was pray and give the whole situation to God.

— 37 —

One day, shortly after the *Daily News* reporter had called, I was walking in the prison yard when suddenly it seemed to me that my worst fears were about to become reality. A voice was heard over the loudspeaker summoning me to the warden's office, and such a summons was rarely good news.

Was the FBI waiting in the warden's office to pick me up? Had that reporter known something, after all? Was I going down? A lump formed in my throat as I walked the distance to the warden's office, as if to the gallows. The whole way I was calling out to God in my spirit. My prayer that day was very simple: "Help me!"

"Franzese," I could almost hear the warden say, "FBI here to see you."

And that would be it. I'd be done at that point. I would spend the rest of my life in prison. No more Cammy. No more children. It would be all over.

Was it God's will for me to finally get what I deserved? I had gained eternity through His grace, but would I have to pay a lifetime of punishment for being part of La Cosa Nostra? My heart sank as I took the final steps toward the warden's office and opened the door.

As I had suspected, there were FBI agents in the office waiting for me that day. They were from headquarters in Washington, D.C. My heart sank further. But I was confused when I walkd in because I couldn't see any handcuffs. Still, as the men introduced themselves, I was dying inside.

Then I realized that their faces did not have the usual sternness of men coming to take me away, and what they were saying was nothing to be upset about.

"Hi, Mike," one of the agents said pleasantly. "We're here to ask a favor. The NBA, MLB, NHL, and NFL are cooperating to produce a video that will deliver an anti-gambling message to the players and personnel of the various leagues, and we'd like you to get involved. What do you think?"

Oh, was I happy to hear those words! In my heart, I was saying, "Thank You, Jesus! You do have a plan for my life." I couldn't have known it in that moment, but the video would lead to my first public speaking engagements and would prepare me to present my testimony to believers and nonbelievers alike. The Lord was laying the foundation from which He would use me in the future. Had my entire life in the mob been a preparation for God's service? Did he really intend to use all that bad for His good? So it seemed.

— 38 —

As the days passed, however, and it got closer to my release date, I must admit that I was still pretty nervous. I had heard nothing more about the George Bush or New York informant issues, and the silence was deafening. I was still terribly nervous on the morning of my release. Cammy and the kids were there bright and early to pick me up, but I kept thinking that something bad was going to happen. I saw them standing outside the gates waiting as I walked through the yard for the last time and received my fellow inmates' good-byes. The men were happy for me and sad for themselves—sad that it wasn't them leaving.

Lance Badgwell, my friend and racquetball partner, was the last to say good-bye that morning. I couldn't believe it when I saw that he was fighting to hold back tears. He had never struck me as the sensitive type, but he was clearly all choked up. It got to me, too, because sometimes you make some good friends in the joint.

When I finally got to R&D (Receiving and Discharging), I was a bundle of nerves. I was looking all around to see where the feds were waiting, and, at the same time, I was praying that they wouldn't be there.

Then I was outside, and suddenly I was in the arms of my beloved wife and my children. What utter joy! But still the conflicting emotions that had assailed me would not let me go.

"Hurry!" I said to everyone. "Let's get in the car! Let's go! Let's get out of here quickly!"

I could think of nothing else. I had to get away.

As we sped away, I turned and looked one last time at the men in the yard. I could see them, but they looked different now. They were behind a fence, and I felt so sorry for them in that moment that I hated to leave them behind.

But I was free. My thoughts ran wild with praise. "God, I thank You. As undeserving and unworthy as I am, You have blessed me yet again. Now, I just want to live to please You."

Prison had been good for me, and I was a much better man for it. I had come through it as a much more dedicated and serious believer. This former Mafia captain had really become a soldier in the army of the Lord Jesus.

— 39 —

For the second time in five years, I had to attempt to rebuild my life after having served a fairly lengthy prison sentence. Once again, I was released on parole. In light of my mob association, past history, and high profile, my parole officer, a lady, politely told me I could expect no favors while on parole.

"Obey the rules. Don't ask for anything. Finish your supervision, and get on with your life," she told me on my first visit.

She was aware of just how disastrous my last attempt at parole had been, and she did not want a repeat performance. Not on her watch.

In reality, she was doing me a favor.

This time, I was able to lay low. The feds didn't have it in for me like they may have had the first time around. And, as for my old mob pals, they had their own troubles to deal with. Most of my former mob associates were either dead or in prison for the rest of their lives. And I hadn't testified against them or put any of them there.

There seemed to be no immediate reason for them to seek retribution. Oh, there were still some ruffled feathers. After all, I had violated the oath and then some, and that would not be forgotten. Not ever. No, they would wait for me to slip up, go back to my old ways, make a run for the presumed buried gasoline money, be in the wrong place at the wrong time.

Or maybe, just maybe, God took care of all of that for me. While in prison one night a long time ago, I was really laboring over the possibility of renouncing my blood oath when I came across a Bible verse that made it all seem crystal clear to me.

Proverbs 16:7 says, *"When a man's ways are pleasing to the Lord, he makes even his enemies live at peace with him."* From that evening on, I can honestly tell you I have never worried about retribution. I gave that problem to God, and He'll decide when it's time for me to enter eternity. All I can do is be ready when He calls me home. But I also realize that it would be helpful not to move back to Brooklyn.

In 1997, I was formally released from parole. No more state or federal supervision. I was a free man at last. It was time to get on with my life. I had made some very nice acquaintances while on parole, people who had given me an opportunity to earn a living. My old Israeli buddy, Moshe Diamant, welcomed me home with open arms and within days introduced me to Howard and Karen Baldwin. The husband and wife team owned the NHL Pittsburgh Penguins and also had a major film production company that was located on the Universal Studios lot, adjacent to Spielberg's Amblin Entertainment offices. With the help and reassurances of my ever-faithful friend and agent from ICM, Jack Gilardi, the Baldwins employed me to help develop some mob-related stories for Universal Pictures, which included a story based upon my own life. I worked with the Baldwins for one year and not only enjoyed a nice working relationship with them, but Cammy and I also developed a meaningful friendship with the couple as well. They are two very gracious people, and I am forever grateful to them for affording this former mob boss an opportunity when I was really in need.

On an interesting side note, I was sitting in my office one day when I received a call from Jack Gilardi. He had received a call from a fellow talent agent who represented a producer by the name of David Chase. He wanted to know if I was interested in going to work as a creative consultant for a television show David was producing for the Fox network about a New Jersey mob family whose boss was named Tony Soprano. I turned the offer down. Goes to show you how smart I was! But then again, Fox turned the show down, too.

The rest, as they say, is history.

— 40—

While I was working for the Baldwins, Howard came into my office one day and asked for a favor. It seemed that a good friend and former fellow NHL team owner had gotten himself into some hot water with the feds. The friend's name was Bruce McNall. The team he had owned was the Los Angeles Kings—then the Wayne Gretzky L.A. Kings. It was Bruce who had lured Gretzky away from his native Canada and engineered the trade that brought him to the Kings just a few years earlier. Many people involved with professional hockey believed this trade had a tremendous impact on the growth of the sport in America. Bruce also played a major role in convincing Michael Eisner and Disney to bring the Mighty Ducks to Anaheim.

Aside from Bruce's involvement with the NHL, he was a big player in Hollywood, having produced some major feature films throughout the years. And now a run-in with the feds had all but brought his empire down.

Bruce was, and is, a classy guy. Once indicted, he almost immediately accepted responsibility for his white-collar misbehavings and accepted a plea agreement from the government that called for him to pay a substantial restitution and to serve seventy months in federal prison. The favor Howard asked me for was to meet with Bruce and give him some advice on how to deal with his impending incarceration. I was happy to oblige, but only after my parole was terminated a few months later. I wasn't about to add criminal association to my violation history. I had seen enough of that in my dad's case.

I liked Bruce McNall. He was one of the few guys I met on the West Coast that I could truly relate to, and in the months prior to his incarceration in 1997, Bruce and I became good friends. Cammy and I enjoyed many great evenings with Bruce, and we remain close to him to this day. On the morning Bruce surrendered himself to the federal prison in Lompoc, California, Cammy and I drove him and his longtime girlfriend, Mara, to the institution. An interesting thing happened that is worth telling.

Bruce had asked me what he could bring with him, and I had told him that very little would be allowed at first. Only the essentials. "Later, you can accumulate things little by little," I told him. But when I picked him up that morning, he had with him a huge hockey equipment bag filled with all sorts of things. He had packed not only many types of clothing but also books, notebooks, and other things he had imagined would be useful to him in prison. One look at the bag and I told him that I seriously doubted he would get it in. "But, we'll try," I encouraged, seeing that the thought of going in with so little bothered him a lot.

As we neared Lompoc, the imposing towers of the fortress-like structure raised their forbidding heads, and Bruce's mood dropped even further. Although an all too familiar sight to Cammy and me, Bruce and Mara were clearly affected by the image in front of them.

Lompoc is made up of three facilities. The camp where Bruce was assigned was a satellite facility of the penitentiary, which meant that he would first surrender to the pen, then be transferred to the minimum security facility. We entered the small reception room and were greeted by a gruff, no-nonsense lieutenant. His very first command to his new detainee was to get rid of the bag and everything in it. Bruce was visibly shaken. We were then ordered to say our good-byes, and Bruce was escorted inside the maximum-security facility.

As we were walking toward our car, hockey bag in tow, I spotted an inmate trustee working on the grounds around the penitentiary. I explained to him that I needed to get the bag inside for Bruce McNall, who would probably be transferred to the camp that evening.

"There's no contraband in the bag," I assured him, "just personal stuff. How do we get it inside?"

Quick to oblige, he pointed to a wheelbarrow alongside the road.

"Drop the bag in the wheelbarrow and I'll take it from there," he instructed.

"Got it!" I replied. "Make sure he gets everything in the bag. He'll be calling us tonight."

I knew how important it was for Bruce to get his belongings. Little conveniences mean an awful lot to an inmate. It is hard to believe just how much a man can appreciate wearing his own underwear.

My instruction clear, I told Cammy I needed her to drive as we approached the car. Seeing the prison hadn't made her nervous, but my plan did. She wasn't about to start visiting me in prison again. She felt very bad for Bruce and Mara, but not bad enough to have me keeping him company for the next five years. She protested, and so did Mara, but I insisted that it would be okay.

Cammy got behind the wheel, and I told her to drive slowly as we approached the wheelbarrow. But she was so nervous that she couldn't take her foot off of the gas pedal. I had to open the door and jump out because she was actually picking up speed. Practically tripping over myself, I ran to the wheelbarrow, dropped the bag, and sprinted back to the moving vehicle.

The moment I jumped back into the car, a siren started blaring, lights began flashing, and a voice yelled out from a tailing prison vehicle, "Stop the car!"

Mara was so visibly shaken that she was gasping for air. Cammy gave me a look that said, *How are you going to get out of this one?* I jumped out of the car and approached the correctional officer.

God was really with me that day because I knew the officer from my days in the correctional facility. I explained to him as quickly as I could what had happened, that Bruce had brought too much and that I had just wanted to get his personal belongings to him.

"There's no contraband in there," I assured him. "You have my word on it."

The officer was a prince. He gave me a nod then told me to get back in the car and get off the grounds "ASAP." I didn't wait around. I jumped back in the car.

I also didn't have to tell Cammy what to do. She drove out of there in a flash. Soon, the color began to come back into Mara's face, and, within a few minutes, the three of us were laughing about the adventure. The women clearly thought I was crazy, but at least I was free.

Bruce called later that evening, and, to no one's surprise, he was sleeping in his own underwear.

— 41 —

My friendship with Howard and Bruce brought Cammy and I together with many NHL players, their wives, lady friends, and agents. One player stands out in my mind as being a great guy, as well as a tremendous player—Luc Robitaille. Cammy and I have enjoyed some nice times with Luc and his lovely wife Stacia. We had the pleasure of vacationing with them and a number of other players and their wives one February in Maui. It was Luc who graciously introduced me to the wonderful world of golf one gorgeous Maui afternoon. You can count me among the ranks of those weekend golfers who have developed a love/hate relationship with that little dimpled demon they call a golf ball. Pat Brisson is Luc's agent and one of the premier agents for NHL players in the business. He's also a premier guy and I consider him a dear friend.

As I was developing these friendships, my accidental career as a speaker was beginning to develop and bear fruit. I was contacted by Major League Baseball and the NBA and asked to come and speak to their players and league personnel about gambling and organized crime. The leagues were becoming very proactive in attempting to educate the players about the dangers gambling and organized crime could present to their careers and to their very lives.

Imagine, a former organized crime member actually standing in the middle of a group of professional ball players and telling them to beware of gambling, bookmakers, and men in pinstriped suits.

"Okay, Barry Bonds, make sure you stay away from guys like me. They'll bring you down."

"And you, too, Shaq. Watch out for that bookmaker. He can put a real blemish on that otherwise untarnished image."

There is truly a dark side to an athlete's involvement with gamblers and organized crime figures, and I knew it firsthand. There was the Norby Walters/Lloyd Bloom fiasco, and much, much more that I could tell these players about. Even though I had never done anything like this before, I agreed to go and speak.

Inviting me was a bold move on the part of the heads of security for both leagues and the NCAA, which also participated in the program. They were agreeing to bring a genuine, notorious mob capo into the midst of their leagues' most prized assets. It was a risk, a huge gamble with a potentially devastating downside. What if I wasn't on the level about this transformation thing from mob guy to good guy? Just let me get the ear of one athlete. Oh, what I could have done.

But I believe it was apparent to them that I now served a different boss. Jesus was my new Master, and He had put it in my heart to glorify Him by ministering to professional athletes. I am grateful that I was given the opportunity to do so.

I continue this ministry today, some seven years after it began. I thank Kevin Hallinan from MLB, Horace Baumer from the NBA, and Bill Saum from the NCAA for giving me the opportunity to serve in this way. And I thank God for allowing me to glorify Him in my ministry to the players.

— 42 —

Never in a million years would I have expected to be invited to speak to professional athletes—or to anyone else for that matter—about gambling or any other subject. When I was still entrenched in mob life, participating in the activities of organized crime, how could I ever have believed that one day I would be addressing professional athletes and informing them of how to avoid getting tripped up by a guy like me? That was never part of the program. It was not on the agenda that Halloween night, 1975, when I was sworn in. Not only am I talking to athletes directly, but also I'm writing a book about it (among other things). Amazing!

Believe me, this was not my plan, and I did not see it coming. My plan when I joined the Mafia was to be the multimillionaire mob capo who beat the system and ruled his own little empire. Why? Because I could! But what an absolute fool I was to believe that I was in control of my life here on earth. I wasn't. And I'm still not.

Are any of us in control of our destinies? Did Christopher Reeve plan to be thrown from a horse and become paralyzed? Did Sharon Osbourne plan to contract a potentially deadly disease? Did Ronald Reagan plan to be afflicted with Alzheimer's disease? Did America's troubled CEOs plan on trading in their Armani suits for prison khakis? Did the people in the World Trade Center plan to get blown up by a plane-turned-bomb on 9/11?

Our plans can be changed at any moment. In an instant! And yet we don't seem to get it unless it happens to us or to someone we know or care about. The Bible tells us that it is God who is in control of our destinies here on earth. The evidence in support of that truth is so visible that we can discount it only if we choose to reject the truth. While I was doing my own thing, God was slowly and methodically setting the course my life would take.

It all makes sense to me now. Growing up idolizing my dad. Leaving college to become a member of the Colombo family. Taking the oath. Experiencing the violence and treachery. All the trials. Searching for evidence. The conflict with Dad in the driveway. Walking into a possible death trap. Falling in love with Cammy. My meeting with Pastor Myron Taylor. Taking a plea. Going to prison. Being baptized. Discovering the Bible and then the evidence—the unmistakable, irrefutable evidence.

Why hadn't God forsaken me? Why did He turn it all around? Why did He save my life and my soul? It was His plan for my life. Not my own. I was in control of nothing.

I can see it all now, very clearly. Thank You, Lord!

He did, however, allow me to make a decision that forever affected the one plan I did have control of—the plan for my eternity!

— 43 —

Now that God is at the center of my life and has so mercifully redirected my misguided plans, you might be curious to know what I am doing with myself. During my second stint in prison, I had the opportunity to meet with many young gang members who had come into the federal system under harsh new drug laws. I'm talking nineteen- and twenty-year old kids who were slapped with ten-, fifteen-, and twenty-year sentences. I really felt sorry for these young men, and I understood their plight.

Most of these young men had grown up under severe conditions and had decided that their best option for survival and success was on the streets. I'm not justifying their actions, and I'm not saying that they shouldn't be held accountable for their crimes. All I'm saying is that I can understand where they're coming from. Been there, done that!

Because of my high prison profile and mob affiliation, these young men would seek me out just to talk. I enjoyed ministering to them and tried to make them realize that they needed to redirect their lives. They paid attention. We would talk about their gang affiliations and how difficult it was to sever their ties with the gang. I told them I understood, but that I had severed my ties with the biggest gang in the world. I told them that with God at the center of their lives, anything was possible. I truly believe that if these men had been given a better option than joining a gang when they were facing life's difficulties, many of them would have taken the higher road and tried to do something constructive with their lives.

I was encouraged by the way these untamed junior gangsters reacted to me. I had credibility with them. I spoke their language, the language of the streets. It didn't matter that I was Italian and many of them were young black or Latino men. We were all the same.

This experience led me to want to do something for young men before they got caught up in gang life. This desire was intensified one evening when I visited a juvenile boot camp in Manatee County, Florida, to speak with about fifty young inmates. It was the spring of 1996, and I was visiting the training camps of Major League Baseball teams, delivering my anti-gambling message to the players, managers, and other team personnel. Kevin Hallinan from MLB asked me to visit the boot camp at the request of the sheriff's department that runs the facility.

When we arrived at the facility, one of the deputies told me that I had twenty minutes to give the juvenile delinquents an anti-crime pep talk. Great! Like I could really turn their lives around in twenty minutes. Almost three full hours later, I'd had the experience of a lifetime, and so had many of the young men. It was a blessed opportunity for all of us.

At the end of the session, many of the young men had tears in their eyes when they were told to return to their dorms. And so did I. I could never have imagined the effect I could have on these young men. It made me realize even more that it is God who deserves all the glory, for I would surely have never reached out to these young men while I was selfishly pursuing my mob interests. It was God who set me up to help these young men and others like them. It was God who changed my heart. I just thank Him for blessing me with the opportunity to serve Him.

— 44 —

My desire to help these young men and women and others like them motivated me to create a program called Breaking Out. Its mission is to reach out to at-risk youth through the sports and entertainment industries. We are developing a program and curriculum that can be introduced in schools, youth centers, and churches throughout the country. The program will inform young people of the hundreds of career opportunities available to them in both of these industries. The idea is to get their attention and direct—or, in many cases, redirect—their focus from the negative influences in life to the goal of establishing a career that they believe is possible for them to achieve.

I have no desire to reinvent the wheel. There are many great programs directed at helping young people, and they are run by dedicated and caring people. I am just hopeful that my approach will be effective and that, along with the information and training we provide, we can create a foundation in the lives of young people that is centered around God.

Aside from developing the Breaking Out program, I continue to be invited to speak and give my testimony to church congregations and men's groups throughout the country. I am very grateful to God for blessing me with this ministry. It is amazing to me just how fascinated people seem to be with mob life. I am always quick to point out how the apostle Paul was the self-proclaimed worst of the worst and that I am at least his equal in that regard. We both had our Damascus Road experiences (Paul's was far more impressive in my opinion), and our testimonies are about repentance, forgiveness, and the blessing of being in the service of the almighty God. While I could never come close to being the amazing servant of God that Paul was, I am thankful that the Lord has provided me with a platform that gets the attention of my audiences.

I love this part of my ministry, especially speaking to the men's groups. At times, I must admit, I do miss the camaraderie among the men in my crew back in the mob days. Part of what attracted me to the life was what appeared to be the bond between men: "You watch my back. I watch yours." The loyalty, the closeness, drew me to the mob. Of course, it didn't prove to be what it was cracked up to be, but the concept was and is very attractive. Now, I talk to a new "crew" of men in church groups. It's like we're all soldiers in the "family" of God. There are books, speaking engagements, and television appearances—and all for the glory of God.

In Mark 16:15, Jesus gave every believer an assignment. The great commission, as it is more commonly known, is for all of us: *"Go into all the world and preach the good news to all creation."* I'm just thankful to God that He is merciful enough to allow me to do my little part. I'm thankful that, in spite of my many faults, my continuous mistakes, and my dreadful past, God has wiped the slate clean and forgiven my sins— past, present, and future. I'm grateful to have come to know and love Jesus Christ, my Redeemer and most trusted and faithful ally.

This former mob capo is honored to proclaim that I am a soldier in the army of Jesus Christ and that He is Lord.

— 45 —

In 1996, Cammy suffered a miscarriage. It would have been our fourth child. This was a very traumatic experience for both of us. We went to her doctor one day for what was expected to be a normal checkup, but the doctor couldn't find a heartbeat. The fetus, he discovered, was dead. The doctor's conclusion, after examining blood samples, was that the child might have suffered from Down's syndrome.

Cammy felt responsible for the death of her unborn child in an odd sort of way, and I, too, was shaken by it because I had never experienced a real crisis with any of my children. I began to feel that perhaps the miscarriage was God's way of dealing with what might have been a serious disability for the child.

But Cammy didn't get over this loss nearly as easily as I did, and her response to the whole situation only caused me to love her even more. How wonderful to see a godly woman treasure her unborn child in this fashion!

I did all I could to comfort her over the next few weeks and months and to try and make her understand that the miscarriage was not her fault. A miscarriage, I explained, was sometimes a natural part of the childbearing process. I also assured Cammy that we would try again to honor God and our marriage by having another child. But, although I was committed to trying again, she was frightened at the prospect. What if something went wrong again? We prayed about this together, and Cammy was able to give the situation into God's hands.

Cammy did become pregnant again, but she was on edge throughout the entire pregnancy, worrying about the outcome constantly. I wasn't unduly concerned. We had given the matter to God, and I was ready to deal with whatever resulted. God had already blessed me with six beautiful, healthy children, and I loved Him for that. I knew His will for this seventh child was good.

As Cammy entered her eighth month of pregnancy, I decided to cancel our annual family trip to Hawaii. I didn't feel that it was wise to travel so late in her pregnancy, even though her doctor had said that it was all right. Instead, we drove a hundred miles to Carlsbad, California, and stayed at the Four Seasons Hotel there for five days. We would have been in Maui for two weeks, but, as it turned out, Cammy went into labor the day after we returned from Carlsbad.

Cammy and I were both very nervous when this happened because the child was arriving a full month premature, but on August 19, 1998, our precious baby daughter Julia was born. She was tiny, only four pounds, but she was absolutely beautiful.

Within minutes of her birth, however, Julia developed a breathing problem. It was severe enough that she was moved into the pediatric ICU unit at Saint Monica Hospital and hooked up to IVs and a breathing apparatus. I was so frightened for her that I was physically shaking.

What a horrible feeling it was! I had never experienced this kind of trauma with any of my children. The thought of Julia not making it was devastating, and I found that I absolutely could not leave her side—except to run to Cammy's room once in a while to comfort her.

I watched every movement of the tiny child's chest and kept reporting to Cammy, who was beside herself with worry, that the child would be fine. We were trusting God, and He would pull little Julia through.

Much of this was sheer bluster. I was feeling very helpless in those moments because I was not accustomed to not being in control. I didn't like the feeling, but I couldn't do anything about it. I had to trust the doctors, and I had to trust God. I prayed desperately.

Slowly, strength came into me, and I gained confidence. Finally, I knew that little Julia was going to be all right.

Cammy and I didn't like leaving the hospital in the days that followed. We stayed as much as we could, holding our baby, feeding her, and playing with her. Gradually, over the course of a week, Julia's breathing got stronger, and she became less dependent upon the breathing apparatus. After only one week, we were able to take her home. What a great miracle!

Needless to say, Julia is very special to Cammy and me. Personally, I love all of my children, but I feel a very special tie to this one because I know that God sent me a message through her. Through Julia, He let me know that if I surrender any situation to Him, He will take care of it.

I had never before prayed with such conviction and such abandonment to the will of God, and I was prepared for the outcome to be different. Julia was the test of my faith, and I came through it knowing that I do trust God—no matter what. I was deeply grateful to Him for the experience.

– 46 –

From the first time I met her (back in 1984), Cammy's mother, Irma Garcia, had played an important part in my life. We were as close as mother-in-law and son-in-law could be. Irma was a true Christian who never held my organized crime background against me. She knew how to look at the heart. She believed in the transforming power of God, and she was convinced that I had a great future ahead of me, despite my background.

Early on, Irma saw that I loved her daughter and treated her like a princess, and that was enough for her. She was on my side. Throughout the ordeal of my trials and imprisonment, she encouraged Cammy to stand by me, support me, and keep our relationship strong. I am convinced that she never said an unkind word about me to her daughter and that her unfailing support of me strongly influenced Cammy, sustaining her through the seven years of my absence.

Irma was a woman of God. She loved Jesus with all her heart, and, in her own simple way, she would express her love and faith to everyone she met. Because of this, she had a very strong impact on me.

She was by my side throughout all of my court battles, and she would encourage me to relax, have faith in God, and let Him work it all out for me. She encouraged me to read my Bible and pray, and she assured me that God would do the work—in His time.

I tended to get stressed out over my court cases, and Irma would say to me, "Stop working so hard. Pray about it. Leave it all to God. He'll take care of everything." I didn't agree with her on this point and would invariably answer her that I just couldn't do it. I felt I had to work hard to make it happen.

One day at church, our pastor related a story I liked very much. A Christian man lived in a village that was being hit with torrential rains. The river overflowed, and the town was being flooded. As the waters rose, the man had to seek refuge on the roof of his house. Still, the water continued to rise, and rescue teams were sent out to find those who were endangered.

First, a neighbor passed by in a boat and called to the man to come aboard before the flood overtook his home. He declined, saying that he was praying to God and trusting Him to save him from drowning. Next, some men came by in a helicopter and called to him to grab their ladder and come aboard before the flood overtook his house. Again he declined, saying that the Lord would save him, and he continued to pray.

Eventually, the floodwaters overtook the house and the man drowned. As he entered heaven and faced God, he said, "Lord, I don't understand. I've been a good Christian all my life. I had a strong faith. I prayed for You to save me, but You let me drown. Why, Lord?"

God's response was, "What do you mean, I let you drown? I sent a boat for you, and then I sent a helicopter!"

I hurried home to tell Irma this story.

"See," I gloated, "God helps those who help themselves. I can't simply leave my troubles to prayer."

With the passing of time, I have come to the conclusion that we were both right. We must give our troubles to God in prayer, but He will often show us a means of escape that we are to follow. We, then, become the vehicle by which our prayers are answered.

At least this was true in my own case. God set the course for me to follow to make a successful break from the mob and begin my ministry. But I had to be proactive, first in seeking His help in prayer, and then in following the course He laid out for me.

I was deeply moved by Irma's persistent faith. She'd had a very difficult life, yet she was always happy, never complaining. Irma Garcia made me want to know Jesus more. She was genuine. She walked the walk and talked the talk, as we say. The one-two punch of Irma and Cammy combined to bring me to this life in Christ.

When I was imprisoned the second time, Irma helped a devastated and discouraged Cammy get through the next thirty-five months. She was always there for her, and Cammy loved her dearly for it. That's why November 1999 was one of the most devastating months in Cammy's life. That month, Irma was diagnosed with breast cancer.

Cammy was not the only one crushed by this news. The rest of the family was equally devastated. The only person who seemed unmoved by it was Irma herself. And that was typical of her. She told us all not to worry. God would work it out—in His time. Whatever happened would be His will for her.

During the days that followed, for the second time in our relationship, I was the one ministering to Cammy and encouraging her to turn to God for strength. The first time had been during my prison term. The time now with her mother's illness was much more significant, though. Cammy desperately loved her mother and didn't want to lose her.

I took the lead role in coordinating the plan of treatment Irma would undergo. First, a tumor was removed by doctors at UCLA Medical Center. Chemotherapy followed and then radiation. The diagnosis was good, because the cancer had not spread to the lymph nodes, so we were hopeful. And, for a while at least, Irma did well.

Then one night in February 2001, I was driving home from a meeting in San Diego when I received two difficult calls on my cell phone. The first was from my mother. She said that Dad had been arrested again for violating his parole. As before, he was accused of associating with known crime figures. This was violation number four. That was not good news, and I felt very bad for Dad because he was eighty-three years old at the time. Prison could not be easy to bear at that age.

I was surprised by my reaction to this call, and it made me realize how much I had changed. Before, I would have cursed the officials who put my father in prison, sure that their actions were unjust. Now, I felt only sorrow for my father as I talked to my mother.

I had no sooner turned off the phone from that call than it rang again. This time, it was Cammy, and she was crying hysterically. My heart began to beat fast. Had one of the children been hurt? Was something else wrong at home?

Cammy's news was about her mother. Irma had been riding with Cammy's sister Sabrina in the car when one side of her face suddenly drooped in partial paralysis, and now she couldn't talk. This lasted a while, so Cammy told Sabrina to take her immediately to a hospital emergency room. Once there, a CAT scan of Irma's brain revealed that she had cancerous tumors—a lot of them. Her cancer had spread, and the prognosis this time was not good at all.

That May, Irma lost her battle with cancer, but not before she had left an indelible imprint upon all our lives. She was ready to "go home," and the two of us spent a lot of time in fellowship together as we drove regularly to UCLA Medical Center for her treatments. I learned a lot from that gracious lady, and I thank God for her.

— 47 —

Since Cammy was the catalyst that brought me to Christ, many have been curious about how our relationship has held up through it all. It has endured now for seventeen years, and I'm certain it will conclude as our vows stated—"until death do us part." But those vows were severely tested when I was forced to return to prison in 1991 for what could have been five very long years. Cammy was devastated by the court ruling that sent me back, and her spirit was weakened.

Even after my release from prison the first time, we felt the need to arrange a renewal of our vows at Westwood Hills Christian Church. The second separation was even harder. Cammy later admitted to me that if it hadn't been for prayer and for her turning to God during those times of uncertainty and lack, she would not have made it through them. It was not that she stopped loving me; it was just that she was emotionally as well as financially exhausted.

This was complicated by the fact that some of her acquaintances were advising that, for her own sake and that of the children, she should think about getting out of the marriage. After all, she was still so young, and being alone for so long with three small children would have been difficult for anyone. Everywhere she went, people asked about her husband, and men tried to take advantage of her loneliness and need.

What should she do? Cammy decided that her marriage vows were important. She had made them before God, not just before people, and not just to me.

As I showed in the previous chapter, her mother, Irma Garcia, was a great help in this regard, constantly reminding

Cammy that I loved her and that if she remained faithful to God and to me, God would bless our marriage and cause everything to work out for us. And, of course, she was right.

Cammy's thinking had to change a little. For quite some time, she was caught up in the excitement of our early relationship, and she started to think that I was invincible, that I could overcome any obstacle in my path. This notion grew until she could not believe that I would ever be imprisoned. I would work things out, she was sure.

Of course, I was to blame for this thinking. I had become Cammy's hero by doing everything for her and by providing her every need—and then some. I had never let her down. This led her to make the mistake of placing me on a pedestal. When I went to prison, the illusion of grandeur she had built up in her mind was shattered, and she had to take a long and hard look at the man she'd married. Obviously, I wasn't invincible.

Then, when I went to prison the second time, things got much worse. Now, Cammy felt that I had let her down, and she was very angry and resentful toward me. Irma explained to her that she had set herself up for disappointment by placing me before God and that this was unfair to me. After all, I was only human. Fortunately, Cammy turned to God, forcing herself to stay in His Word and praying regularly for His strength to sustain her. There is no question that her faith in God pulled her through that very difficult time.

For my part, I had not originally believed that my faith had anything to do with our marriage. I loved Cammy to death, and I didn't need God to enforce that love. I know now that I was wrong in that I loved her more than I loved Him. Even though I had accepted Christ, I could not yet fully comprehend how I could love a God whom I couldn't see, touch, or feel more than this wonderful woman whom I absolutely adored.

My love for Cammy was unselfish in one sense. I would do anything and everything for her, and I was willing to share everything I had with her, without ever having to be asked. But my love for her was also selfish in that I wanted all of her attention. I was older, had been in other relationships, and knew that Cammy was the woman I wanted to grow old with.

But, at the same time, I was the one causing all the problems: my trials, my imprisonments, my parole complications, my death threats. It was all because of my mob ties. Cammy had never caused me a minute's grief when I was going through all this. Every trouble we endured was the result of my actions. I had put every effort into keeping her as comfortable as possible, but I had failed to give God His rightful place in our lives and in our marriage.

Belatedly, I came to realize that what I was giving Cammy was not enough. Even though she knew that I loved her dearly, other influences in our lives would have been too much for her to withstand without God's help. I had been relying on myself, but Cammy turned to God. In the end, it was His love and grace that kept our marriage together, nothing that either of us had done.

After I came home from prison the second time, I found myself desperately needing God to help me with the marriage. Cammy now reacted differently to me and was sometimes distant. She lived in constant fear that something would happen, that I would fail her again and have to go back to prison. And, because she didn't want to be hurt again, she put up a kind of shield that wouldn't allow me to get as close to her as I had before.

This was very difficult for me to understand. Cammy and I had been so much in love and had shared such a special closeness. Now, I began to mistake her protective mechanism for a loss of the special love we shared, and I felt betrayed. How could she do this to me after all we had been through these past years? Our love should be stronger than ever, I reasoned.

Of course, what Cammy was feeling was normal. I just didn't get it at the time. I needed to work through it, and, in time, I came to realize that she had never lost her love for me. Fortunately, my biblical foundation had become strong enough to direct me to God to find the answer to our dilemma. If He could get me out of prison, He could heal whatever was wrong with our marriage. If He had been able to speak to me while I was still behind bars, He could answer us now and show us what to do.

My faith was developing in other areas, and now I asked God for guidance and enlightenment in matters of the heart. Over the coming weeks and months, I found the counsel I needed in His Word, and Cammy and I listened intently to messages that preached and taught about God's will for marriage. Our marriage was sacred to us, and we had to find solutions to the things that separated us. Neither of us thought of giving up or of ending the marriage.

Now, after some years of growing and learning, I can honestly say that our love has grown deeper through the trials. It may be somewhat different today than it was when we were younger, but it is battle-tested and true. And, best of all, I have strengthened my relationship with God as a result of my love for Cammy and her love for me. Turning to Him helped me to remain in love with her, and that, in turn, has manifested itself in my greater love for Him. I no longer place Cammy above God.

Our love is now God-centered, and, as a result, it is strong and continues to grow through each transition we make. Without a strong foundation, a marriage cannot survive, and what better foundation than God Himself?

— 48 —

Well, we're getting to the end of the story now. I hope you know me better than you did when you first picked up the book, and I also hope that by now you have gotten the message. The message isn't about me, and it isn't about the mob, my father, or even my relationship with Cammy.

The message is about YOU.

God can be pretty creative, you know. You might have noticed some of His work. He can create an entire lifetime for a person for the sole purpose of using that life to deliver His message to one person. Or two. Or ten. Or maybe even a million.

The story of my life can be thought of as a parable, a story Jesus would tell when He wanted to simplify a message He was attempting to deliver to His disciples. The message in my parable is simple. It's not, "Read my lips" or "It's the economy, stupid." No, this message is all about your salvation. It's about where you will spend eternity. Nothing in your entire existence should matter more to you than the answer to that question.

Every human being, regardless of race, color, or religious belief (or the absence of the same), will one day die. The evidence to support that conclusion is as concrete as any cinder block the mob ever used. And what then?

Eternity! An ageless, endless, boundless FOREVER! This is not just a word created to describe something we humans cannot comprehend and, therefore, need not concern ourselves with. Eternity is a place we will all enter one day that is not limited by time as we now know it. You won't find an alarm clock, a wristwatch, or even Big Ben there. Still, it's the very last stop on the train. Take a moment or two, or even an hour, and let that sink in. But I caution you, don't take much longer than that, because none of us knows for sure when he will enter that final zone. The people who entered on September 11, 2001, certainly didn't know the timing of their departure.

Eternity! Jesus, Himself, tells us in John 5:28–29, *"Do not be amazed by this, for a time is coming when all who are in the graves will hear his voice and come out—those who have done good will rise to live, and those who have done evil will rise to be condemned."* He was saying that every man, woman, and child will have to face eternity—some with Him (*"to live"*) and some without Him *("to be condemned")*. It's real, people. As real as the bloodstained hands of a one-time Mafia prince!

In prison, Death Row is a horrible place. So are the cell blocks that house those inmates who have been condemned to spend the remainder of their natural lives in prison. I got a taste of both places during my incarceration. I spent twenty-nine months in isolation, eleven of those months on Murderers' Row in the Los Angeles County Jail. And I can tell you right now, in all sincerity, I would rather be put to death than to spend the rest of my life in either of those places.

Still, I thank God that He allowed me to experience that hell on earth. It was a wake-up call, a smack in the face, a bullet to my soul. It made me think about the possibility of spending all of eternity in some cell block. I don't mind telling you that it scared me, and it scared me bad. It caused me to intensify my search for my true purpose in life. I opened my heart and soul and searched for the truth, and, as promised, God revealed Himself to me through the evidence presented in the Holy Bible and in all of creation. He then saved me from everlasting imprisonment as a condemned man on eternity's Death Row. I love God for that.

I now believe with all of my heart and soul that Jesus Christ is our only hope for salvation, a belief based totally on the evidence, a belief that really narrows the gap between what we can see, hear, and touch, and what we need faith to believe is real. And I am so passionate in my belief that I needed to share it with you. If I could, I would be your personal guide on a trip through Death Row, in the hope that you, too, would hear God's wake-up call and believe. Please focus on where you will spend eternity. I don't want to see anyone condemned to eternity's "Death Row," a place far worse than the nightmarish federal prison in Marion, Illinois, where I feared to go when I was serving time. Hell is a place the Bible describes as a *"fiery furnace where there will be weeping and gnashing of teeth"* (Matthew 13:41–42). What's worse is that it's forever; there are no possible paroles when it comes to being sentenced to life in the *"eternal fire"* of hell (Matthew 25:41).

To those of you who are not yet believers, I wrote this book for you. I don't judge you or condemn you for your current beliefs. God tells us that no man has the right to judge what is in another's heart. Remember, I was one of you, and I assure you that I was no better person than anyone who has read this book—and probably a lot worse than most.

I'm not attempting to impose my beliefs on you. In reality, they're not my beliefs; they're God's truths. Please do not be offended by my boldness in asking you to open your mind and heart to the evidence and to allow the one true God to reveal Himself to you. Embark on an honest, sincere search for the Savior, and, because He is faithful, He will reveal Himself to you. Then you, too, will be guaranteed your rightful place in eternity. I submit to you that there is nothing more important in this life than that decision.

This was my hope in writing the book, and it is my hope for you today. It is my prayer for you always!

Epilogue

The summer of 2001 will remain among the most memorable and rewarding times in my life. For five years, I had coached my son Michael's Little League baseball teams in the Los Angeles suburb of Encino. Encino offers parents and their kids one of the best Little League baseball programs in the country, if not the world. That particular year, I was selected by the league president Mark Rutter to manage the major league all-star team, which consisted of eleven- and twelve-year-olds. For three months, the boys and their parents were my extended family. I really came to love the entire group, and Cammy and I remain close friends with many of them today.

Try as I did to be a normal, everyday suburban Little League dad, I couldn't keep my former mob affiliation out of the dugout. A reporter from the *New York Times* thought it pretty amazing that a former mob capo was coaching eleven- and twelve-year-old all-stars, so he decided to write a story about it. "From Captain to Coach: Ex-Goodfella's New Life" read the headline. Within a day of the story appearing in the sports section, Encino Little League officials were bombarded with requests from *ESPN, HBO's Real Sports*, and other media outlets wanting to cover the story for television. The headline on the front page of L.A.'s *Daily News* read, "Ballpark Hit."

Then came movie requests and magazine articles. I couldn't believe the fuss being made over my coaching a youth baseball team. I had managed to keep a pretty low profile until then, and I became concerned that the League and the parents of my all-stars would not appreciate all the unnecessary attention I was bringing to their beautifully maintained diamonds. To my relief, everyone was terrific about it. The camera crews showed up, and parents and kids were interviewed, along with the league officials. The reporters even interviewed the umpires.

"How do you feel about a former mob boss coaching your kids?" the parents were asked.

"How does he conduct himself on the field?" the officials were asked.

I can get pretty emotional when I think about the wonderful things all of these people had to say about me. Both Cammy and I love our Encino baseball friends, and the summer of 2001, along with the six great years we spent in the League, will always have a special place in our hearts.

Why tell a Little League story in my Epilogue you might ask? For me, it's all about redemption, forgiveness, and a second chance in life. Once again, God blessed me with the opportunity to be out there on that diamond with those kids and their families. We have a tendency to take life's little pleasures for granted. It's understandable but actually quite foolish since none of us is guaranteed even the next breath of air. That reality became crystal clear to me as a mob soldier, and it should be abundantly clear to you. Being out on that field, among those young boys and girls, is an opportunity to glorify God through the manner in which I conduct myself. It's a reminder that, in everything we do, whether big or small, public or private, we have an opportunity to glorify the Savior just by being the people He wants us to be.

So whether you eat or drink or whatever you do, do it all for the glory of God. (1 Corinthians 10:31)

I suspect there are many people out there who are not convinced that I have been born again into a new life, born again a second time, this time into the light of the Savior. When I began writing this book, I was very hesitant to use the term "born-again" to describe my acceptance of the Christian faith. Many people hear the term and immediately roll their eyes, thinking, *These born-again Christians are nothing but a bunch of Bible-toting, fanatical hypocrites.* I don't consider myself to be among those ranks. I am anything but fanatical. I don't purposely expose my Bible for all to see, and please don't label me a hypocrite because I readily admit that I always have been and always will be a sinner. I am a Christian sinner, but a sinner nonetheless.

That's no surprise to God. The Bible tells us that ever since Adam sinned in the Garden, man has a sinful nature, and all of us will sin, and sin again. He's been telling us that for six thousand years now. And nowhere in the Bible does it say that Christians become perfect and never sin again. So why should it surprise you when Christians sin? Every Christian is, by definition, born-again. In fact, the term "Christian" is of human origin, used to describe those who have accepted Christ. The calling to be "born-again" is of God. Jesus Himself told us that in order to be forgiven of our sins—past, present, and future—we must be "born-again" into a new life with Him, the Savior.

Jesus declared, "I tell you the truth, no one can see the kingdom of God unless he is born again." (John 3:3)

People, don't make the mistake of judging the perfect Creator by the sins of His imperfect creations.

For all of you who do not believe that God can reach into the heart of a "family man," an organized career criminal, and reveal Himself in such a way that that man is made to believe in Him with all his heart and soul, have you ever searched for God? I

379

Michael Franzese

mean really searched for God with a desire to find out who this almighty Being, this Creator of all mankind really is? If your answer is "no," why not? It's the most important matter in your life, hands down! I would lay odds that more than half the people who have known me throughout my lifetime believe I am either trying to con someone (I don't know who or for what purpose), that Cammy somehow hypnotized me, or maybe that I have gone soft in the head. And the Lord only knows what my former mob associates believe happened to me.

I have tried to explain what happened to me in the pages of this book. However, God needs no justification! He will reveal Himself to those who truly seek Him. It doesn't matter under what circumstances you open your heart to the Lord. Just do it! Your eternal life depends on it!

> *The LORD is faithful to all his promises and loving toward all he has made.* (Psalm 145:13)

It is my hope and prayer that, in reading this book, those members of my family who have not yet accepted Jesus as their personal Savior will immediately invite Him into their hearts. For a lifetime now, my father, mother, brother, and sisters have suffered the devastating side effects of the mob life. The mob is not just a business; it's a way of life that affects everyone it touches. That "backward thinking" that Dary Matera talked about in the Foreword has dominated the thought process of my family for as long as I can remember.

I am both encouraged and grateful to God that my younger brother John appears to have defeated a lengthy battle with drug addiction. He has been clean for over a year now. He found his strength in Jesus, and I want to encourage him to stay in the Word and seek the Lord even further. He can become a true warrior for Christ, and I am confident that God will use him in a powerful way.

For over twenty-five years, my mom has been a wife to an imprisoned husband. To say that her life has been difficult would be a gross understatement. She did her best to provide her children with something of a balanced family life, but, without God at the center of her life, it just never seemed to work. It's time, Mom—time to put all else aside and open your heart to Jesus. I guarantee that you will find the peace and happiness you have been lacking all these years in the arms of the Savior. Don't wait any longer.

To this day, I love and respect my dad. I will be forever thankful to him for the way he treated me as a child. The man he is has had so much to do with the man I have become. My prayer is that he begins to realize that he will not be a "made man" in eternity. The legend of Sonny Franzese will not survive into the next life. The oath he took that bound him to the mob life for some fifty years will become a far heavier cross for him to bear in eternity than it has been for him in this life. You have a powerful testimony, Dad. You are one of the most dynamic men I have ever known. Please, open your heart, and discover what I have found in my life. Allow God to reveal Himself to you as He has to me. You are too intelligent to reject the evidence that proves beyond all doubt that Jesus is Lord and that the only way to eternal life is to open your heart to the truth that is Jesus Christ. You will be an even more powerful force in the army of God than you were in the army of destruction.

My eldest daughter, Tina, is a lovely and talented young woman of whom I am very proud. We have struggled over the years to repair a father-daughter relationship that never had a chance to fully blossom. I can give a million reasons why this is so, but, in the end, they all lead back to me. I take full responsibility for that. I only hope you can look beyond all the difficult times you endured as a result of our separation and heed the advice Daddy is giving you now. Please, look past all the times I failed you as a dad and look toward the only Father who will never let you down, almighty God. I promise that if you open your heart to Him, He will bless you with a gentle spirit, a fresh perspective on life. I love you, honey, but nothing I can do for you can ever compare to what God will do if you let Him into your heart. You are in my prayers always!

My prayer for my son John and daughter Maria is that they, too, will understand that Dad is deeply concerned with the condition of their lives when I ask them to allow Jesus into their hearts. I want you to allow God to do what I was never able to do—be with you constantly, through good times and bad. If you put your faith and hope in Christ, He will never let you down, either in this life or the next. I love you both, more than I can express in words or than I can show in deeds.

Lastly, my prayer is for the friends and associates I had when we entered into the blood covenant that bound our lives to La Cosa Nostra. I ask that God will allow you to open your hearts to the truth so that you may be set free by the blood covenant the Almighty made possible through His Son, Jesus Christ, the Lord and Savior of all mankind.

And as for what the future has in store for me, well I'm just heading down the path that I believe God has laid out for me. I take one step at a time, one day at a time, and pray that the course I am taking is God's will for my life. I live each day to praise Him, and, hopefully, in doing so, I *will* please Him. I ask all of you to view my life as a testimony of God's infinite mercy and power and not as an accomplishment of my own doing. For He alone deserves the glory.

Be blessed!
Michael

From Cammy

When Michael asked me to write something for this book, I was reluctant at first. I am normally less inclined than he is to speak out about what goes on in our personal lives—even when it concerns our faith. And so much has already been said about it. But he felt it important that I contribute my thoughts on what the Lord has done in his life, not as a testimony to him, but as an awesome testament of God's unlimited power to transform a life. In that context, I do feel it appropriate to share my thoughts.

I believe the transformation Michael has made from the man he was to the man he is today is nothing short of a miracle. I watched the change take place, ever so slowly over the years. It was a real process. At times, I had my doubts—not about God's ability to change Michael, but rather about Michael's sincerity in wanting to change. For a while, I thought the influence of his former life was just too powerful for him to overcome. When I would see him slip and fall, I would remind him that God knew what was in his heart. I guess I never really quite understood the battle that was raging within his heart and soul as he struggled to allow God to take control of his life. It was very difficult for him. He had always been the one in control of his life. Or so he believed.

At times, I lost patience with him. I even lost patience with God, as it seemed to take Him forever to answer my prayers concerning Michael. But He was answering my prayers all the while. God knew He had to break Michael to prepare him for what was to follow in his life. The Bible shows that God can never really use a man unless He first breaks that man's will. That was certainly true in my husband's case. I thank God for blessing me with a mother who never lost patience, neither with God, nor with Michael. She was confident that one day Michael would become a soldier in God's army and serve only one Master. I believe that it was largely through her faith and constant prayer that Michael has reached his current level of experience with God. God truly answered her prayers.

Today, I am absolutely confident that Michael's faith is deeply rooted and strong. Of course, he is not perfect. None of us are. And my hope is that people will not expect too much of him, so that, if he stumbles or falls in his ministry, he will not be judged too harshly because of his past life. I know that he is sincere in his desire to rightfully give God the glory for his amazing transformation. He is a wonderful father, and he has been an amazing husband. I am blessed and honored to be his wife. I will support him forever in his efforts to glorify God in whatever way the Lord has planned—until death do us part.

My dad has been a true warrior in his own right. For as long as I can remember, he has always been a champion for the rights of those whom he feels are his people, especially the children. Sometimes, I questioned his methods, but never his motivation. He really cares about people. As a child, I can remember him opening his arms (and our home) to any neighborhood people who were in need, no matter what it was. We didn't have much, but whatever we had, he would give it. You have a good heart, Dad. It would make a great home for Jesus. It's time for you to let Him in. He's waiting. It's what I want. It's what all your children want. It's what Mom prayed so hard for, for so long. Our prayers were answered with Michael, and now it's your turn. Let God in, and I assure you, our family will be reunited again for all eternity. It's God's promise!

My mother's prayers took root in a little brick building in Anaheim that is now the home of Agape House of Prayer. I am so grateful to my brothers—Dean, Joaquin, and Che—for devoting their lives to Jesus and helping him answer Mom's prayers for all of them. I am so proud of you guys and the wonderful work you are doing for the glory of God. I would never have believed that you would put more effort into praising God in that church than you all did trying to score touchdowns, run track, or hit three-point shots. But I am seeing it with my own eyes, and I am just amazed at the power Jesus has to change lives.

First Michael and now all of you guys. I feel so blessed to be the big sister to all of you. You keep building that church and expanding your ministry, and someday God will allow you to ful-fill Mom's prayer of seeing a million people saved. Michael and I are with you all the way.

There's a void in my heart for someone I love so very much—my brother Cuauhtemoc, who seems to be fumbling a bit, trying to find his way. He was always independent, never a burden to anyone. He's really a very kind soul. I miss you, brother. Even though you're around, you're still not here with us, and we all miss you. My prayer for you is that you, too, will open your heart and let Jesus in. Dad's knocking at the door, Themo. Please be the next to knock, and Jesus will be there to answer. Then we can all be together with Mom for all eternity in the pres-ence of God.

It took the passing of my beloved mother to make me realize just how much of a blessing my sisters Sabrina and Raquel are to me. You are both so close to my heart. I pray so hard for God to heal your broken hearts, to take the pain away. I know the hurt is unbearable at times, but we have to be strong, press on, and continue the work Mom was so passionate about. She left us with each other and all the wonderful memories of our times with her. Let's never forget the lessons she taught us, the strength she gave us. We are Irma Garcia's daughters, and we must continue the wonderful legacy of our godly mother. Let's seek comfort in knowing that we all are a part of that beautiful woman and that we have each other. I promise that I will always be there for you in any way I can. I love you both with all my heart.

I honestly cannot write these next few words without feeling a lump in my throat and my eyes beginning to tear. It's because I love you both so very, very much. My dearest Nana and Ta Ta, you did so much to make my life special. I'm forever grateful to you both, and I will always cherish the beautiful memories of our times together. Nana, you gave me the best mom in the whole world, and I know why she was the best—because her heart was as beautiful as yours. I love you so much for that. You are my best friend. I am truly blessed to be your granddaughter. I pray every day for God to heal your heart. May God comfort you and keep you well. I love you, my dearest Nana.

I feel so strongly in my heart that my husband's ministry is the fulfillment of my mother's prayers. She was a true prayer warrior, and she prayed as hard for Michael as she did for everyone she knew and for many people whom she didn't know. I know that nothing would please her more than to know that those of you who have read Michael's testimony will be touched enough to want to seek comfort in the person of Jesus Christ. That was her mission, to bring people to Jesus. That was Michael's hope and prayer in writing this book. It is my prayer for all of you. I thank you for allowing my husband to speak to you and for giving him the opportunity to glorify God through the work of his ministry.

God bless you,
Camille

Afterword

"I'll make him an offer he can't refuse."

It's one of the most famous movie lines ever spoken. Vito Corleone, the man who spoke those words in *The Godfather*, was subtly referring to the power the godfather had to force someone to accept his offer, like it or not. You can be certain that the offer being made was not for the benefit of its recipient, but rather for that of the mobster or his mob family. I am very familiar with the mob's persuasive power. When I was in the life, I took advantage of that power when I needed to.

Our Creator has likewise made us an offer that none of us should refuse. He has offered to all of us the gift of eternal life, not by way of force, but by way of simply accepting His Son Jesus Christ into our hearts. Unlike the godfather, God the Father makes us an offer that will benefit our lives, both here on earth and for all of eternity.

Today, I am making an offer to all of you who have not yet come to know your Savior and also to all those believers who still might have some doubts about the Christian faith. Take the time to "intellectually examine" the claim that Jesus Christ truly is the Son of God and that the Holy Bible truly is the Word of God. Examine the evidence in support of these claims, and I guarantee that you will arrive at only one conclusion—a conclusion that will leave you wondering why you didn't accept God's offer long ago.

How do you begin this intellectual examination? First, if you don't already have one, get yourself a Bible. My experience has been that most people who reject the idea that the Bible is the word of God have never even read it. I recommend the New International Version. It is a simple translation and very easy to understand.

I don't believe there is any specific formula for studying the Bible. It is certainly not necessary to start from the book of Genesis and read all the way through to the book of Revelation. In the beginning, you might want to skip around and look for a book that is of particular interest to you. God will get your attention as you begin to find your way. I began my examination with a thorough reading of the New Testament. I was very interested in learning about Jesus. The entire Old Testament was written in preparation for the coming of the Messiah, and I wanted to know who He was right from the start. I became fascinated with the four Gospels and the epistles of the apostle Paul. I kind of worked backwards from there and began to study the Old Testament. The books of Proverbs and Psalms were of particular interest to me. The writings were so profound, so intelligently written, that I was really inspired by their teachings.

From there, God seemed to just take over. He instilled in me a genuine desire to prove to myself that all of this amazing material I was reading was factual, reliable, and worthy of my belief. The Bible itself was convincing me of that, but I wanted more proof, more independent evidence that I could rely on to establish the authenticity of the book itself.

I realized that the Bible, among other things, was actually a history book. It contained the history of the world from the beginning of creation to the establishment of the Christian church after the death and resurrection of Christ. I began to search for additional written materials that would help me form an objective conclusion concerning the authenticity of the writings of the Bible. I was amazed at the volumes of information that were available in bookstores concerning the authenticity of the Holy Bible.

I then expanded my search to include information concerning the authenticity of the writings of other religious beliefs and objectively compared that information with what I had learned about the Bible. For me, the conclusion was simple. Hands down, the Bible was truly the Word of God. I am confident that an honest, objective examination will lead you to arrive at the same conclusion.

Be certain that, by no means, is it my intention to attempt to establish myself as an authority on the doctrine of the Christian faith. I am neither an authority nor an expert in that regard. There are many learned and knowledgeable Christian scholars who are far more qualified than myself to teach and explain Christian doctrine. It was not necessary for me to be a scholar, however, to process the evidence in support of the reliability of our Christian faith. I trust it will not be necessary for you, either.

I have provided for you a list of reference materials that have helped me establish beyond any reasonable doubt that Jesus is Lord and that the Holy Bible is truly the Word of God. The following information is taken from these reference materials and offered to help you get started on your intellectual examination of the evidence, an offer that no one is really in a position to refuse.

Remember, this is an intellectual examination, a search for the truth. Examine the information carefully, objectively. Weigh the evidence. Only when you are totally convinced of the deity of Jesus Christ can you give your heart completely to Him. Do not deprive yourself of the amazing gifts such a commitment will bring to your life.

The Uniqueness of the Bible

The Bible stands alone among all other books ever written. It is different from all other books in the following ways, to name just a few:

Unique in Its Continuity

The Bible is the only book that was

1. Written over a span of about 1500 years.
2. Written by more than forty authors from every walk of life.
3. Written in different places and on three different continents.
4. Written during different moods.
5. Written in three languages.
6. Written in a wide variety of literary styles.
7. Written to address hundreds of controversial subjects.
8. Written (in spite of its diversity) to present a single, unfolding story of God's redemption of human beings through one central character, Jesus Christ.

Unique in Its Circulation

The number of Bibles sold reaches into the billions. More copies have been produced, either in whole or in part, than any other book in history. If you were to line up all of the people who received Bible or Scripture selections last year and then hand a Bible to each one of them every five seconds, it would take more than ninety-two years to distribute what just the United Bible Societies gave out last year alone.

Unique in Its Translation

No other book in history has been translated, retranslated, and paraphrased more than the Bible. According to the United Bible Societies, the Bible has been translated into more than twenty-two hundred languages, which represent the primary vehicle of communication for well over ninety percent of the world.

Unique in Its Survival

The Scriptures have never diminished in style or correctness, nor have they ever faced extinction. Compared with other ancient writings, the Bible has more manuscript evidence to support it than any ten pieces of classical literature combined.

Unique in Its Teachings

Prophecy:

Among the evidences put forth by the Bible for the truth of biblical Christianity, fulfilled predictions (prophecies) are especially important. According to Deuteronomy 18, a prophet was false if he made predictions that were never fulfilled. No unconditional prophecy of the Bible about events up to the present day has gone unfulfilled. Hundreds of predictions, some of them given hundreds of years in advance, have been literally fulfilled. The time (Daniel 9), city (Micah 5:2), and nature (Isaiah 7:14) of Christ's birth were accurately foretold hundreds of years earlier in the Old Testament, as were dozens of other things about His life, death, and resurrection. The ancient world had many different devices for determining the future, known as divination, but not in the entire gamut of Greek and Latin literature, even though they use the words "prophet" and "prophecy," can we find any real specific prophecy of a great historic event to come in the distant future, nor any prophecy of a Savior to arise in the human race. No other religion or religious writing outside of the Bible can claim the absolute existence of fulfilled prophecy.

Character:

The Bible as a book focuses on reality, not fantasy. It presents the good and the bad, the right and the wrong, the best and the worst, the hope and despair, the joy and pain of life. And so it should, for its ultimate author is God, and *"Nothing in all creation is hidden from God's sight. Everything is uncovered and*

391

laid bare before the eyes of Him to whom we must give an account" (Hebrews 4:13).

Unique in Its Influence on Civilization

Civilization has been influenced more by the Judeo-Christian Scriptures than by any other book or series of books in the world. The influence of the Bible and its teachings on the Western world is clear to all who study history. It has been the most available, familiar, and dependable source of intellectual, moral, and spiritual ideals in the West. After some two thousand years, the centuries themselves are measured from the birth of Jesus. Calendars in India and China, like those in Europe, America, and the Middle East registered the dawn of the third millennium from the date of His birth. The Bible presents the highest ideals known to men, ideals that have molded civilization up until the present day.

Historical Accuracy of the Bible

The Old Testament has been shown to be reliable in at least three major ways: (1) textual transmission (the accuracy of the copying process down through history), (2) the confirmation of the Old Testament by hard evidence uncovered through archaeology, and (3) documentary evidence also uncovered through archaeology.

Evidence from Archaeology

The Old Testament:

Not only do we have accurate copies of the Old Testament, but the contents of the manuscripts are historically reliable. The evidence in support of these facts is not credibly refutable.

Archaeology, a relative newcomer among the physical sciences, has provided exciting and dramatic confirmation of the

Bible's accuracy. Whole books are not large enough to contain all the finds that have bolstered confidence in the historical reliability of the Bible.

William F. Albright, reputed to be one of the greatest archaeologists, states, "There can be no doubt that archaeology confirmed the substantial historicity of Old Testament tradition."

Other experts have also spoken as to the evidence supporting the Bible:

It may be stated categorically, that no archaeological discovery has ever controverted a biblical reference. Scores of archaeological findings have been made which confirm in clear outline or exact detail historical statements in the Bible. And, by the same token, proper evaluation of Biblical descriptions has led to amazing discoveries.
—Nelson Glueck, renowned Jewish archaeologist

Archaeology has confirmed countless passages which have been rejected by critics as unhistorical or contradictory to known facts....Yet archaeological discoveries have shown that these critical charges...are wrong and that the Bible is trustworthy in the very statements which have been set aside as untrustworthy....We do not know of any cases where the Bible has been proven wrong.
—Dr. Joseph P. Free, professor of archaeology and history, Bemidji State College

Professor Merrill F. Unger, who received his A.B. and Ph.D. degrees at Johns Hopkins University, says, "Old Testament archaeology has rediscovered whole nations, resurrected important peoples, and in a most astonishing manner filled in historical gaps, adding immeasurably to the knowledge of biblical backgrounds."

I have not even scratched the surface here in providing you with the volumes of discoveries archaeologists have uncovered to quiet the Bible's critics and prove its authenticity and reliability as an ancient manuscript. In short, even the stones have cried out in praise of the word of God as it appears in the Holy Bible.

The New Testament:

The primary sources for the life of Jesus Christ are the four Gospels contained in the New Testament. Aside from the numerous archaeological discoveries that provide clear and convincing evidence of the New Testament's authenticity and historical accuracy, there are considerable reports from non-Christian sources that supplement and confirm the Gospel accounts. These come largely from Greek, Roman, Jewish, and Samaritan sources from the first century. These reports corroborate numerous accounts of Christ's life that are reported in the Gospels, including the accounts that: (1) He performed unusual feats that *they* called "sorcery," (2) He was crucified in Palestine under Pontius Pilate, (3) it was believed by His disciples that He was raised from the dead three days later, (4) His small band of disciples multiplied rapidly, spreading even as far as Rome, (5) His disciples denied polytheism, lived moral lives, and worshipped Christ as divine.

The twenty-seven books of the New Testament proclaim and verify the historicity of Jesus Christ. A careful review of the evidence proves that these books are historically reliable as previously indicated. We can see that their testimony about Jesus provides significant, irrefutable evidence that He really lived and, in fact, still does.

Consider for a moment how tradition says the apostles met their deaths because of their absolute refusal to renounce Jesus Christ as the Savior and the one true God:

Philip:	Stoned to death, A.D. 54
Barnabas:	Burned to death, A.D. 64
Peter:	Crucified, A.D. 69
Andrew:	Beheaded, A.D. 70

Luke:	Hanged, A.D. 93
Thomas:	Speared to death, A.D. 70
Mark:	Dragged to death, A.D. 64
James:	Clubbed to death, A.D. 63
John:	Abandoned on Patmos to die, A.D. 63

Having walked with Jesus during His public life, these men had to make a determination as to whether Jesus was actually the Son of God and the Savior as He claimed to be, or else a liar, madman, or demon, and, on top of it all, an absolute fool.

Consider this: if Jesus really knew He was not God, then He was lying. But if He was a liar, then He was also a hypocrite, because He told others to be honest, whatever the cost, while He, at the same time, was teaching and living a colossal lie.

If Jesus really believed He was God when, in reality, He was not, then He had to be a lunatic—a madman. God is either God, who knows all things and cannot be mistaken, or He is not.

More than that, He would have been a demon, because He deliberately told others to trust Him for their eternal destiny. If He could not back up His claims and knew they were false, then He was unspeakably evil.

Last, Jesus would also have been a fool, because it was His claim to deity that led to His crucifixion.

If Jesus was a liar, a con man, and therefore an evil, foolish man, then how can we explain the fact that He left us with the most profound moral instruction and powerful moral example that anyone has ever given? Could a deceiver, an imposter of monstrous proportions, teach such ethical truths and live such a morally exemplary life as Jesus did? The very notion is beyond belief.

The reliably documented evidence that is the New Testament account of Jesus' life, death, and resurrection and of the apostles' activities after His resurrection, allows us to reasonably and rationally draw only one conclusion: these men went to their deaths believing what they reported, that Jesus was the Son of God and Savior as He claimed to be.

Consider What Some of Our Great Leaders Say about the Bible

"It is not possible to rightly govern the world without God and the Bible."

George Washington

"A Bible in every home is the principle support of virtue, morality, and civil liberty."

Benjamin Franklin

"There is a Book worth more than all the other books which were ever printed."

Patrick Henry

"I say to you, search the Scriptures! The Bible is the book of all others, to be read at all ages, and in all conditions of human life; not to be read once, twice or thrice through, and then laid aside, but to be read in small portions of one or two chapters every day, and never to be intermitted, unless by some overruling necessity."

John Quincy Adams

"The Bible is the rock on which our republic rests."

Andrew Jackson

"I am profitably engaged in reading the Bible. Take all of this book upon reason that you can and the balance by faith, and you will live and die a better man. I believe that the Bible is the best gift God has given to man. All the good from the Savior of the world is communicated to us through the Book."

Abraham Lincoln

"The best religion the world has ever known is the religion of the Bible. It builds up all that is good."

Rutherford B. Hayes

"The more profoundly we study this wonderful Book, and the more closely we observe it's divine precepts, the better citizens we will become and the higher will be our destiny as a nation."

William McKinley

"I plead for a closer and wider and deeper study of the Bible, so that our people may be in fact as well as theory 'doers of the Word and not hearers only.'"

Theodore Roosevelt

"The whole inspiration of our civilization springs from the teachings of Christ and the lessons of the prophets. To read the Bible for these fundamentals is a necessity of American life."

Herbert Hoover

"Within the covers of the Bible are all the answers for all the problems men face. The Bible can touch hearts, order minds, and refresh souls."

Ronald Reagan

Much of the information contained in this chapter was taken from the following books:

The New Evidence That Demands a Verdict by Josh McDowell (Thomas Nelson).
The Evidence Bible compiled by Ray Comfort (Bridge-Logos).

In addition to the books listed above, I recommend the following books to help you in your "intellectual examination" of the evidence in support of the Holy Bible:

The Revised & Expanded Answers Book by Ken Hamm, Johnathan Sarfati, Carl Wieland and edited by Don Batten (Master Books).
The Case for Faith by Lee Strobel (Zondervan).
The Case for Christ by Lee Strobel (Zondervan).
101 Answers to the Most Asked Questions about the End Times by Mark Hitchcock (Multnomah).
The Evidence of Prophecy edited by Robert C. Newman.

Appendix
My Ministry

The apostle Paul said in his first letter to the Corinthians, *"So whether you eat or drink or whatever you do, do it all for the glory of God"* (1 Corinthians 10:31). God had no greater soldier than Paul, and his ministry has been my inspiration. Imagine...if all Christians strived to do what Paul directed in this verse, what a difference we could really make in the world. Doing everything for the glory of God is really not that difficult when you are truly one of His children.

In 1 John 5:3–4, we read the words, *"This is love for God: to obey His commands. And His commands are not burdensome, for everyone born of God overcomes the world."* Think about that for a moment. It's really not a burden to glorify God in all that we do during our day, provided that our hearts are truly God-centered and not self-centered. Christians need to acquire a God consciousness. It comes by remaining in His Word, in prayer, and in fellowship with other believers. It means that God is on your mind throughout the day, in all that you do. He must never be an afterthought. He must be our first thought. Then, it's almost as if God has you on autopilot, and the only time you can go wrong is when you try to fly the craft of life manually.

This doesn't mean that we spend our days preaching to anyone and everyone who will listen. Please! Surely, you've heard the expression "less is more." When it comes to preaching, sometimes we Christians should take that saying to heart. Our actions always speak a whole lot louder than our words. As St. Francis of Assisi said, "Preach the Gospel at all times, and when necessary use words."

For my speaking ministry, God has directed me to address diverse groups of people, both believers and nonbelievers. The many experiences I had in the mob have afforded me the opportunity to share some valuable information with people from all walks of life. Sharing my testimony, of course, is a no-brainer. But even when it would be "politically incorrect" to praise God in my speech, well, I praise God in my speech anyway. And I don't even have to mention His name. People just know.

Kevin Hallinan, head of security for Major League Baseball, has described me as "a pound of prevention," among other things, before introducing me to deliver my anti-gambling message to the players. The common theme that runs through every message I deliver to any audience is that I've been there and done that, and here's what you need to watch out for.

In addition to speaking to athletes and young people at risk, allow me to share with you some of the other subjects I am invited to speak about. Please do not be offended as I give a brief overview of some of the illegal activity I engaged in as a member of organized crime. I remind you that what man intended for bad, God can now use for His good:

- **Gambling:** When you are a member of organized crime, you are always somehow connected to gambling. I was, and in a fairly substantial way. In addition to having bookmaking operations under my control, I infiltrated casinos in Las Vegas and on the island of Haiti and defrauded the companies out of several millions of dollars. I have shared this information in speeches to Indian Gaming Casinos throughout the country.

- **Insurance fraud:** I defrauded a major insurance company of more than five million dollars. The company was called Union Indemnity Insurance and was a subsidiary of the brokerage firm, Frank B. Hall. I had inside information that the company was planning to file for bankruptcy rather than pay a $50 million claim on behalf of the MGM Grand in Las Vegas. The hotel had suffered a major loss as a result of a fire. The fraud involved an executive of the company, a corrupt CPA, and a cooperative banker.
- **Bank fraud:** I defrauded several banks in New York out of substantial amounts of money: Apple Bank, Citibank, and Chase Manhattan, to name just a few. I also defrauded the Small Business Association (SBA) out of more than $500,000.
- **Tax fraud:** I defrauded federal and state governments out of hundreds of millions of dollars in taxes from the sale of gasoline. The scheme was quite sophisticated and required the use of more than twenty-five separate corporations formed in several states and in Panama. It required payoffs to bankers, government employees, and others. I also formed a major alliance with members of a Russian crime syndicate.
- **Corporate fraud:** I defrauded General Motors Corporation, Beneficial Leasing Company, and Mazda Motors of America—always with the help of people on the inside, executives on the edge.
- **Prison:** People are curious. What is prison really like? Death row? Isolation? They seek my opinions on possible reforms, how the system can save taxpayers money, how the system can better prepare convicts for release back into society, and how the system can protect society from repeat offenders.
- **Criminal justice system:** I have more than thirty years of experience with all aspects of the system and have spoken with law enforcement groups throughout the country.

- **Organized crime:** It seems that people from all walks of life have a fascination with the mob life. This is even more true now that *The Sopranos* have found their way into our living rooms each week. I am open to all questions, and the question-and-answer sessions are always a highlight of my visit.

I have been blessed to become part of a team of knowledgeable, dedicated professionals led by my dearest friend, Pastor Barry Minkow, whose mission is to educate and inform corporate America on how to prevent its companies from becoming victims of corporate fraud. I am excited about this latest addition to my ministry and pray that God will be glorified in the services the company provides.

My ministry is very important to me. God has blessed me with an opportunity to give back a little after having taken so much during my years in organized crime. I am grateful to Him for that. I do my best to make myself available to those interested in having me visit with their group or organization. For further information about my speaking ministry, please visit my web site at www.michaelfranzese.com.

My ministry, Breaking Out, has been described in greater detail in a previous chapter. Directed toward at-risk youth, the ministry is a special undertaking for both Cammy and myself. For further information about the ministry, please visit our web site at www.breakingout.net.

The Agape House of Prayer is a place of worship that is particularly dear to my heart. It is the church in Anaheim (only a stone's throw from Disneyland) that was founded on the prayers of my beloved mother-in-law, Irma Garcia. My brother-in-law, Joaquin Garcia, is the founder and senior pastor of the church. God has truly blessed this young man in his transformation from a street-tough, hard-living, high school star athlete to what he has become today—a true man of God.

He often tells the story of the church's early days when he was preaching to nearly empty pews and was ready to give up. But Irma wouldn't have it.

"I'm here," she would tell him, "and as long as there is one person in this building that wants to hear the Word of God, you get up there and preach."

So he preached, and Irma prayed.

Irma is no longer with us to sit in one of the pews, but Pastor Joaquin also no longer preaches to an empty church. His mother's prayers were answered. In just a few short years, the ministry of the church has grown to include a home for men who are in need of shelter and sound biblical instruction, a youth ministry administered by the youngest Garcia brother, Che, and a neighborhood outreach that provides dinners and gifts to more than three hundred needy children and their families at Christmas.

The oldest Garcia brother, Dean, is in charge of a music ministry that is reaching out to the young people of Anaheim. His worship team has already ministered to thousands by leading them into the presence of God. It is my belief that God will expand this ministry far beyond the walls of the the Agape House of Prayer.

On the one-year anniversary of Irma's death, the newest addition of the church ministry was unveiled. Irma's House of Prayer is an interim home for women and their children who are in need of food, shelter, and biblical instruction as they attempt to put their sometimes broken lives back in order, God's way.

My father-in-law, Seferino Garcia, has joined his sons in providing his support to the church's mission. A driving force in the community for many years, Seferino has dedicated his life to directing neighborhood youth away from gang violence and negative influences and has taught them to make getting a solid education their primary goal. Now, he's directing them to the church to be nourished with the Word of God.

Pastor Joaquin's belief is that if he stays faithful to the little matters that are part of their daily ministry, the Lord will bless them, and their congregation will continue to grow. The doors are open to anyone who wants to know Jesus.

As part of my ministry, I will continue to support my wife and her brothers in their efforts to glorify God through the church's ministry. For more information about the Agape House of Prayer, please visit the ministry website at www.michaelfranzese.com.

Please remember to keep my ministry in your prayers, and if you have a special prayer request that we can join you in prayer for, please click on the "Contact Us" or "Need Prayer?" links on the website.

Contact Information

Dear Friends,

Should you have any questions or comments regarding *Blood Covenant*, or if you would like to contact me, please visit our website at:

www.michaelfranzese.com

I encourage you to contact me directly at my e-mail address in the website contact section with any concerns you might have—and trust me, I've heard it all. Anywhere I speak, I offer those in attendance my contact information and invite them to write. Whether collegiate or professional athletes, businessmen at a conference, or youth and parents at a church, I read and respond to those who write.

On the website you can also find information about our foundation, Breaking Out, created to educate, encourage, and empower youth and young adults, particularly as it regards gambling. More than half of my time is spent speaking about this critical issue with collegiate and professional athletes, Greeks, and Res Life students. We teach them about the pitfalls involved in the *business* of gambling, a business I knew all too well. Our foundation is designed to take this message to those in middle and high schools, where more than one million teens are addicted to gambling. On our site we have more information about gambling, as well as ways to recognize a problem gambler.

Should you prefer writing, you may contact me at:

Breaking Out Foundation
P.O. Box 11045
Marina Del Rey, CA 90295

If you are interested in speaking opportunities or for more information on Breaking Out, I encourage you to get in touch with my managing partner, Rob Michaels. His contact information is on the website also.

Thanks,
Michael Franzese